'YOU KNOW THE FAIR RULE'

Strategies for making the hard job
of discipline in school easier

BILL ROGERS

LONGMAN

First published 1990 by The Australian Council for Educational Research Ltd
Radford House, Frederick Street, Hawthorn, Victoria 3122, Australia

First published in Great Britain 1991 by
Longman Industry and Public Service Management
Longman Group UK Limited, Westgate House, The High, Harlow, Essex CM20 1YR
England; Tel Harlow (0279) 442601; Fax (0279) 444501

Reprinted 1992

This edition is not for sale in Australia, New Zealand or Canada

Line drawings by Kevin Burgemeestre
Edited by Writers Reign
Designed by Pauline McClenahan, Bookworks
Printed in Malaysia by PA

British Library Cataloguing-in-Publication Data
Rogers, Bill
    'You know the fair rule': Strategies for making the hard job of discipline in
    school easier.
    I. Title
    371.5

    ISBN 0-582-08672-8

Contents

CHAPTER 4
Rights and rules in the classroom   85

The author

Bill Rogers' concern with discipline in schools began in the classroom. As a young teacher he was troubled by the absence of training in discipline strategies and by the lack of support given to teachers in this difficult aspect of an already demanding job. As his career and studies progressed, he began researching the issues of discipline, classroom management and teacher stress. His Masters degree concentrated on conflict and conflict resolution among pre-adolescents.

Bill now works as a consultant in all areas of education (primary, post-primary and tertiary), running in-service programs for teachers, lecturing at Colleges of Education and Universities, and working with parent groups and students. He lectures widely on discipline, classroom management, stress and teaching, developing peer-support programs for teachers, and developing community-based policies on discipline and student welfare. He has worked with a large number of teachers throughout Australia in the last four years. He is currently researching the issue of teacher stress as it relates to classroom management.

Bill Rogers holds degrees in Theology and Education, and was a parish Minister in the western suburbs of Melbourne for eight years, a role which included chaplaincy in hospitals and schools. He has published several books and a video package on discipline.

Preface to the British edition

In 1987 I visited the UK as a recipient of a Research Scholarship. I was looking at teacher stress in the UK. Apart from some formal lecturing I visited several schools in England, Wales, Scotland and Belfast. I returned to the UK to lecture again in 1989. It was obvious to me that when teachers and students are together in a classroom it could be anywhere – local accents notwithstanding!

In Western cultures, at least, teachers face much the same environment. They are busy people, who spend most of their day with 'minors', in a *naturally* stressful environment. TV has given a 'universal' culture to the young (as McLuhan said it would). The natural resistance to mere role-status of teachers by the young is no different in Melbourne or Sydney compared to say Glasgow or London. Students are more conscious of 'their rights', less 'compliant' to adult authority *per se*, more 'street-wise'... all of which present significantly different climates for discipline in schools.

I've written this book as a teacher, for teachers, at every level in schools. You will easily recognise and tune-in-to the student/teacher scenarios described here.

Some of the terms may need some explanation. When, for example, you read *Good On You* you're reading a common (perhaps the most common) Australian phrase; it is a cross between 'well done' and 'I'm pleased with your effort'. It is meant to engender a rapport in the working relationship between teacher and student.

Fair Dinkum in the mouth of a student or teacher alike is akin to, 'Oh come on, is that true, you're not serious are you!?' and can encompass mild to strong frustration.

Titles like 'post-primary' mean students from 12/13 years of age. Many Australian schools use the term 'year – level' to describe a students year place in the school. So, prep grade equals $4\frac{1}{2}$ to $5\frac{1}{2}$ years of age; followed by years 1 to 12 (year 12 equalling sixth form). 'Relieving' teachers are the equivalent of supply teachers, and 'patrol' time is break time.

Apart from these few qualifications you can easily read, enjoy, laugh at and adapt the descriptions and solutions outlined here.

Good on you!

Bill Rogers
December 1990

Preface

Nobody actually taught me to discipline. Of course I've *been* disciplined; everything from repeated canings and a 'thick ear' to the occasional wearing of a dunce's hat in the corner of the classroom. When I went to Teachers' College and University I expected to learn *how* to discipline. Regularly I asked my lecturers questions such as 'Well, what do you do when students persistently call out in class or rudely butt-in on your delivery?'; 'What do you do with kids who hoon around, swear, or say the work is boring?'; 'How do you deal with those who are regularly out of their seats and are chattering away to their friends during teaching time?'. When I asked such questions, few answers came.

Now, as a consultant, I spend my time, along with others, trying to give answers to those questions and offering possible solutions to the discipline problems of today's classrooms. This book came about as a result of countless hours of in-servicing and peer-support work with teachers. In order to share discipline concerns widely across the school, support groups (see Chapter 9) were formed to explore common concerns and begin to build better solutions. These were established in a wide range of schools from kindergarten to Year 12 and the results of that work are collected here. This book seeks to answer, in the most practical way, the question: How can I discipline more effectively, positively, less stressfully, in that busy place called a classroom?

- This is not a book about curriculum — although curriculum plays a significant part in discipline.
- This is not a book about particular discipline theories — although certain theories are alluded to in the text.
- This *is* a book about practical classroom strategies for use both in individual classes and across the school. It is written for those who take on one of the most demanding of all jobs — teaching.

Chapter 1 defines the concept of discipline used throughout the text and argues for some fundamental protocols (accepted practices) that ought to form the bottom line in our practice of discipline. The central protocol is that all discipline should proceed from the due *rights*, *rules* and *responsibilities* of all members of the classroom group. Discipline is explored as a function of teacher leadership that aims to give students maximum self-control. The goals of discipline are also outlined.

Chapter 2 explores disruptive behaviour as a phenomenon occurring in the group as well as the individual. Disruptive behaviour is explored as a function of attention-seeking, from clowning and 'notice-me' behaviours through to provocation. (This is further explored under 'Conflict in the classroom' in Chapter 8.) Teacher style has a significant effect on disruptive behaviour, its frequency and duration. Three basic styles are explored (Lewin, 1948) in terms of the degree to which teachers seek to obtain *compliance* from students.

Chapter 3 is devoted entirely to classroom management skills and explores the fundamental premise that positive discipline is rarely fortuitous, or accidental — it needs to be planned. A range of discipline strategies are explored which adopt a decisive but positive stance enabling the goals of discipline: self-control, on-task enjoyment, respect for rights, personal accountability and self-esteem to be realised. The chapter argues that teachers need to make a clear discipline plan.

Chapter 4 explores how rights can be realised in a classroom setting without sacrificing clear, positive rules which are the essence of preventative discipline. Examples of how to form classroom rules are given.

Chapter 5 explores effective support structures for classroom discipline which are needed on a school-wide basis. These include: a time-out policy (for on-going disruptions); the use of logical or behavioural consequences (helping students to 'wear' the consequences of their actions); the writing of contracts as a mechanism for behaviour change; classroom meetings to discuss common concerns with students and achieve some 'ownership' of classroom life.

Chapter 6 concentrates on a fundamental goal of discipline and of teaching — self-esteem. This is explored through the concept of classroom 'tone' and argues that supportive discipline is all about the way we build the tone. This includes:
• how we speak to our students
• the quality of our interaction
• room organisation

Chapter 7 examines the place of reinforcement as a form of discipline that can both achieve the aims of self-esteem and respect for rights, yet enhance self-control in students by providing a consistent and controlled structure. Individual and group programs are detailed for use in a wide range of classroom settings.

Chapter 8 explores the issue of conflict. This may not be an issue for some teachers, however, many of us have struggled with quite extreme (sometimes bizarre) student behaviour. To integrate such students more successfully, we need an understanding of how conflict can arise in a group setting; a clear plan to deal with it (rather than react to it); an understanding of our own frustration and anger; and clear collegiate support. Some essential protocols of conflict resolution that are effective with a wide range of conflict situations have been included.

Chapter 9 examines how support groups can not only give moral and structural support (in discipline and classroom management), but also aid the professional development of staff.

The Appendices contain:
• Personal running record (noting discipline incidents)
• The 4W form (a student's contract)
• Formal contract form and picture contract form
• Observation information record
• Gentle, assertive role-plays (GARPs)
• Discipline survey

Putting a book together takes a long time and, apart from the personal effort involved, requires the assistance of many people. From the outset, the Australian Council for Educational Research were especially supportive. I then had the good fortune of working with two editors who, over much coffee and many a laugh, enabled me to fine-tune the manuscript. Brigid James and Leonie Keaney, for your professional good will, many thanks. My typist, Joy Draper, has (once again) transformed multi-coloured biro-covered sheets of paper into a readable script. Well done, and thanks, Joy.

I doubt whether the many hundreds of students in schools where I have taught will ever read this book (who knows, some of them may want to teach!), but I thank them for the times we had together. As well as 'disciplining' them, I've discussed the mechanics and purpose of discipline and why they prefer one sort rather than another; some of their stories are in this book. I've also been teaching the skills covered here to teachers (and trainee teachers) in Australia and overseas for the last five years. My thanks to those who now are slogging it out with skill and good humour at the 'chalkface'.

I wish to acknowledge too, the article (anon), 'A memorandum for your child', which I have adapted and used to illustrate self-esteem as a child might see it. In the section on rights, rules and responsibilities (Chapter 4) I have included part of a school-policy document on discipline from Moonee Ponds West Primary School (Victoria), one of the many schools who have successfully developed a school-wide policy.

As an example of how first-year teachers generally respond to peer support I've let some of them tell their own story in Chapter 9. I thank them for their contribution.

Lastly, special thanks to my wife, Lora, and my two daughters, Elizabeth, aged 14 and Sarah, aged 2, who endured many discussions about, and practical demonstrations of, the sort of discipline espoused herein, and who supported me all the way.

Bill Rogers
Melbourne
January 1990

Introduction

Form 5, 1960

When I was at secondary school, Millar was the school tough, the
school bully, the 'sometime him-against-them' and the bane of the
teachers' lives. He once (and this is all true) half-hanged a Form 4 boy
upside down by a rope from a tree just for refusing to do a job. Millar
was caned in front of the whole school on several occasions. Every
child watched while Millar, and his crew, received their canings on
both hands by the principal or the senior science master. On the last
occasion he was publicly caned, 800 children watched Millar walk on
to the school stage (after public singing, school anthem and motto —
1960 remember?). Mr Johnstone (the 'boss') in his black gown, twitch-
ing eyes behind his thick glasses, lifted the cane to belt the impassive,
obsidian Millar who stood facing the school. It happened so quickly!
Down whooshed the cane. As it hit Millar's hand, he grabbed the cane
from the principal and with great aplomb broke it across his knee,
threw it on the floor and marched off stage. A few seconds later the
Form 4, 5 and 6 classes began to cheer. It took the school staff five

minutes to finally restore order and that was mostly by yelling threats. Who won?

It was our weekly music class. I was fourteen at the time. The music teacher was a thin, hirsute man; nervous, with a shock of Beethoven-style hair. He had a reputation in the school for being a weak disciplinarian — his classes ranging from moderate to extreme disorder. There was 'muzak' noise, butt-ins, task-refusals, shouting . . .

From time to time, during music, I managed to score a seat next to a rather pretty girl (in 14-year-old terms). Okay so far, except for Millar. Millar was nearly as tall as our de facto Beethoven, but twice as broad. He smoked like a chimney, had freckles and flaming red hair and a punch like a heavyweight boxer.

It was the first few minutes of settling in before we were to begin another frustrating, boring music lesson. Millar came over to me and said, 'You sit over that side Rogers. I sit here.' Very cool. Not only did you not say 'no' to Millar, you also didn't waste time with discussion. I did as he said.

The music teacher saw this 'seat cross-over' and called out to Millar to get back into the seat from whence he had come. He, of course, just refused. He sat and smiled at the girl and at me. (I gave a 'It's nothing to do with me, sir' look.) Believing he had real power over Millar and that he must win to prove this, the teacher marched up to Millar's seat and demanded that he move, 'Now . . .!'. Freckle-faced and fearless, Millar simply replied, 'Make me'. So calm, so cool. 'Don't you defy me!' screamed the teacher. 'If you don't get out now, I'll make you!'

'Yeah, you and who else?' replied our boy version of Clint Eastwood. The teacher grabbed Millar and tried to pull him out of the seat. In the ensuing scuffle, chairs went flying and soon a ring of Form 5 children watched as teacher and student actually wrestled on the floor. A couple of girls raced to the staff room in tears and the science and geography teachers managed to drag them apart.

The music teacher left at the end of term. To get back at him, Millar let the tyres down on his car. Millar was finally expelled and ended up in a boys' home.

Public canings, I recall, diminished within weeks following the famous Millar incident.

How would Millar fare in the 1980s, in a society that aims for social justice with its elimination of sexism, democracy in schools and the abolition of corporal punishment? Psychologists and social workers would, no doubt, explain his behaviour as the result of social or emotional deprivation, or economic disadvantage.

Fortunately there are few students like Millar in our schools though the level of socio-emotionally disturbed (and disadvantaged) students may be as high as from three to five per cent across the school population (Wragg, 1989).

There are, however, many students who are more 'up-front' with their disruptive behaviour these days. Whether it is in the private girls' secondary school or the local 'reputation' technical school, there are many students who will not do what they are asked the first time, or simply because the teacher said so. They will argue, answer back, challenge, procrastinate, debate ... In the Elton Report on Discipline in Schools (1989, U.K.) it was indicated that 'talking out of turn', 'distracting others', 'making unnecessary (non-verbal) noises', 'getting out of seats without permission', and 'general rowdiness', most concerned teachers, and that these behaviours occurred right across the school spectrum.

What is certain, in the 1990s, is that the protest song of the 1960s has borne fruit: 'Your sons and your daughters are beyond your command'. The relative power and authority that teachers once 'enjoyed' is being easily eroded by students whose behaviour demonstrates that they want fundamental rights, such as the right to fair treatment and a say in what happens to them at school.

7B, 1990

It's just after lunch. The bell has rung and 7B charge down the concrete path to their home room.

Mr S. is nearly knocked down by a dark-haired runner wearing jeans and a vest bearing the motif 'Acid heads do it better'. ('Than what?' thinks Mr S.) 'G'day Sir ... gonna let us in?'

Already, half a dozen kids crowd the door so Mr S. has to push through them to open up. 'C'mon fellas, give us some air!' he pleads. Once open, the teacher and the half dozen move smartly, *en masse*, into Room 17. The students *appear* to have no manners whatever as they yell, cavort, tap, hoon and swear for five minutes or so until their teacher says, 'Can I have your attention please'.

Calling out is legion. One boy is half lying across the desk. A boy with a crew-cut and rat-like features has been tapping loudly with his pen for what seems ages; 'Get f _____!' is directed at the 'Acid heads do it better' boy by the crew-cut minor (who is now sucking a lolly on a stick). More abusive missiles are hurled around the room between these charming lads: 'liar', 'crap', 'shit', 'dickhead', 'Don't you sit near me you prick!'. Mike, a lad with terminal acne and a jean-jacket bearing a swastika and other motifs jumps up and runs after a small, fat boy who has apparently taken his sunglasses. 'Gimme them back now!' he yells, 'or I'll kick your arse!'.

Either the teacher is oblivious, deaf, powerless, having a bad day, or feels he can do nothing except yell again, 'Now settle down! I'm trying to mark the roll!'. This is Mr S.'s regular burden. They never prepared him for it at university.

'Hey Sir! Sir! Paul's away.' Apparently David cannot speak at a normal pitch. He shouts across the three metres separating him from the teacher's desk. Paul spits his chewy, loudly and with gusto, across the room and misses the bin. He grins. Mr S. doesn't. He's had it. 'Look, shut up you lot, you can see I'm trying to mark the roll!'

All this in the first 10 minutes of the session. Why do these kids act so rudely and disruptively? Perhaps you have never had a class like 7B or had to contend with someone like Millar. Perhaps the disruptions in your class are minor ones — a bit of calling out, a few students without pens or some low-level answering back. Spare a thought however for those like Mr S.

Of course the kids described here come from emotionally, socially, and economically depressed areas. Of course they watch hours of T.V. (much more than the time they are on-task at school). Of course many of the kids think school is a wag — perhaps they're right in some respects. Of course many of them act disruptively as an expression of belonging to the social group. They've found that A grade hooning (attention-seeking, defiance, teacher-baiting) gives them a fundamental sense of place in classroom life. But when kids regularly muck up in a class like this, something else is happening.

Sane order, purpose and management of a class is significantly related to the method a teacher employs and to the presence they have in the daily classroom interaction. Kids are not naturally well ordered or well mannered or well anything in a group. Without clear direction from a teacher, the class members will find ways to take over. It's unfortunate, but children are not naturally democratic, and ideologues who have either forgotten what a robust Year 7 class is like or, more likely, never been in one, don't help by peddling slogans of relevance-in-the-curriculum, democracy in learning, and student participation — as if these were, *simpliciter*, the answer. They are not.

While student rights, a democratic curriculum, cooperative learning, participation and equity, access and success are worthy goals of education, those goals need a clear structure. Discipline is one way to develop that structure. Not autocratic discipline, not the martinet-style that many of us knew in our education, but democratic leadership. Times have changed, students no longer easily or naturally respect the teacher role *per se*. Even that universal culprit, society, no longer rates teaching as a significant profession.

Many teachers, finding discipline difficult, complain that their college or university did not adequately prepare them for what they were facing. Many teachers plan well for curriculum but tend not to plan rigorously for discipline even though they know what the common disruptions are.

I believe we ill-serve trainee teachers if we do not give them discipline and management skills. While thorough preparation of curriculum is essential, so is preparation for discipline. We need to discipline even if it's only calling out, chattering and 'mobility' we have to contend with. With some of the 'worst-case' scenarios discussed later in this book, a thorough, detailed discipline plan is vital.

When I became a teacher, I soon realised the need for discipline skills. I read, I practised, I evaluated, I failed, I revised, and, in time, I began to discuss successes and failures with interested peers. One of the more optimistic signs in the current educational climate is the stress on peer support; a move away from that assumption that a teacher is weak or inefficient in wanting to discuss discipline concerns and to access mutual solutions. Teaching (unfortunately) has the structural potential to be a lonely profession.

When I became a consultant, I continued this approach in schools through peer-support groups, team-teaching new ideas and skills with teachers in their classrooms, and through professional development at in-services, seminars and at university.

Discipline (as a major facet of classroom management) is not easy. It is taxing emotionally, straining relationships between staff and students and between members of staff. To make discipline a *positive* feature of teaching practice, and school life, such that students have maximum self-control and responsibility with minimum damage to self-esteem and the due rights of all, is no mean feat. It requires skill, planning and team support.

There are no magic ways of achieving effective discipline. It takes hard work. But that work is made easier with knowledge and skills — practical, achievable skills. I have seen countless teachers use the approaches developed in this book with success. That success has required changes in organisation, as well as changes in behaviour and approach by the teacher, which in turn has changed the working relationship between students and their teacher.

It is my hope that any teacher, however long they have been in the game, will benefit from using the ideas, skills and resources in this book to build more positive, workable relationships that enhance the educational climate of our schools. After all, isn't that the fundamental goal of discipline?

CHAPTER 1

Discipline: definition and protocols

I am the decisive element . . . my personal approach . . . creates the climate . . . As a teacher I possess tremendous power to make a child's life miserable or joyous. I can be a tool of torture or an instrument of inspiration. I can humiliate, humour, hurt or heal.

Ginott, 1972

It's worth defining discipline

When I sported thin white legs with knobbly knees, a baggy pair of shorts, and blazer with cap to boot (circa 1950), *discipline* was a 'thick ear', respect for our masters, a cane across the hand or legs, or the dreaded trip to the principal's office. *That* trip was a narrow flight of stairs, a pronouncement of doom by this fearsome, awesome, black-robed stranger and the holding back of tears as he lashed out across the back of the knees or across the open hands. Ten times I was caned at school, for lateness, breaking a pencil, 'answering back', and going out of the school grounds to the shops at playtime. It did not teach me to respect my elders, the system or authority.

The application of corporal punishment may have relieved the frustration of my teachers but their behaviour totally disenfranchised my due rights. Children of the 50s were not aware they had such things as rights.

Corporal punishment

Corporal punishment (hitting, striking, pulling of ears or hair, pushing and shoving, beating, teaching-him-a-lesson-down-the-back-of-the-bike-shed) is now abolished in most democratic countries. Most states in Australia have abolished such 'discipline'. This does not mean that frustrated teachers do not occasionally hit, strike or poke their students when they display disruptive behaviour. It does mean that such behaviours are against the law. By 1985, Victoria had followed the lead of England where the prevailing opinion was that physical pain and fear were incompatible with democratic education. This was in tune with the 1982 report to the General Assembly of the United Nations on a student's right not to be physically punished as 'an educational or disciplinary measure' (Boer and Gleeson 1982).

The abolition of corporal punishment coincided with the emergence of a more open, less repressive society in the West. However, there are still principals and teachers who pine for the 'good old days' when they had 'real' power over children, when they could 'teach' them via the strap or cane. I still hear the asinine statement, 'They've taken our power away'.

There is an illusion about corporal punishment still common in the media, and amongst some teachers and parents, that it is a needed, fundamental tool. Whenever I speak to parents (especially fathers) about discipline, I often hear statements like 'I know what I'd do with some of these kids ...'. The suggestion is that control by force is a *necessary* ingredient in discipline. The basic argument still tendered for corporal punishment is that it *shows* the child he is wrong by associating pain with unacceptable behaviour. It is also supposed to act as a 'red light' to the other students and, of course, it relieves the frustration of the teacher. It *looks* as if something is being done.

Corporal punishment may solve the situation temporarily but it is ineffective in the long-term, especially with those students whose background is already one of socio-emotional deprivation or aggression and hostility and who are under stresses often not of their own making. If a child is already being maltreated or emotionally 'bastardised' at home, how will further adult punishment help the effective resolution of inner turmoil? What do students learn of problem solving if teachers use force to deal with external conflicts? Is it not teaching them to solve a problem *by force*? Corporal punishment does not work for the 'harder' student — the recidivist. It teaches such students nothing about the *resolution* of inner turmoil or conflict. It teaches students nothing about the positive social or task behaviours that they should be employing. A policy of accepting the consequences for one's actions, as distinct from punishment by pain, seeks to enhance accountability and self-control. Even if corporal punishment stops them and temporarily works, it doesn't make such discipline *right*.

In schools with serious behaviour problems some teachers will still say that corporal punishment is necessary, 'because it's the only language those kids understand!'. Again, what does such a teacher attitude convey about power relationships between an adult and a minor? About the nature of authority? About 'class' attitudes towards children whose background predisposes them to poor social behaviour patterns?

When physical pain is being used as a form of control, the recipient needs to be passive. The degree to which, in the past, even recidivist children submitted to hair-pulling, caning, belting round the ear, was staggering. Such behaviours exhibited today would not only be (rightly) resisted by students, they would be tantamount to child abuse. It is very difficult to smack a struggling, resistant child. The old teacher 'con' of, 'It'll hurt me more than it hurts you' only conveys the message that the adult has a legitimacy (endorsed by the State and society). It legitimises the arrogance of a power relationship based on coercion, force and degradation. It may also see the student getting back at the teacher in other ways and will certainly produce students adept at avoidance mechanisms.

It is my view that those who still hark back to the 'good old days' forget how degrading it is to hurt another human being in order to 'discipline' them. Are there no other options? Are we so bereft of discipline and management skills that the touting of physical punishment is still seen, by many, as a panacea for behaviour problems? There is no convincing evidence to demonstrate that physical punishment (as distinct from correction, leadership and applied consequences) leads to self-control and self-discipline. It has been my experience that teachers (and parents) who call for the reintroduction of corporal punishment often betray a singular lack of skill in the area of discipline, classroom management and curriculum planning. I have seen teachers fly into a rage because one or two students dared question sines and cosines in a maths class, who dared to 'answer back'. Such teachers make little effort to cater for mixed abilities, to speak respectfully to students ('Listen you, who the hell do you think you are? I spent ages preparing this work!'), to exercise any classroom management skill. Punitive style is the easy option.

We can no longer expect to walk into a classroom and automatically be given respect. Many children *will not* just sit still and do as they're told. We have to learn to work with them and discipline them in such a way as to make clear that self-control and respect for rights are the norm and the expected outcome in the classroom.

The three types of discipline

When discipline is used as a verb, it is common to associate it with correction or punishment. The word 'discipline' is used in this book in three ways.

Preventative Discipline: where there is concern with clear rules and consequences, contracting with students, room organisation, curriculum planning, time-out etc.

Corrective Discipline: where teacher actions are carried out to correct disruptive, anti-social or deviant behaviour.

Supportive Discipline: where 'correction' can be received as fairly as is possible and working relationships with corrected students re-established.

Discipline is a teacher-directed activity whereby we seek to lead, guide, direct, manage, or confront a student about behaviour that disrupts the rights of others be they teachers or students. This teacher behaviour has *goals* beyond retaliation or punishment. It aims to lead a student towards self-control and personal accountability. In fact, the *test* of 'good' or positive discipline is this: how does what I do and say enable a student to reach socially responsible goals?

The prep teacher has the choice to *teach* shoe-lace tying or daily, frustratingly, tie up 15 or 20 pairs of laces or buckles. The same goes for nose wiping, use of equipment, cleaning up, etc. With any age group, we have the choice of nagging, or teaching students independence, cooperation and responsibility.

Goals of discipline

- To develop students' self-discipline and self-control.
- To enable students to be on-task with their learning.
- To enhance students' self-esteem.
- To encourage accountability for behaviour.
- To encourage the individual student to recognise and respect the rights of others.
- To affirm cooperation as well as responsible independence in learning.
- To promote the values of honesty, fairness, respect for others, etc.
- To enable rational conflict-resolution.

Discipline is concerned with the following:

1 *The socialisation process* of individuals

It is important that children see stability, and develop stability, in social conduct. Respect for the rights of others, accountability for one's actions as they affect others, cooperation, self-direction, the balance between freedom and restriction, tolerance, and fair restriction are important social realities that can be usefully learned in a classroom. One of the essential skills of life is the ability to get on with others. We, as teachers, need to model that and teach it. We need to teach some students how to live with inner conflict and tension. Of course we don't always have a lot of time to do this but by the *manner* of discipline we choose to exercise, we can give students better options to take some control of their behaviour.

2 *Personal maturation*

Children need to develop responsibility, tolerance to the frustrations of learning and social relationships, a sense of individual effort, and fair pride in themselves and their potential.

3 *Moral development*

This is bound up with the socialisation process. Manners, standards, rules, boundaries of right and wrong are required to enable all members of a group to enjoy their rights. This assurance comes about when children know what the clear, fair rules are. Children care very much about justice and discipline will be better received when it is seen as just.

4 *Emotional security*

Discipline can provide that sense of security which enhances effective learning. We learn best when we feel good about ourselves which is why self-esteem is an important goal of discipline. Encouragement, positive reinforcement, helpful guiding, questioning and listening are the sorts of teacher behaviours that assist the achievement of this goal. Even when a teacher needs to be firm, assertive or angry, it is possible to discipline and still affirm these laudable goals.

Discipline is not merely an end in itself. It is a process to enable a student to come back on-task with their learning, allow self-control and give a sense of choice over their own behaviour. It is more than mere punishment. If we want to punish someone, let's call it by its right name; discipline is interested in longer term goals.

Discipline is needed in a classroom for the security and protection of the rights of all its members. It is necessary that a class run as smoothly as possible so that all students can benefit from the learning environment. Discipline technique is not the answer. Technique is only as good as the human relationship in which it occurs, and techniques are not value-free; if we believe that the dignity of the individual is important, we will eschew techniques like humiliation, sarcasm, ridicule, verbal aggression and put-downs.

Discipline occurs in a dynamic relationship where relationships are sometimes strained (at times seriously strained). 'Technique', without due consideration to the fact we are dealing with individuals, will often increase the conflict and further strain the relationship. I once saw a teacher drag a Year 4 student out of his class, pin him by his arm and repeatedly push him against the corridor wall. He yelled at this admittedly difficult child, 'I'm sick (thump) and tired (thump) of your stupid, idiotic, (thump) behaviour . . .'. Across the passage, my class went deathly silent.

I've seen teachers put children in rubbish bins and tell them they're 'rubbish'! I've witnessed countless acts of deprivation and had many more drawn to my attention. Surely no one who understands anything about child development and teaching can sanction *that* kind of teacher behaviour.

Protocols of discipline

Everyone has a view about discipline, everyone has been 'disciplined' at some point in their life. The case for discipline can be argued on a continuum, from punishment to maximum freedom. It means different things to different people. Even within the teaching community, within faculties of education, there can be wide variation of opinion. When we act to correct or address unacceptable behaviour in our students, we act on the basis of certain beliefs or philosophical assumptions. These assumptions may be stated or unstated but they are certainly there in our actions.

If we believe children *must* respect their teachers, our behaviour will be different when a student says 'This work sucks!', from that of a teacher who believes that we earn respect from our students by the kind of leadership we display. The teacher who believes that embarrassing students in front of their peers is okay, will act very differently from the teacher who believes in giving students their due rights, especially the due right of respectful treatment.

There are several major approaches taken to discipline in the published literature, for example: Gordon, 1974; Dreikurs, 1968; Dreikurs and Cassel, 1972; Glasser, 1965, 1969, 1986; Canter and Canter, 1976; Kounin, 1977; Ginott, 1972; Lewis and Lovegrove, 1985; Dobson, 1970, 1974.

These reflect the degree of intervention teachers believe they ought to exercise and how that intervention is practised. Behind each 'position' is a philosophy of human interaction. This book is not a discussion about those approaches or philosophical positions.

It is my argument, an argument that will be sustained through every practical example of discipline given, that there are central protocols of discipline that signal effective practice. These protocols are, in a sense, the 'bottom line' when it comes to *how* we discipline. They reflect the kind of discipline that endorses and maximises the due rights of all parties in the education stakes.

Of course there is a philosophical position behind these protocols. (No teacher's professional practice is free from values. Even if they are 'unstated' they can be seen in the characteristic practice.) I will need to leave my philosophical position undefended at this point and allow the protocols and practices to defend themselves, save to say that I hold the dignity of the individual and the fundamental nature of human rights to be pivotal in the practice of effective discipline (see Chapter 3). The protocols outlined here enable a value position to be held even if, for example, a behavioural approach (say behaviour modification) is used. As long as we embrace due rights, ensure the minimising of embarrassment, maintain respect, and give 'choices' we maintain the dignity of the individual. Even if we have to be highly assertive with a student or display anger, if we embrace these protocols we have done the best we can do in the human transaction.

There are teachers who will say that discipline depends on the circumstances or personality of the teacher or that any discipline is okay as long as it gets results (utility). Does it really matter what methods we use in discipline? Does that nippy little phrase, 'it all *depends*' mitigate the worst excesses of teacher behaviour?

Essential protocols of discipline

These protocols are the starting point for a positive teacher-student interaction that makes corrective discipline more likely to achieve its goal. It does not make such discipline *easier*. It makes the practice of discipline with dignity achievable.

1 Approach all discipline from the perspective of joint *rights, rules* and *responsibilities*. This means that the focus of discipline is not merely the teacher's relative power and authority (earned rather than imposed), but the joint rights of all members of the class. The most fundamental right of a classroom member is that of respect. These rights are not automatic. They relate to due responsibility, and fair and agreed rules (see Chapter 4). This 3Rs focus provides a positive and just basis for any corrective discipline. Teachers discuss, 'upfront', the basis of classroom life and how due rights will be enjoyed in the classroom. A clear understanding and practice of rights, rules and responsibilities is the basis of preventative discipline.

2 When engaged in corrective discipline, it is important to speak and

act in such a way as to *intentionally* minimise embarrassment, undue confrontation, and hostility. Sarcasm, put-downs, critical or caustic language, are unfortunate features of some teachers' disciplinary style. When verbal and non-verbal hostility (slamming hands on desks; snatching up objects such as pens, food, toys; waving a pointed finger; yelling; throwing objects; waving fists at students etc.) is an intentional feature of discipline style, it not only reveals a tragic professional weakness, it models a distinctly lousy approach to conflict-resolution. Witness the teacher who screams at the student with an outstretched, pointed hand, 'Don't you dare scream at me!'.

Not only does such behaviour fundamentally remove the right to reasonable treatment (dignity), it betrays a singular lack of skill. Emotional management is never easy but it is possible to speak firmly and assertively without unnecessary or intentional hostility, even when frustrated or angry. It is a basic maxim of respectful conflict-resolution that one person can assert their rights without trampling on the other party's rights (see Chapter 8).

3 Teachers ought to promote the use of appropriate choices in disciplining their students. It is an important feature of positive discipline that teachers seek to direct students to responsibility for their own behaviour. Teachers can do this by using language that emphasises the student's choice rather than the teacher's threat. Even when speaking to a child aside from the group, the teacher should seek to enable the child to:

- examine her behaviour and seek to act responsibly, and 'own' her behaviour
- move into a solution-oriented focus that puts primary responsibility on the student choosing the better options

When we give appropriate choices, we develop an approach to discipline that emphasises self-control rather than merely teacher control. 'I said move!' is different, in kind, from saying, 'David, you either work quietly here or I'll have to ask you to work over there'. Expressed as a choice, it gives the student an option, or options, within the rights/rules framework. Apart from students involved in physical fighting or unsafe behaviour, it is better practice to give a choice before imposing isolation, removal, logical consequences, or 'exit-ing' from the room. Our interaction style ought to try to help the student choose the better option or 'wear' the consequences of his or her actions.

4 In disciplining students, especially the annoying, frustrating, ones, it is important to discipline respectfully. It is easy when faced with difficult, testy, 'pain-in-the-neck' children to act from feelings of dislike. Conversely, it is easy to act fairly, kindly, reasonably, affirmatively towards those we like. This is natural. It can be observed in countless classrooms and often guides actual teacher behaviour. Some teachers rationalise their different treatment of students by saying, 'Why shouldn't I give Jason a hard time. He's a pain in the neck! He deserves it'. To discipline *respectfully*, however, we must concentrate not so much on our feelings or likes and dislikes but how we can discipline (guide, direct, motivate, lead) without submitting to rancour, sarcasm, the put-down, or embarrassment. Respect means employing verbal repertoire that models what we want, and expect, to see in our students.

Respectful discipline also means making an effort to notice (affirm, encourage or merely speak humanly as we pass by their desk) the normally 'painful' disruptive students when they show evidence of on-task behaviour. In this way, the student can begin to relate to the teacher at times other than when he's being disciplined. If the only time I visit Jason is when he is a 'pain' then I have a very limited and unproductive working relationship with him. To speak regularly, individually, with every student, takes a lot of effort — especially the effort of respect. It is worth it.

Ultimately respect is a relational exercise that seeks to:
- model dignity in treatment
- not hold grudges
- re-establish positive working relationships as soon as possible with the disruptor
- give the student a 'right-of-reply' when it is appropriate

Even when a child has to be removed from the room for significant disruptive behaviour, such an exit can be carried out respectfully without screaming, yelling or last-minute grandstanding.

5 Positive discipline is aware that we often get what we expect. 8D can be painful on Friday afternoon; 9E are no picnic either and a prep class, first term, is equivalent to digging the roads from 6 a.m. until sundown! Notwithstanding pay, conditions, and public perception,

if we expect 8D to be dreadful we may well find our expectations returning to us. The maxim 'children rise to the level of our expectations' is not a plea for Pollyannaism but a recognition that what we may be saying, believing and reflecting about our students has a 'boomerang' effect. Expectations can so easily be communicated unconsciously by the teacher. Children pick up fairly quickly what we expect of them from our actions. Better surely, to communicate expectations more reflectively, purposefully, even overtly in a positive way.

We have a difficult and at times demanding job. A judicious sense of humour is clearly needed (and appreciated by our clientele) to keep mind and sanity together. A smile, a joke, a laugh now and

Defuse conflicts

then says we are human. Even when we have to discipline, judicious humour can have a place. Certainly self-humour, not taking it all *too* seriously, is a useful antidote to the routine stress of the chalkface life. And there is plenty to laugh about in our profession.

6 Positive discipline follows up issues beyond the classroom. One of the marks of consistency is keeping track of on-going disruptions. If we say to a child we expect her to stay back after class (for detention, logical consequences, behaviour contract, or time-out) we must ensure it happens. It's so easy when the coffee break looms to ignore it or leave the issue to a senior teacher. Follow-up is important because ultimately, the disturbance of Trish in *my* room, while benefiting from senior personnel intervention, is still a problem to be resolved between Trish and *me*. We are the ones who have to work together in Room 17 three times a week, or all day if it's a primary setting.

Following up with consequences demonstrates concern as well as consistency, justice as well as accountability, and models the fact that we care and will not easily give up on them even when they are a 'pain'. At this level of discipline, though, we will often need support beyond the classroom.

7 Discipline and classroom management need collegiate and parental support. If we are struggling with a particular student, or a group or even the whole class, and our personal 'plans' are not working, it is in the interests of all to:
- seek help from a trusted colleague
- seek out senior teacher support
- call on parents to assist by mutual resolution

There is no virtue at all in isolation and pretending all is going well. A good deal of teacher stress arises because, as teachers, we tend not to communicate our feelings, problems and concerns. When we do, we often find how similar our problems are. A *whole school* approach to discipline will provide regular opportunities to share problems, identify needs and have a shared focus in exploring solutions and support. There are nearly always one or two teachers that we can share with.

These protocols are at once a guide, and, coupled with the skills discussed in Chapter 3, a means of 'testing' how positive our discipline stance is. In fact, where teachers seek to build such protocols into their

PREVENTATIVE DISCIPLINE

- clear rules established with the class
- clear expectations about work, tasks etc.
- attractive environment
- well planned room organisation (seating, movement capability, access to equipment, clearly labelled cupboards etc)
- setting up of time-out area in the room (age appropriate)
- adequate resources
- organising curriculum to cater for mixed abilities

CORRECTIVE DISCIPLINE

- what we say, how we say it, when a student is disruptive or off-task
- tactical ignoring of some behaviours
- casual or direct questioning
- simple directions or warnings
- defusing or re-directing potential conflict
- reminding or restating classroom rules
- giving simple choices
- taking students aside from the group
- using in-class time-out

SUPPORTIVE DISCIPLINE

- following up disruptions later when the initial 'heat' has subsided
- encouraging students wherever possible
- re-establishing working relationships with a 'disciplined' student
- developing contracts with a student
- developing and maintaining a climate of respect
- building a positive classroom 'tone'
- applying a team approach to solving discipline problems

Fig 1

consistent practice, they find their working relationship with students is more positive, less demanding and more productive for all concerned.

Summary

The concept and practice of discipline has suffered roundly from an over concentration on punishment. By contrast, discipline is better seen in terms of what it is trying to achieve, namely self-discipline, self-control and respect for others' rights.

Such 'discipline' requires a conscious effort by teachers to embrace a philosophy and practice of teaching and discipline that:
- emphasises due rights, responsibilities and rules
- minimises hostility and embarrassment in teacher-student interaction
- develops and maintains respectful treatment.
- develops a climate of choice
- provides due right of reply to the student
- follows up and follows through with disruptive students
- includes as wide a support base as is necessary to improve and enable a positive working and social environment for student and teacher alike.

Some questions to consider

- How can I be corrective, and appropriately confront disruptive behaviour, while giving due rights to myself and students alike?
- How do I define appropriate authority and status differences between teacher and student?
- How do I exercise that fundamental humanity that children of all generations have wanted in their teachers, yet still maintain a well ordered classroom that enhances learning?
- In disciplining students, how can I enable them to get back on-task as quickly as possible:
  — without long-winded discussion?
  — without intentional embarrassment?
  — with minimal audience attention?

- Am I conscious of the 'steps' I use in disciplining children? What are they?
- If someone were to observe my characteristic discipline style, what sort of things would they note?
- What is my school's working definition of discipline?
- Do I consciously discipline students with particular *goals* in mind?
- What are these goals?
- In what way do I modify my behaviour (discipline behaviour) to make the reaching of those goals (say self-control) a possibility?
- What sort of things can I *say* (for example) that are likely to lead a student to self-control?
- What are the protocols by which I discipline? How do they relate to the protocols discussed here?
- What support structures or processes do we have in our school for persistent, on-going, disruptive students? Who can I call on?

What approaches to classroom discipline enable these goals to, in any way, be realised? Before answering this question it will be necessary to look at the effect of teaching styles on disruptive behaviour and the effect of disruptive behaviour on teaching styles.

CHAPTER 2

Disruptive behaviour and teacher style

*Somewhat on the tabasco side
as a young man . . .
Carry on Jeeves,*
P. G. Wodehouse

Disruptive behaviour

Every classroom has its share of disruptions. Of course it may only be low-level disruption such as calling out, not having equipment, or uniform misdemeanours. This will be a long way from some schools where seldom are heard the respectful and dulcet words of 'please Sir', or 'yes Miss'. More likely, we'll hear, 'This work sucks!', 'Gees this is boring — fair dinkum!', and 'You can't make me!'. Add to this aggressive sulking, insolence, swearing, defiance, and one can see why teaching is often rated as a highly stressful profession.

The causes of disruption

Children disrupt for a number of reasons: boredom, immaturity, inability to master the curriculum, low tolerance to frustration, or an emotionally disturbed home situation. These days we are seeing more and more children in classrooms whose home environment is seriously affecting their ability to cope in a formal social setting like school. If

23

Johnny's father is unemployed, belts him regularly, is an alcoholic and often 'shoots through'; if mum has five other children under 15, if there is regular screaming, shouting and put-downs at home, this will have an effect on Johnny's social behaviour at school. If he comes to school with significant inner conflict he can hardly comprehend, and then meets an intransigent, petty teacher whose verbal repertoire is limited to hostile and embarrassing interaction, there is already a context for disruption. This is a particularly bleak picture, but variations of this situation will be found in many schools.

Johnny comes to school late (yet again) and meets Mr D. at 9.20 a.m. for maths. 'Listen,' says the teacher, 'I'm sick and tired of you coming late to my class. Where's your late pass? I suppose you haven't got one again. What's your excuse this time?'. Of course, by this time, the whole class is focused on these two (it's much more interesting than maths). Johnny is feeling 'screwed up' inside. Already that morning, his mum has screamed at him about his mess in the bedroom, he's had a lousy breakfast, he's fought with his younger brother. He had to run to the chemist at 9.00 a.m. to get some pain killers for mum who had another of her headaches. He reacts angrily to Mr D. 'Don't shit me — you're always picking on me. What about the other kids who are late?'. He throws his bag on the floor. Mr D. yells back, 'Who the hell do you think you are speaking to me like that — get out, go on, get out now!'. Johnny turns and when he is three metres away, slyly pokes his finger up at Mr D.

Who won? Was it worth it? Johnny doesn't have the social skills to say, when he's angry, 'Excuse me, I'm late for a good reason. I do wish you wouldn't speak to me like that'. The situation could have been handled differently and the level of the disruption would have been changed by the approach used. Further, how is Johnny going to fit into a class where the teacher has no interest in the problems that contribute to his poor performance? How is Johnny going to sit there and lap up square-root tables when all he's thinking about is home problems? Some teachers argue that kids like Johnny shouldn't be at school. Where should they be? At home? Of course we have little or no control over our students' home environment. Some students' backgrounds are pitiful, even tragic. We can rarely step in and modify that but we can modify the environment that we have relative control over.

There are many students like Johnny attending our schools and they don't all go to the local 'tech'. St Smiggins private girls school has its fair share of emotionally stretched students too. Defiance, persistent tantrums, even swearing are not the behavioural prerogative of the so-called disadvantaged schools.

Attention and audience

Whatever the precipitate causes of disruption, when a student comes into a group she immediately seeks to find some sort of place, to belong in some way to 'the classroom'. One of the central needs a person has is to be noticed: to be attended to, to have contact with others. Most students fulfil this need in socially acceptable ways: they put their hands up, they ask for equipment instead of snatching, they wait their turn, they gain attention from the production of acceptable work, they participate cooperatively — they 'belong'. Their teachers and peers reinforce this acceptable mode of attention seeking.

> Mary gets her attention differently. If she is asked to 'settle down', she pouts and tosses her head around like an irate horse. It works. Her teacher comments, 'Look, I asked you to be quiet, not to snort like a horse! What's wrong with you?'. Mary answers back. 'Others are talking as well, why d'you have to pick on me?'. 'I am not picking on you. I am telling you to be quiet or you can move out of that seat now!'.

What a lot of words. What a lot of attention. Mary got what she wanted. Procrastination is something she learned in the supermarket trolley: the attention-seeking whine, the sulky 'notice-me' pout, the extended 'come-over-and-pity-me' sulking routine.

The attention seeker

Primary and secondary behaviour

Another way of looking at attention-seeking behaviour is to view the behaviour cycle as progressive: from the primary disruption through to secondary attention-seeking behaviours.

Cameron has secretly brought his expensive ultra-light *Walkman* into class and hidden the cassette deck in his bag by his feet. The teacher notices his nodding, hears the faint music, and 'twigs'. She asks him to take the *Walkman* off; she addresses the primary behaviour. Now Cameron (even though he's in year 10 at a private school) does not say, 'Right Miss. I'll take it off straight away. Thanks for pointing it out'. Cameron employs typical secondary behaviours. He grunts, sighs (to increase the feeling of, 'notice how annoyed I am!') and says, 'Gee, Miss Davies lets me play it in art — fair dinkum' (more sighs). His secondary behaviour is designed to remove the responsibility for his primary behaviour (having a *Walkman* on in class — or whatever).

The problem with secondary behaviour is that it is so easy to get caught up with it, speak to it, and never really direct ownership to the real issue. 'Cameron, this is not Miss Davies' class. Now why have you got it on?' 'Gee Miss, I can still work with it on! I'm even quieter with it on aren't I Harry?' (here he turns to his mate for extra back up). And so it can go on. Procrastination, more secondary dialogue; avoidance of behaviour ownership. It can happen in almost any discipline trans-action — if we let it.

Secondary behaviours include sighing, pouting, sulking, a range of 'tantrumming' behaviours, and eyes rolled to the ceiling. They are employed purposefully, or are the result of frustration, but they will almost certainly cause:
- over-attendance to the student (and 'over-servicing')
- avoidance of responsibility for the real issue at stake; their primary behaviour (out of seat, calling out, having a comic on the desk etc.)
- a feeling of guilt in the teacher as if they shouldn't even be address-ing the student about this behaviour. (This is where pouting, sighing, shoulder-shrugging, kicking-the-chair-in-passing are used for great effect as secondary behaviour — 'I'll make you feel sorry!').

This teacher is well meaning, but, through over attention to Cameron's antics, her behaviour reinforces the very thing she is trying to eliminate. Even if the child does stop disrupting (having got his dose of attention), it is likely he will employ similar behaviour next time he's after attention. Some children make a career of it! It's easy to fall into the trap of just reacting to such attention seeking because we feel frustrated, angry, or anxious. What we often end up doing is just what the child wants — 'Notice me!', 'Attend to me when I want attention!'.

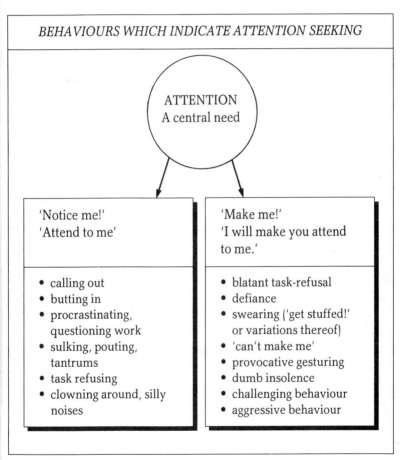

Fig 2

Attention-seeking children, in a group, find it easy to get teachers into an indecisive mode when they become embroiled in long and fruitless discussions or pleadings, in front of the class.

Three girls are chatting about their favourite television show during maths. 'Girls, girls, really it's too loud.' 'We're only talking Miss. We're not doing anything wrong!' comes the reply. 'But I can't teach with that noise can I?' 'You're always picking on us,' says a spokesperson for the trio. 'Oh, be fair, I am not. All I ask is for a little quiet.' 'But you do pick on us Miss,' says another.

And so it goes on. All work has stopped and the teacher is still 'playing it by ear' and over attending to the semaphore of 'notice me'. If we have to go back several times, for example, to the 'task-refuser' to see even a few sentences of work completed we are falling into the trap of over-attention: 'How can I keep my teacher busy with me?'. The repeated question, 'What do we have to do again Miss?' may elicit our anger or pleading but it gives the child a sense of belonging. 'I'm noticed, I'm attended to.'

Our frustration with such children

Teachers will note how frustrated they get with children when they call out, make silly noises, tap and the like. This is both a problem and a clue for what we can do when dealing with such behaviour. Because we are frustrated by the child's purpose ('Attend to me, spend time on me.') it is easy to act in accord with the child's goal. In fact, the child may have learned how to trigger such attention from adults even if such attention is anger. 'Gee I can get him angry just by calling out!' 'I can make him come over to me by pleading.' It is essential in dealing with such behaviours to use our frustrations and internal dialogue to marshal appropriate discipline responses.

Power seeking is another form of attention seeking. The power-seeking child is out to 'belong' by using challenging behaviour: 'Can't make me', 'Not gonna do this work', 'This work is boring', 'I hate you'. When such a child throws out a challenge, he is inviting the teacher to a contest. His belief may register as 'I belong when I'm as powerful or more powerful than the teacher' or 'I must win, she must lose'.

When the teacher uses more force, 'You'll do this work or else!', she easily endorses the child's purposeful behaviour. There is also the added problem that there is a sense in which a teacher cannot make a child do any work. She can invite, ask, direct, apply consequences but cannot merely make. We can, of course, make a small child move from one place to another by physically 'helping' him. We can hardly do that with a robust Year 7 student who responds by saying, 'No, I'm not gonna move and you can't make me'. What are we going to do? Drag him out? Fight him? There are much more effective ways of dealing with power-seeking students than merely giving them the contest they want.

Power-seeking children 'feed' off force which is why it makes good sense not to use such a reaction. The teacher's response (rather than reaction) will determine and reinforce a child's behaviour as much as anything else. 'Notice me' and 'make me' are the two key expressions of disruptive behaviour.

The importance of disruptive patterns

If we are aware that some children's misbehaviour is *purposeful* in seeking attention or an exchange of power, we can better plan how to manage disruptions that arise from their behaviour. If a child is actively seeking attention in off-task, clownish, annoying ways, it is counter-productive to let him achieve such a goal at the expense of our frustration: 'I won't tell you again!', 'Just sit down will you!'. If we are aware of the behaviour that signals attention seeking, we need to be consciously prepared not to over-attend or fall into power plays. Our behaviour affects the level and degree of disruption as much as the disruption itself does. If Johnny is purposefully baiting the teacher with 'This work sucks', it is clear, an angry retort from the teacher will only reinforce such behaviour. This child may never have successfully learned cooperative ways to belong but he gets an 'A' for being a 'pain'. We give the marks! Ultimately, we have to decide how we will deal with the disruptive behaviour such children utilise to gain teacher or peer attention.

Effective discipline approaches will seek to minimise a child's inappropriate ways of belonging through attention-seeking and power-play and maximise appropriate ways to belong. The way we do this will depend on our teaching style and what skills we bring to bear. Such skills need to be developed in a planned and purposeful way. The combination rarely occurs accidentally.

Styles of teaching

Teaching style significantly affects classroom climate. Any visitor to a classroom could, after several visits, pinpoint a teacher's style; harsh, decisive, autocrat, martinet, wimp . . .

In the late 1930s Kurt Lewin experimented with teacher style and classroom leadership and observed and documented three basic approaches: the autocratic; the *laissez-faire*; the democratic (Lewin, Lippitt and White, 1939; Lewin, 1948). He hypothesised that all teachers fit somewhere along a continuum embracing these positions.

The autocrat basically tells children what to do, with most children being compliant (not necessarily happy, but compliant). This approach relies on overt power and constant teacher control. The trouble with the autocratic teacher is that all is 'under control' (no noise and heads down) but only when the 'boss' is there. In extreme cases of autocratic control, the vertical tyranny of the adult is often accompanied by rough or unthinking verbal treatment.

The *laissez-faire* teacher lets the children do virtually what they want. There are no effective rules, guidelines or directions. There are many classes where this occurs, that experience the lateral tyranny of the peer group. The result can be chaos.

The democratic leader tends to be very clear in direction and goals, involving the children wherever possible. Children are challenged, spoken to, assisted in such a way that independence, self-motivation and self-control are the likely outcomes. The democratic leader seeks to win cooperation rather than demand compliance, is prepared to discuss and assist in a child's own decision-making even when the child is being 'disciplined' (corrected, challenged or directed about off-task or disruptive behaviour).

Another way of looking at Lewin's categories is to assess the manner in which the teacher seeks to gain compliance from students when they are disruptive.

Hoping for compliance: the indecisive teacher

'I've got to teach number and line today — how can I do it?' Ms A. is in her second week at Styx Rd, a large post-primary school in an area of low socio-economic status. This was not the school of her choice.

Because she is new to the school she has been given four periods of maths with 8E in a portable classroom! (This is an unfortunate practice in some schools where the last teacher in gets the worst classes and classrooms. It says a lot about teacher welfare.) The portable is a 1970s reject, has lousy seats and desks, cupboards that don't open properly and windows that jam.

8E are filing in as Ms A. seeks to start a new day, another lesson. She is nervous. She knows what she wants to do in the lesson but is uncertain about how to handle the inevitable disruptions. With the best of intentions, she wants these students to like her. It is quite noisy at the beginning of the lesson; that's normal. Her eyes dart around the room. Several times she says, 'Shh please,' or 'Settle down now'. One boy calls out, 'Miss, can I go to the toilet?' and grins. The question races through her head, 'What will I do?'. 'Oh Craig, can't you wait please? I'm trying to start the lesson'. 'Gees Miss, (grin) I didn't get a chance before. I'm bustin'. He looks around and grins again. She wants to keep the peace, she doesn't want to lose face, she doesn't want to be aggressive but is equally unsure about how to assert her due rights. 'Craig, can't you wait till I've finished this explanation?' Ms A's body language communicates defeat. She is hoping (against hope) for compliance. Craig folds his arms and, in mock frustration, sticks his legs out: 'humph!'.

Bravely Ms A. soldiers on with the up-front teaching. Drawing a train line across the board, she proceeds to draw a train on the tracks. She puts a zero on the tracks and then the negative and positive numbers on either sides. Each time she faces the board the students start talking. She is getting more and more concerned and edgy. As she completes the drawing she begins to explain the theory of negative numbers. The class wag notices she hasn't drawn any wheels on the train and leaning back in his chair calls out, 'Hey Miss, can't you draw wheels on a train or something?'. She turns and says, 'Who said that, come on who said it? Be fair. What does it matter that I left the wheels off? Was it you who said that Richard?'. 'Me (stupefied look) Miss? Me? Why do you always pick on me?' 'I don't Richard, but why do you have to be rude?' And so it goes on.

Ms A. finally manages to write up some problems on the board, answers several students who call out and then sets them to work. During the on-task phase of the lesson, Maria calls out. 'Miss, can you come here? I need your help.' She is already working with Richard who displays no interest in number lines. She walks across to Maria and says, 'Maria, please (plead), can't you see I'm trying to work with Richard?'. At this juncture Richard calls out, 'Yeah Maria, can't you wait your turn?'. She turns back to Richard, 'Please Richard *I'm* talking to Maria not you!'. She's starting to get very frustrated. 'Gees, I was only asking a question' says Maria who pouts and folds her arms. 'Well, can you wait please?' 'Doesn't matter now' comes the reply as Maria again pouts at her teacher.

'Why did I choose teaching?' thinks Ms A., as she goes back to Richard. Paul gets out of his seat to wander over to his mate Dimi. She can see and hear that they are way off-task. Her shoulders slump, a signal of her herculean task. Not another problem. 'Paul, why are you out of your seat?' 'I'm only asking Dimi for a pencil, Miss.' 'But you've been talking Paul, I heard you. I'm trying to teach over here.' 'Fair dinkum! Other people get out of their seats and you don't tell them off.' (Now it's Paul's turn to pout.) 'Now be fair, Paul. I wasn't picking on you. I only wanted to know why you were out of your seat (sigh, sigh).' Dimi chips into the fray now. The rest of the class are watching. 'Yes you do Miss, you do pick on Paul!' She turns; now she *is* frustrated. 'Look Dimi, all I asked was a civil question. Now be reasonable . . .'

Apparently Ms A. is unaware that each time she opens her mouth she reinforces these attention seekers by falling for their procrastination. When pushed to the limit with children like Paul or Richard she will say things like, 'Do I have to get angry with you Paul?'. Inside, Paul will say 'Yes — of course you do!'. In many of the discipline transactions Ms A. is engaged in, she never really believes the student will be compliant. She hopes they will, but her behaviour, verbal and non-verbal, clearly signals a lack of assertion, uncertainty and often indecision.

It doesn't help to simply label her an ineffective teacher when her training has not prepared her for the type of discipline problems she encounters. Her heart is in the right place. She just is not sure *what* to do. She plans well for her lessons but not for the things she needs to say and do when students are disruptive. She plays it 'by ear'; ever a dangerous stance in teaching especially with 8E.

Indecisive teachers are characterised by:
- a non-assertive stance (passivity)
- an overly discursive means of settling disruption especially when concentrating on secondary behaviours
- the belief that it is wrong to impose their will on students and the tendency to over-compensate for this by a tone of voice and body language that indicates vacillation

- the belief that it is wrong to use force in words or action, but when pushed to the limit will get angry and yell and then later feel guilty about this behaviour
- their fear of failure
- the tendency to allow the student to decide the agenda in a discipline transaction
- their hope for compliance based on the belief that good will and friendliness is enough (It isn't.)

Demanding compliance: the overly authoritarian or demanding teacher

In his Year 6 class Mr B. has a reputation for toughness. He's not one to mince words. At the beginning of the lesson Mustapah is silly enough to call out twice. Mr B. sits on this 'rubbish' quickly. 'Listen, I'm not going to tell you again. Don't call out! You got that?' Mustapah says, 'Yes!'.

While he is explaining the lesson material, two students are talking up the back. He calls out to them, 'You, yes you two! Don't pretend you didn't hear me. You're not deaf are you? Stop talking — now'. Mission accomplished. He carries on. The two at the back are silly enough to try to whisper. It's time for a scene. He walks over and all eyes focus on him and the two students. 'Listen, didn't I just tell you to be quiet? If you can't shut-up now, then you can stay in and write out why you have the right to interrupt my lesson.' 'Yes Mr B.!' He has 'won'.

There is little calling out in his class but when there is, he will remind them, 'Don't call out in my class. I'm sick and tired of telling you'. If anyone dares make a smart alec comment or butt in, he'll probably say, 'Listen smart alec, who's running this class? You or me?'. He will often bear down on a student using his size to intimidate. As he's walking round the room he can be heard saying things like, 'Look, I'm not going to tell you again. I've told you how to do this before, surely you can understand it by now!'.

Such teachers may disguise churlish or petty behaviour as 'discipline'. Kylie is wearing rather large earrings. In seeking to 'discipline' her Mr B. goes up and says, 'What do you think these are?', in a rather loud voice. Kylie is one of those students prepared to stand up for her rights. 'Just my earrings.' 'You know they're not regulation, now get them off — now!' Kylie is prepared to stand her ground. 'There's nothing wrong with them — Miss D. said they were okay.' 'Listen, I don't care what Miss D. said, she's not your teacher, I am! Get them off.' Kylie is determined. 'No, they're all right.' It's a power struggle. Mr B. cannot afford to lose face, he's in too deep by now. 'Right, get out now. Go to the principal. Go on — move!' Kylie sullenly leaves the class jangling her earrings as she goes. Who has won?

Most of the time, during the on-task phase of the lesson, Mr B. is at his desk. Now and then he'll move out to help a student. If he hears giggling or talking he'll tend to be over-corrective. 'You, yes *you*. Got a private joke have you?'.

I've heard teachers call girls 'sluts', 'cheap' or make snide remarks about a student's home background. Embarrassment and humiliation are among the worst forms of teacher discipline and, as research shows (Lewis and Lovegrove, 1985), among the most disliked of teacher behaviours. Jacob Kounin (1977) coined the term 'ripple effect' to describe what happens when the impact of a teacher's discipline on one student 'ripples' out to others. When Mr B. argues with Kylie, using straight humiliation, his 'discipline' has an effect on the other students. Some sit up straight, some are frightened or concerned, others are clearly off-task, most are angry inside at his unjust treatment. One of the sad features of the overly demanding teacher is their lack of respect and basic humanity as they insist on the power-status relationship.

I have seen petty, demanding teachers send Year 7 students to the back of the room with the direction, 'Right, if you're not going to listen, you can move to the back of the class. Go on! You're not part of my class! Now stand and face the wall'. What amazes me is how many students still put up with this kind of rubbish.

I've seen teachers throw books in the bin, slam their hands on desks or the metre ruler across the desk to intimidate a child or create the impression of power. The defensive stance often sees the teacher defining the transaction as *me* and *them* (the enemy) and win or lose as the nature of resolution. Such teachers get angry quickly. Sometimes the anger may not even be connected with the child's behaviour but arise from the demanding beliefs that the teacher must win in all discipline transactions and that students should obey and respect their teachers. Further, a good teacher must be able to control his class at all times. He is a failure if he doesn't or can't. The hidden agenda of these beliefs is the degree to which they demand from reality that which reality (8D, 6A, the testy little preps) may not easily care to conform to.

'Look he *should* just listen and that's that! I've set the work — he should do it!' 'But he doesn't listen does he?' 'But he should dammit!' But the reality is he doesn't (yet). How does your 'belief' in any way help your emotional coping or increase the likelihood of student compliance?

If I say, 'He *must* not swear. Children *should* not swear.', I will feel differently and act differently than if I say, 'I dislike, even strongly dislike, swearing but it is *not* the end of the world. I can cope. It is only awful if I allow the awfulness to overwhelm me'. This does not mean we excuse swearing, it does mean our working beliefs are realistic enough to recognise reality and respond appropriately even thoughtfully. Social reality (those students!) has no obligation to conform to our demands.

Of course, a *demanding* belief, as distinct from a flexible and more realistic belief, creates as much stress as the disruptive situation itself. When a student fails to respond to the threat, the demand, or the power stance, then the belief creates stressful emotions of intense frustration or anger. It's a short step to then get into easy blaming. 'It's his fault, that little creep; he made me so angry when he refused to do the work. Cocky little bugger!' It's almost impossible to embrace this style of discipline and still maintain a *rights* focus in teaching.

Teachers who are highly demanding are often hostile and overly critical, rude, or in some cases plain aggressive. They make little or no effort to manage their own frustration, apparently not caring about the effect of their behaviour on others. Some are even proud of such a stance. The strap may have been abolished but the power of the tongue to damage should never be underestimated. An easy option is to explain away teacher style in terms of personality. While it is obvious that we differ in personality, we have a professional duty to eschew the reactive styles of discipline not because they don't work but simply because of their in-built capacity to disenfranchise the due rights of students.

There are degrees of demandingness of course, but these are the characteristics of the authoritarian demanding teacher:

- demands compliance (I must have it.)
- has demanding beliefs about their role and student behaviour, rather than preferential or flexible beliefs ('I must win.' rather than 'It's preferable to resolve this with minimal heat.')
- tells rather than asks or directs
- threatens rather than gives choices
- will resort to humiliation, sarcasm, even verbal aggression
- minimises or disenfranchises students' rights
- uses a sharp, even caustic tone of voice
- employs an unreflective, unplanned verbal repertoire in discipline: 'If I have to tell you one more time . . .' 'I'm sick and tired of telling you.' 'You dummy!' 'What's wrong with you?' 'I've told you a thousand times!' 'Can't you get it by now? Are you thick or what?'
- makes snide comments such as: 'What kind of home do you come from?' 'Were you brought up or dragged up?' 'Don't they teach you any manners at home?' 'Wipe that smile off your face!'

Expecting compliance: the decisive teacher

Ms C. is a second year teacher at a secondary school. It's term one, week four. The students are still testing her out somewhat.

In the first week she developed clear rules for each of her classes, she explained the need for rules (to protect rights) and involved the students in the process of formulating them. In her Year 7 class, she has the rules written up on large cards displayed on one wall. Like the previous two teachers she faces a common range of disruptions from calling out, butting in, out-of-seat behaviour through to teacher baiting and defiance. However, unlike Ms A. and Mr B. she has planned her discipline repertoire ahead of time. She knows, all too well, the disruptions which are, in a sense, inevitable and has developed a 'discipline plan' in concert with her lesson plan.

Her lesson on multiculturalism will include a class discussion, small group work and a written exercise. She settles the class down by consciously encouraging the quieter members, not in an obsequious way, but simply with, 'Thanks for settling down — good on you,' as she looks in their direction. Finally only a few are still talking. 'Okay, time to start.' This arouses their attention. The class is looking 'up front'. She welcomes the class with a 'good morning everyone' and explains carefully what they will be doing that lesson. She regularly uses phrases like 'we will', 'our class', 'our assignments'. This is not accidental. She believes that each class is a community and this affects the way she relates to them.

During the class discussion on multiculturalism there are several disruptions. Michael, the class clown, can be seen building up his breath for a burp. Ms C. too can see it out of the corner of her eye. He lets out a loud, attention-seeking burp and looks around grinning. Without even looking in his direction the teacher extends her hand, palm open, and says, as if in passing, 'Best thing you've said all day'. This is followed up by a welcome titter of laughter. Ms C. has not been embarrassing; she has used defusion or repartee. This tasty little *bon mot*, delivered quickly, enables her to press on without giving Michael any *undue* attention which is, after all, what he is after.

The inevitable calling out is prefaced by a general rule reminder. 'Okay you all know the rule for communication. Let's use it thanks.' Ms C. then quickly looks for a hand up to reinforce the rule. If a student is persistent in calling out she will ignore, give a brief, clear reminder of the rule, or simply direct the student to act fairly. 'Richard you know the rule for communication, use it thanks', or 'If you want to ask a question put your hand up. Good on you'. The little phrase, 'Good on you,' is used to communicate, 'I know you'll comply. I expect you'll comply'. She speaks firmly, with eye contact, *expecting compliance*. Most times, a simple direction or rule reminder is enough. She doesn't preach or over attend but is economical with her words. She has learned it is important to be:

- brief (minimal attention)
- clear
- rule-focused
- calm but expectant
- assertive where the situation requires it

When Jason starts dropping his book she ignores it for a while. When it doesn't stop she addresses him. 'Jason I'm trying to teach. I can't teach with that noise. Ta.' That's all. No big deal. Just a hand extended and then very quickly she focuses on on-task students to bring attention back to the lesson.

Maria comes in late for the third time in two weeks. Ms C. knows there are some home problems. Maria slams the door, throws her bag down. The class, naturally, turn to check this out. Ms C. walks over. Maria quickly blurts out, 'The bloody bus was late, I tried to get away early!'. Ms C. doesn't waste time arguing about the veracity of the story or the 'bad' language. 'Look, I can see you're uptight. Grab a seat, I'll be with you in a sec.' Later in the lesson she'll have a quiet word with Maria about a late pass.

There are several more calling out episodes. Most she plainly ignores, a couple of persistent ones she gives brief directions to. Winding up the class discussion she explains the set written activity and sends them off in groups. Nicko comes up immediately, as the class reorganises itself and says, 'Miss, I haven't got a pen!'. 'What are you going to do then Nicko?' 'I can go to my locker Miss! Won't take a minute (grin, grin)!'. Is he after a free five minutes? 'Well, you know the routine Nicko. You can borrow from a mate or borrow one of mine.' 'But Miss, it won't take a minute!' 'Your choice Nicko.' 'Gees! It's not fair.' He walks off sulkily. She ignores him, having already moved off *expecting* compliance. She makes no comment about his sulky behaviour. She doesn't feed his procrastination. She leaves him with a clear, simple, choice.

Ms C. would like to sit down and have a break but she realises the importance of moving around the room to direct, encourage, assist, redirect, correct and support her students. She will muster as much enthusiasm and humanity as she is able. At all times she seeks to model respect even with those few students she doesn't actually like. Walking past Damien she sees him (out of the corner of her eye) leaning back provocatively on his chair. She could simply direct him, 'Sitting thanks Damien.' or remind him of the rule, but has decided to *tactically* ignore him. She uses a lot of tactical ignoring for low-level attention seeking. Because she has that crucial teacher skill of being able to notice what students are doing without making direct eye contact, she is able to see *when* Damien stops leaning back on his chair. She then walks over and casually asks him, 'How's it going then?'. In other words, she looks for as much on-task behaviour as possible and *then* visits the student to encourage them.

If she wants to see a student's work she doesn't snatch it, poke at it, or even just pull it towards her. She asks politely, 'Can I have a look at your work?' or, 'Where are you up to?' or, 'Having trouble, need a hand?'. She doesn't invade a student's 'body space' or 'territory', but respectfully asks them to turn the book, or work, so they can both see it. If she meets a rare student who says, 'No, you can't see it', she simply says 'Okay, when you're ready', and moves off. She doesn't over-attend to such students who often use tactics like this as a form of attention seeking, rather like the child who says 'I'm dumb!' wanting the teacher to then say, 'Oh don't say that, of course you're not'.

As the teacher continues moving around the room, Jason, keen to get her help, employs his get-the-teacher-here-quick routine. 'Miss, hey Miss!' He calls out across the room as the teacher is assisting two other students. Ms C. decides to rigorously ignore the behaviour. Why should she go over to Jason or ask him to wait? If she does either she may easily be saying to Jason 'Your calling out will be noticed and attended to any time you try it on'. She decides to tactically ignore Jason. She neither looks in his direction (though she can see him out of the corner of her eye) or comments on his behaviour; she continues working with the other two students.

Jason calls out again. 'Miss, come on Miss. I need your help!' The teacher decisively continues the tactical ignoring. She moves off to work with another student. Coming up to Boris, she says, 'How's it going then Boris?'. As she's talking to Boris, Jason starts clicking his fingers and sighing. 'Gees, Miss, what's wrong? I only want to ask a question.' By tactically ignoring Jason, the teacher is seeking to send a message saying, 'Yes *when* you are on-task, quiet, I'll come over.' or 'When you put up your hand without calling out then, yes, I'll come over. I am not at your instant beck and call'. The teacher seeks to communicate all this by her tactical presence. Students quickly pick up this silent, but decisive, semaphore.

Jason sulks for a while. The teacher keeps on doing the rounds. She notices, in passing, that Jason is now writing. She goes up to him and casually asks, 'Can I have a look at your work?' and reaches down to turn the exercise book so she can view his work. Jason moans, 'Why didn't you answer me before?'. Instead of getting into a debate with Jason, she simply, quietly, reminds him of the rule. 'When you put up your hand and wait, then I'll come over.' She then quickly directs Jason back to the written work.

If this calling out routine had occurred in a primary setting with prep to Year 3 students, the teacher may have said firmly, 'Jason *when* you can put your hand up and wait, then I'll come over and help', and *then* tactically ignored any subsequent calling out.

Ms C. is also conscious of a contingency plan for Jason's calling out. If tactical ignoring and positive reinforcement is ineffective, she will give a firm rule reminder or restatement or a clear, simple direction. 'Jason, if you want to ask a question, use the rule please.'

As she continues her rounds she sees Sally and Marisa teasing Marcia about her boyfriend. The noise level rises quickly and can't be ignored. Seeing Marcia crying, she calls across firmly, decisively, to the other two. 'Sally, Marisa, I'll see you over here *now*.' She pauses, establishing eye contact and extending her hand as if directing them to the rear of the room. '*Now*, thank you.' The teasers sullenly move off down the back of the class, the rest of the students either resume work, watch, or whisper.

The teacher has taken the students aside to minimise any embarrassment to Marcia, but also to reduce blame shifting and hostility with the teasers! Ms C. walks to the back of the room and asks the question, 'What's going on? You can see she's upset'. She uses an approach that puts responsibility quickly on them by asking 'What are you going to do about your behaviour?'. She doesn't have time for the full story but simply asks the question firmly to engage responsibility now. By taking the students aside, she can afford to be more discursive.

Later in the lesson, Michael wanders out of his seat to talk with Alex. The two of them are talking quite loudly. She finishes what she is saying to Maria (the student who came in late) and decides the Michael/Alex noise incident can't be tactically ignored. Walking past a gum chewer, she merely indicates with her hand to the mouth 'In the bin thanks'. She winks at Paul who drags himself off to spit his chewy into the bin. As she comes over to Alex and Michael she establishes eye contact by firmly saying, 'Michael, what are you doing?'. Most students say 'Nothing!'. Michael, however, is a bit of a 'hot-shot'. 'What's it look like I'm doing?' She doesn't take his bait. She focuses in on his behaviour. 'It looks like you're out of your seat and talking loudly to Alex.' 'I was just getting a rubber — fair dinkum!' Again, she doesn't take the bait, she merely asks, 'What should you be doing?'. 'I told you I was just getting my rubber.' Rather than argue, she simply repeats the question, 'What should you be doing?'. She knows all too well the fruitless, pointless, procrastination game. She asserts by her question, the clear implication of responsible behaviour, expecting (not demanding) compliance. Michael gets up to move off. The moment he moves, she walks away as if to say, 'I knew you'd cooperate, I'm not going to stay around to push you!'. He could, of course, refuse to move. I have had many students say, 'No, you can't make me.' Like Ms C. I usually say, 'That's all right — it's your choice. If you don't move now, I'll have to ask you to stay back and explain why later'. Most students do move.

This is an important stance to take with older students. If we merely stand with folded arms and foot tapping, we communicate that we believe they'll only move, obey or respond because we are there. With younger students, kindergarten to Year 2, we may need to stay close, establish eye contact, repeat the rule if necessary. But, again, the moment they go, move off to work with other students.

When he gets back to his seat Michael sulks and folds his arms. Now and then he grunts and scrapes his chair on the floor. She ignores this regressive sulky behaviour. In fact, she will ignore it until he picks up his pen again. She knows that if she goes back to either coerce or plead or 'make' him work, she is giving attention at the wrong time.

Ms C. combines several approaches in a dynamic way. At one moment a simple direction, another time a rule restatement. She may distract or divert a potential disruption by moving alongside a student, asking a question, or giving a task. If behaviour becomes disruptive beyond a simple direction, warning or question, she will then give a simple choice or 'take' the student aside. It is not easy. She has to think ahead to ensure that her behaviour is appropriate for the disruption. For example, when Bill drops his pencil case and swears, she will deal with it differently than when Bill swore at her in one of his temper tantrums.

Maybe it would be easier to shout, yell, intimidate, be sarcastic, cruel or immature towards her students but she realises that giving in to mood, chance or circumstance creates a bad learning environment and models the very thing she is trying to work against. There are no short cuts to good discipline.

Ms C. also works hard at establishing good working relationships with her students. It is easy to miss the significance of this. If we only ever visit the difficult students to 'discipline' them, then the relationship becomes lopsided. We need to be scanning the room to pick up those times when a student *is* on-task. In doing this, we encourage the student to build on small successes and consolidate those appropriate behaviours.

Like the other two teachers (authoritarian/demanding and indecisive/*laissez-faire*) Ms C. still gets frustrated and angry from time to time but she has learned to utilise those emotions to her advantage. She doesn't deny them or bottle them up inside but uses the emotions to respond. She has learned to recognise how the emotion comes and to then quickly reassess the threat as she perceives it and respond appropriately.

Dean, the class 'toughie', swore at her on the second day. She communicated her anger assertively. 'Dean, I don't speak to you like that, I don't expect you to speak to me like that!'. She was tense, but controlled. There was anger in her voice. Later, at the end of the lesson, she called him over to discuss his behaviour and obtained the apology she would not have got if she had demanded it, at the time of the outburst.

Uncontrolled, irrational anger ('You idiot, you dummy you!' 'I'm sick and tired of your stupid, idiotic behaviour — get out!') or internalised, repressed anger is damaging to both health and personal relationships. We can't eliminate the emotions of frustration and anger but we can learn to utilise them. We can only do this if we plan the discipline environment rather than react to disruptions as they arise.

Decisive discipline is marked by these characteristics:

- a focus on the due rights of all
- an assertive stance

    (Assertion is distinguished between aggression and hostility on the one hand, and passivity or capitulating to student demands on the other. Essentially, assertion communicates one's own need and due rights without trampling on the other parties' rights.)

- refusal to rely on power or role-status to gain respect
- speaking and acting respectfully even when frustrated or angry
- choosing to respond to discipline incidents (from prior reflection and planning) rather than reacting to incidents as they arise
- preparing for discipline as rigorously as any aspect of the curriculum

    When actually disciplining, a decisive approach engages the student by:

- establishing eye contact
- speaking clearly with appropriate firmness
- speaking briefly, addressing primary behaviour and ignoring as much of the secondary behaviour as is possible
- distinguishing between the child and his or her behaviour
- expecting compliance rather than demanding or merely hoping for it
- re-establishing working relationships as soon as possible

CHAPTER 3

Classroom management: planning and skills

A theory must be tempered with reality.
Jawaharlal Nehru

Creating a positive environment

The specific skills advanced here follow on from those explored in the case study of the decisive teacher. They are based on *expecting* compliance rather than demanding it or merely hoping for it. For these skills to be effective in the dynamic setting of a classroom, a teacher will need to recognise the crucial importance of discipline protocols. These skills are discussed in the context of typical classroom disruptions from 'low-level' to 'high-level'.

It is worth restating that the purpose of these skills is to enable the teacher to act in a more decisive, non-aggressive way; to use those forms of discipline that are more likely to encourage some degree of self-discipline in the student and enable on-task learning to take place. Discipline has an educational focus; its aim is to create the least stressful, most positive environment for learning. Decisive approaches aim to direct the student back to the task quickly, fairly and positively.

Levels of disruption

It is not easy to rate a disruption as 'low', 'medium' or 'high-level'. To one teacher, pen-tapping may be no problem; something which can be ignored. But if it is persistent, pen-tapping, on a hot day, in the middle of an important explanation by the teacher, can be quite a different matter. How disruption is perceived is important. 'Do I perceive it as a threat to me personally?' 'Is my authority in question?' 'How seriously does it affect my right to teach?' 'How frustrated am I feeling when . . .?'

Teachers have different levels of tolerance to frustration. One teacher may effectively deal with calling-out by the use of reinforcement, while others feel compelled to 'shh' every instance of rule breaking or constantly remind those who call out of the rule. Teacher ability to effectively manage disruption will depend on the degree to which they can effectively cope with frustration, the sort of discipline skills they possess, and how confidently they can use those skills when required.

Developing a plan

Few teachers would enter a classroom without some sort of lesson plan. It is surprising that many teachers, even some of the very experienced will enter a classroom knowing that calling out, butting in, students with 'no pens', mobile behaviour, are to be expected yet not *strategically* plan for them in the sense of seeking answers to the fundamental questions.

- What will I do when . . . ?
- How best can I deal with 'x' behaviours?
- When is the best time to intervene in a disruption?
- What will happen if my first approach is ineffective?
- What are my contingency steps?
  Imagine these situations:
- You've completed your description of metric number on the board and you ask for questions. Five students call out, two call out with their hands up. *What do you do?*

- You've asked two students to settle down, and one of them starts to argue. *What do you do?*
- David starts flicking elastic bands at his girlfriend during maths. *What do you do?*
- A student wanders out of his seat for the fourth time. *What do you do?*
- Andrew throws a tantrum. *What do you do?*

It is helpful to have a kind of hierarchy of possible steps in mind; a repertoire of possible actions that will enable us to take a decisive stance in the demanding context of a classroom. It stops us falling into that unnecessary, faltering or reactive stance when someone butts in on our fantastic exposition up-front, or when a student starts the game of 'let's see how long I can keep you discussing the merits of my case'.

The possible steps are best thought of as definitions of possible actions to use given certain disruptions. These steps would range from *least intrusive* teacher action to *most intrusive* teacher action as the circumstance demands; that is, the degree to which the disruption is affecting others' rights. Each step or suggested action is set in the context of common disruptive incidents occurring in the classroom. The language of each step can be modified to suit the age or maturity of the child but the basic purpose of each step is generally relevant at any age level (see Figure 3).

Attention seeking and tactical ignoring

Nothing is more annoying than disruptive behaviour that seems set on raising a teacher's frustration level. Attention seeking is a well developed, learned behaviour pattern in some students.

> Little Dean in Year 1 is an expert at home at getting his own way. He starts with a whine and builds it up into a tantrum. He's 'trying it on' with his new teacher. He starts off by calling out across the room while she is assisting at another table. 'Miss . . . (he whines as if he's in pain), come here, I need you!' He puts his hand up and down, up and down, to pretend he's within the class rule. 'Miss, Miss!'

What will she do? If she just accedes, what does he learn? Whistle dog — and she comes? Miss D. cannot decide what Dean will do, only

INCREASING LEVELS OF DECISIVE TEACHER ACTION

An example of how the steps might appear as a sequence of teacher actions. Each level describes:
- the degree of assertion used
- the appropriate thing to say
- the element of choice given to the student

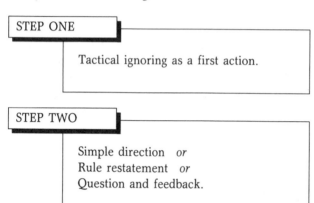

STEP ONE

Tactical ignoring as a first action.

STEP TWO

Simple direction   *or*
Rule restatement   *or*
Question and feedback.

STEP THREE

Repeat step 2 if the child resists or argues. Either take student aside or give a clear choice.

STEP FOUR

Follow up the choice by isolation within the room   *or*
time out in the room   *or*
exit from room (in extreme cases).

The 'chain-of-action' will depend on the disruption being addressed.

Fig 3

what she will do. She has thought out, in advance, how she can best deal with attention-seeking behaviours. She gives:

- minimal (at times none at all) eye contact and verbal direction when the student is off-task
- significant encouragement and attention when the student is on-task

This is sometimes called 'negative' and 'positive' reinforcement and is found in its most systematic form in behaviour modification (see Chapter 7). It is discussed here as part of normal classroom discipline; as a form of *tactically* ignoring the child's off-task behaviour until they stop seeking attention in that way and elect to seek it in socially appropriate ways.

> Miss D. looks across to Dean (without going over to him) and says firmly, with eye contact, 'When you put your hand up and wait'. No more. That's enough. She then ignores him. He calls out again, 'Miss. Miss!', and grunts and snorts in a sulky fashion. She continues moving around the room helping, encouraging, directing. She can see out of the corner of her eye (without giving eye contact) what Dean is doing. 'How's it going Maria?' She speaks to a student at a table near Dean. She is rigorously, tactically, ignoring Dean, hoping that he will then decide to seek attention by putting up his hand and waiting. He doesn't. He drags himself out of his seat and follows her around, pulling at her dress. Without looking at him, or saying anything to him, she firmly pushes his hand away and continues working with the other students. He tries again. 'Miss, Miss.' He's nearly crying now. He can't bear not to be the centre of attention. She tactically ignores him, gently, firmly pushing him away. After all, he *knows* the rule. If she starts preaching, yelling or pleading, she will only do what mum and dad do: reinforce his game.
>
> He finally gives up and falls on the floor crying in tantrum style. She walks over to him and around him. He finally goes back to his seat, head in hands and sobs. When a few children say, 'Miss, Dean's crying', without looking at Dean she simply says, 'I know', then distracts them by redirecting them to their work. The other students are secure in the knowledge that their teacher knows what she is doing.

It takes a lot of effort to tantrum and keep it up. This regression to the cot routine doesn't end in Year 1. 'Tantruming' is a behaviour many people use all their lives to get their own way. Tactical ignoring is one way of saying to a child the following:

- 'Yes, I'll notice you, talk to you, help you, when you're on-task with

your social behaviour and your learning. I will not simply accede to your pouting, sulking, clowning, tantrums, or baiting.'
- 'When you are off-task, I will firmly ignore you (my decisive choice) or I'll give you a brief, clear, simple direction (I won't argue, or procrastinate) or I may refer you to the class rules. You can't make me argue with you. You have no infallible magic to ruin my day.'
- 'In extreme cases of attention seeking, I will ask you to cool off in "time-out", or ask you to leave the room or even have you removed.'

The students in a class are not foolish. They are astute enough to know when a teacher is tactically ignoring attention-seeking behaviours. They know why teachers will let some behaviours continue for a while (calling out, butting in, sulking, clowning, tantrums). Tactical ignoring has to be exercised confidently for the rest of the class to go along with it. It is not an easy skill to use. To be effective a teacher needs to:

1 Use eye-scanning to monitor the disruption without actually looking at the disruptor: looking round or past calling-out students until they put up their hand. This is crucial because tactical ignoring is only a means to an end. When Allison stops her silly noises, then we can include her in the lesson; when the sulker finally gets back to work, then we go over to speak to him; when the low-level clowning stops, then go over and ask how things are going. Teachers need to use eye-scanning effectively to make ignoring *tactical*.

2 Know what behaviours to tactically ignore. Never, for example, ignore defiance, blatant swearing, high-level noise or unsafe behaviour.
3 Know how long you will ignore before you need to say or do something. Know beforehand what secondary steps you will use when tactical ignoring is not working. It is only when we are in control of ignoring that it becomes a tactical and useful tool in discipline. Tactical ignoring is often combined with other steps and, though a difficult teacher skill to develop, is a powerful strategy for effective discipline.

There are teachers who object to ignoring because it looks like the child is getting away with 'it'. 'I'll teach him!' they say. What will you teach him? That your shouting stopped his calling out, that your slamming of a hand on his desk and berating him proved you could get back at him? That every time he calls out you'll attend?

'He shouldn't call out!' But he does, he did and will probably continue to do so. 'I've got to make him learn?' Yes, but how? If teachers struggle with tactical ignoring because they have difficulty tolerating frustration, they are better served by using simple directions or rule reminders. Note, too, that tactical ignoring can often be employed with other verbal strategies.

Diversions and distractions

Part of effective discipline is preventing potential or likely problems from getting out of hand. If you know that Sean is first off the mark when you ask questions, divert possible calling out by saying something like, 'I know some of you will know the answers almost before I've finished speaking. But I want you to hold off for a while to give others a chance. Okay?' Then, if they do hold off, 'Thanks Sean and Jill for waiting. I see you know the answer but I see Vlado has his hand up'.

Other ways of distracting or diverting possible disruption are to give a job, rearrange seating, modify routines, have work available for early finishers or, if there is disruption in the early phase of a lesson, call the child aside to speak quietly about their work. 'Sean, are you having any problems? Do you know what to do next?' Invite another student to work with Sean; stay close without giving due attention (tactical ignoring). Use the 'when' statement: 'Sean *when* you've finished your maths, I want you to give me a hand with this please'.

> Sean is supposed to be engaged in a 'cooperative building game', putting a large wooden car together. He picks up one of the wheels and throws it against the wall. The teacher quietly calls him over. 'What are you doing Sean?' 'Nothing' as he hangs his head. 'You threw the wheel against the wall Sean. What are you supposed to be doing?' No answer. 'Come on, show me how you can put the wheel on with Maria and Simon'. This diverted his attention to the task at hand.

Non-verbal directions

With some low-level disruption, a wink, nod, frown or brief stare is enough. It is a form of non-verbal direction that says, 'You know that I know you know'. It works effectively when the teacher has a good working rapport with students. The non-verbal gesture acts simply as a reminder or reinforcer. One useful non-verbal gesture during calling out is to direct an extended hand towards the calling-out student (an open, extended hand like a traffic controller) without looking at the student, and continue on. It can often be combined with tactical ignoring.

Simple directions and desists

A simple direction conveys a message to a student that you are directing them to do something about their behaviour. A desist is a direction to the student that you are telling them to stop doing something. To be effective, they should specify the expected behaviour clearly and simply with appropriate firmness.

If Paul, aged 5, is out of his seat forgetfully we will direct him differently from Nick who has spilt acid on the floor for fun in a Year 8 science class. For Paul it is enough to say, 'Paul, back to your seat, thanks'. For Nick, one of those rare, and consequently powerful, desists is needed. A raised voice is used to establish contact. 'Nick! Put that jar down — now!' Get the others settled and then get Nick to clean up.

Where students engage in dangerous or unsafe behaviour, don't waste time discussing. Direct as a command. Most simple directions, however, can be delivered as reminders to self-control. Deliver the direction quickly and firmly, a few times if necessary. Keep the same form of words. Use the child's name. Mild desists are effective if the teacher has a good working relationship with the children. 'Michelle, don't play with the scissors like that, use them properly' is better than 'Michelle! I'm sick of telling you . . .'.

In a busy classroom with competing demands on a teacher's attention, we don't, generally speaking, have time for extended discussions when we need to correct misbehaviour or lead students towards appropriate behaviour. Here are some simple directions which focus on particular behaviours.

- 'There's mess on the table.' (Describe the situation.) 'Clean it up now — thanks.' (Direct and expect compliance.)
- 'I can't work with that tapping.' (Teacher expresses need.) 'Pen down, now — thanks.' Look back to the class after the direction.

Two students are busily, and annoyingly chatting over a comic while the teacher is up-front teaching. It is too loud to be tactically ignored so the teacher gives a clear, simple, direction. She addresses the behaviour she wants. 'Michelle, Lisa (direct eye contact, her hand extended towards them) do me the courtesy of facing the front and listening thanks. Put the magazine away too, thanks.' She immediately resumes control of the lesson; expecting compliance she doesn't invite discussion.

If these had been Year 2 students instead of Year 10, a simple 'Facing the front and listening thanks' would be enough. With older students, we can often add an 'I' message with the direction to emphasise the non-confrontational but just nature of the direction.

- 'David stop tapping with that pen, thanks.'
- 'Lisa get back to your seat, thanks.'
- 'Zlato put that toy in your bag now, thank you.'
- 'Simone clean up that mess before you leave, thanks.'

Use the child's first name, and a please or thank you.

Sally is fiddling noisily with her ruler during the teacher's up-front explanation. He tactically ignores for a while but it is too distracting. He eye-balls her and says, 'Sally, put the ruler down, I'm trying to teach. Good on you'. The implicit expectation is clear but also positive.

He throws in the 'good on you' as a mitigator to the direction and as a statement of belief that says, in effect, 'I know you'll cooperate'. He then briefly smiles and turns immediately back to the class and continues the lesson. It is surprisingly effective.

With younger children

If small children are over excited and appear not to hear the first time, it may be necessary to repeat the direction. Establish eye contact and repeat the reminder, or correction. Small children need very clear rules for behaviour and brief, clear reminders; not nagging dialogues. If the boundary is uncertain and unenforced, the children will be insecure and act out their insecurity via their disruptions. A teacher will need to regularly enforce routines for safety, movement, tidying up and so on especially with small children. But, again, respectful treatment is the key; staying calm, but speaking and acting firmly.

There is no point arguing, discussing, debating with a 5-year-old who is uptight, frustrated, anxious, angry or confused. What children need most from their teacher when they're in such a state is direction, even if such direction means removal from the scene of frustration for 'time-out'. Remember:

- keep the direction simple and brief
- expect compliance
- if necessary stay close and repeat
- stay calm

Restating or reminding via the rules

Refer the individual, or group, back to 'our' rules. 'Michael, you know the rule for lining up.' If the child starts a discussion, repeat the rule and follow up later. Many low-frustration-tolerance children go into sulk mode when they have been disciplined firmly. If they do, give them a healthy dose of tactical ignoring until they choose to work productively. If they don't, follow up with consequences later.

'Simone and Maria, you know our rule for safety with the scissors.' Keep the reminder brief, just the rule, the voice, and firm eye contact. If necessary, show assertion by hand emphasis (outstretched but open and emphatic, making the point). Michael is calling out during the up-front part of a lesson. 'Michael, you know the rule for asking questions — use it thanks.' No more. Keep it brief and then refocus attention on others.

Rule reminders can be used with students of any age. They can be said quietly, humorously or assertively as the situation requires. If John, out of his seat, argues about it, we can reassert the movement rule. 'But you know the rule John', 'Okay, but you know the rule'. 'John, you know the rule for asking questions. Use it thanks.'

Restating of the class rules can also be effective with the whole group if noise levels are too high, although the effectiveness of this approach diminishes with frequency. If there is a regular problem with class noise, it is better discussed at a classroom meeting (see Chapter 5).

Rule reminders and prep to Year 3 students

One way of giving rule reminders to younger, primary-age students is use of a word that briefly and concisely expresses the required action implicit in the rule. For example, 'Don't run in the classroom Sandra' becomes 'Sandra (to gain attention use the child's name), walking'. If two students are arguing, the teacher walks by and says, firmly, 'Mike, Paul, sharing thanks' or 'Helping' or 'Asking'. Rude behaviour receives a, 'Manners Dave' and a student who keeps interrupting is simply told, 'Waiting Anna'. The required action, expressed as a verb or participle, reduces the likelihood of long discussion. Make the point clear, firm and non-threatening, and expect compliance. If the disruption is low-level, forgetful behaviour, say it with a smile. It is a reminder of the rule, and acts as a simple direction. Rule reminders or restatements of the rule enable us to be more positive when disciplining.

If two students are talking loudly while you are working close by with other students, it may be enough to turn, extend the hand, and say, 'Excuse me Maria, Michelle, you know the rule for working noise. Thanks.', and turn back to the students you were working with. Establish eye contact, speak briefly, clearly, expectantly. So, expectantly, you will turn away as soon as you have restated the (fair) rule. If the noise continues, then use more decisive steps. It is surprising, though, how effective brief rule reminders are. They are effective because the student is referred back to *our* rules. This puts the responsibility back where it belongs — with the child.

Two ways of saying something

Ill considered	Considered
'Didn't I tell you to put a margin there — goodness, do I have to *keep* reminding you?'	'What's missing on the page Dave?' (Said casually.)
'Can't you walk? What do you have to run for, I've told you before.'	'Walk, don't run' or just 'Walking, Dave' — a rule reminder said firmly, with a smile if appropriate.
'You spilt the paint! Can't you be careful? Look at all that mess. Go and wash your hands — you're not doing any more painting now.'	'How can we fix up this mess Paul? Okay, grab the cloth over there.' (Well-planned classrooms have cleaning materials handy.)
'You're not supposed to be playing with the M.A.B. blocks! You're supposed to be grouping them. If you can't use them properly, don't use them at all!'	'That's an interesting shape Maria — now see if you can make them into 2 groups of ten, as well.'
'Don't grab those scissors! What are you — can't you see he's using them?'	'David, you can use the scissors *when* (ever a useful word with younger children) Paul's finished. Okay Paul?'
'Look, I've shown you how to cut out on the line before (sigh, sigh). C'mon Simon give it to me — I'll show you again!'	'You've started to cut out the shape — well done. Show me how you can cut closer to the line.'

'Oh, Richard, yes you! You know I mean you — get over here — now! Listen son, I don't care how you speak at home, in my class . . .'

'Richard, I want to see you now — now! You know the rule about swearing.'

'Every time I walk past you two you're talking. I'm fed up with it do you hear. Now get out, Danielle and move over there!' (She argues.) 'Don't you argue with me. I said go!'

'Keep the noise down thanks, I'm trying to work over here with Michelle and Denise.' The noise continues. 'Danielle and Simone, you know the rule for working noise — if you can't work quietly, I'll have to ask one of you to move.'

Verbal interruptions

The teacher is starting a new unit on vectors. She had touched on it when she taught directed numbers the term before. Standing before the class she greets them and says, 'Okay, today we will be studying a topic on vectors'. One of the attention-seeking boys in the front row calls out loudly in his best 'notice-me' voice, 'Not vectors again!'. The teacher, without looking at the student, calmly continues and says, 'Some of you may be wondering why we're doing vectors and directed numbers again . . .'

The butting-in child has not been noticed, nor has he stolen her thunder. What the teacher has done is use a form of tactical ignoring, while still addressing the class about the lesson. She has not given the attention-seeker what he is after, nor has she allowed a minor conflict to escalate.

When children butt-in or call out and say, 'I know the answer to that!', thus attempting to disrupt the lesson flow, a teacher can effectively use a form of tactical ignoring by speaking *around* such students, making no direct eye or verbal contact. 'Some of you know the answer to this problem already but what I'd like you to do is hang off for a while because we'll be discussing these problems in small groups.' The teacher chooses not to be drawn by such attention-seeking and diverts potential disruption. If the student continues to be disruptive by butting-in, the teacher could use a rule restatement, or a brief, simple direction. Tactical ignoring is used up to the point where it becomes difficult for the teacher to teach or for the children to learn because of undue noise or movement.

> Paul has had his hand up and is vigorously clicking his fingers to get the teacher's attention. The teacher's first step is to try tactical ignoring. He becomes more insistent and calls out, 'Look I'm asking a question, why don't you answer!'. The teacher turns, makes direct eye-contact, and with an outstretched hand, palm out, says, in a decisive voice, 'Paul you know the fair rule for communication, use it thanks'. No more. She then turns back to the group and continues her discussion.

This is a brief, decisive rule reminder. If Paul has continued being overly disruptive he would have been given a choice to work within the fair rules or face isolation within the room. When moving from tactical ignoring to more decisive action, a number of key elements should be kept in mind.

- Know broadly what you are going to say ahead of time.
- Know at what point to move from tactical ignoring to more decisive steps.
- Be brief and decisive when the child is off-task. Don't labour the verbal direction or descend into nagging.
- Even tactical ignoring is a form of decisive teacher behaviour. *You* decide what, and for how long, you will ignore certain attention-seeking behaviour.
- Re-establish working relationships as soon as possible when the child is on-task. Look for opportunities to give some basic reinforcement by teacher assistance, encouragement or direction.

Getting feedback by asking questions

Two children are talking about a television show during social studies. The teacher is three metres away helping another child and their noise is well above 'working' noise level. Instead of running across to settle it, or ignoring it (the noise is too loud, too disruptive), the teacher calls across the room in a firm voice and asks, 'What's going on Grace and Nick?'. 'Nothing' they say. (Most children do.) She replies with an explanation and direction, 'We can't work with that loud talking — please get back to your work now. I'll be with you in a moment'. Her hand gesture is firm and direct. Her facial message is as assertive as her voice. They know if they keep talking they'll be given a choice to work by the rules or be separated.

Another form of gaining feedback is to intensify the question.

Simon is out of his seat and has decided to sit and talk with Vlado in the desk behind. The teacher walks up beside the desk and uses firm eye contact directed at the off-task Simon. 'Excuse me, Simon, what are you doing?' 'Nothing, just sitting here — not doing anything wrong!' 'Actually,' says his teacher, 'you're out of your seat talking loudly to Vlado'. Simon whinges on, 'Gees, I'm just talking'. He grimaces and pouts (behaviour that the teacher tactically ignores). 'You're always picking on me!'. The teacher asks another question, not taking this new 'bait' for discussion. 'What should you be doing?' 'My work.' 'I want you to go back to your seat now, thanks.' (Simple direction.) If he argues, she will reassert the direction or give a simple, clear, choice.

What questions are more effective than *Why* questions. They place the responsibility for some sort of feedback on to the student. (Glasser, 1965, 1969.) 'Kerry, what's happening with this M.A.B.?' challenges the child to give feedback. Because most children say, 'Nothing', to the question, 'What are you doing?', it's better to tell them what they are, in fact, doing. Not a lecture, but clear feedback by the teacher. 'Actually, you're playing around with it. What should you be doing Kerry?' This asks Kerry for more feedback by directing her back to the task as it were.

Teacher baiting

Some children give smart answers as their response to *What* questions. 'What's it look like I'm doing?' Children who try this approach are often baiting the teacher. It is generally better to say, 'It looks like you're mucking around with the science equipment. What should you be doing?' If they say, 'Don't know, do I?', tell them. If they say, 'Nothing' simply remind them of what they should be doing and redirect them. Be sure to follow these children up later but at the time, minimise unnecessary heat by keeping the dialogue task-focused.

Giving in to the temptation to take the bait ('Listen smart alec, don't come the raw prawn with me!') is hardly worth it. Keep the transaction brief and focused on the rule and/or task. If the child's agenda is a contest, why give him an audience and a contestant?

Noises, gesturing and posturing

They sometimes squawk like a crow, bark like a dog, snort like a pig or raspberry at a high decibel rate. Certain children will gesture with fingers behind the teacher's back (the two-up finger sign is a common one), or throw their hands up in acted anger when asked to move away from desks they shouldn't be sitting in.

Another form of attention seeking

All children, in some way, seek attention; some children seek to get it in ways that are frustrating and annoying to their teachers. The provocative child gets his or her attention by posturing at the teacher.

The teacher directs Michelle to move because she and her partner are too noisy. She procrastinates. The teacher has already given a choice to the student to work quietly or face the option of moving. 'Why?' says Michelle. 'She (turning to her friend) was talking as well. Why are you always picking on me?' The teacher is decisive and doesn't get dragged into an interminable debate about natural justice. He redirects by re-asserting. 'Take your books and work over there.' If the child wants to argue, the teacher merely reasserts the simple direction, 'I gave you a choice, take your books and work over there'. Firm, non-argumentative and non-aggressive.

Michelle stands up, stamps the foot, snorts, goes over to the desk she should have been at, slumps down, glares and folds her arms. Dramatic posturing is another form of secondary behaviour. The teacher has finished this little discipline transaction and now tactically ignores the student. The teacher walks around, working with the other (on-task) students, reinforcing, commenting, chatting briefly, marking, teaching. The sulker waits until the teacher's back is turned and blows a raspberry and then gives a 'two-up'. One smart alec calls out loudly, 'Sir,

Michelle just stuck her fingers up at you' and then quietly sniggers. The class goes into quiet mode as the teacher quickly replies, without looking either at Michelle or the smart alec. 'Well, I'm glad I didn't see it' and moves on. Thus, the teacher does not get drawn into a new debate with another student or rekindle the sulker's 'He's not fair to me — I'm going to get back!' attitude.

If the sulker picks up her pen, the teacher, with his regular eye-sweep, will casually walk over and give her some respectful treatment by commenting on her work: 'How's it going?', 'Need some help?', 'Oh, I see you managed that part'. Many sulkers, when spoken to normally in this way, often speak back, or grunt back, as if to say 'I don't like you at the moment. Why don't you comment on my sulking and pouting and give me attention for it — others do!'. Of course, if the teacher starts saying, 'Look don't speak to me in that tone of voice' or words to that effect, it only feeds the attention-seeking. The teacher just speaks normally, gives some respectful attention and moves on. He may keep Michelle back later to discuss her behaviour.

Some noises can be tactically ignored. If they continue, a teacher can try a firm, simple direction, rule restatement or defusion. For teachers who can use repartee (not sarcasm), they can defuse such attention-seeking by a quick aside, bowled smartly, with minimal attention.

For rude noises, some of these one-liners may be useful: 'Dave, the Pidgin English class is at 4 o'clock. Okay?'; 'I didn't know you were French.'; 'Oh, they're nesting earlier this year.'; 'Traffic warden?' (this to the gesticulator who has used a provocative finger gesture). The teacher may actually deliver these without looking at the student. It is another form of tactical ignoring — giving minimal attention. If the noise continues, give a choice or remind the child of the rules or perhaps even take the child aside and quickly discuss their behaviour. 'David, either the noise ends now or we'll have to discuss it later. Okay?' (move off). 'Cathy, you know our rules'. If the child is young, the teacher may need to withdraw him and explain firmly that crows make nests, they don't do cut and paste in Room 17.

Teacher follow-up

Persistent crowing or snorting or 'I'm going to get your attention one way if I can't get it another' routines cannot be ignored and are best handled with a clear, firm choice. Be sure to follow up later with the student and sort out what the problem is; that is the time to give right of reply. In some cases, it may require a discussion with the home-group teacher or year-level coordinator.

Choosing appropriate discipline

It is important, as in all discipline, to work within the context of the disruption. If the noise level is minimal, use tactical ignoring. If it looks like a one-off, use a simple direction or defusion (if such a tactic is comfortable). If it looks heated, direct the child aside from the group. If the child is aggressive in their posturing and loud, give a firm choice to remain within fair class rights and rules or to leave. (The language of *rules* is best used with younger groups, prep to Year 6.) Have a clear exit plan if the child continues. (See Chapter 5.)

Some children can be incredibly persistent with their noises. I've seen Year 3 children crawl under tables and bark persistently in order to gain attention. The most successful strategy with such children is to minimise attention when they are off-task, use tactical ignoring, brief, simple directions, firm rule reminders, time-out in the room, beckoning the child aside and giving maximum attention when they are on-task. Even when removing loud, persistently noisy children from a room, a teacher can give minimal attention to the disruptive child while talking calmly to the other children. All this *while* the teacher is firmly removing the child. Similar behaviour can be used by other teachers acting on the classroom teacher's behalf.

A specific problem

What to do with flatulators?

Several boys down the back of Ms H's humanities class were abusing the olfactory organs of most of the class members. She wasn't exactly sure who the culprits were. After a couple of sessions of this, she decided on a rather novel deflection. Armed with a spray deodorant, she went in the following Tuesday and both heard and smelt the attention-seeking rubbish. A decisive five-second spray and she walked off. There was laughter but it soon settled down. Before the end of the session she quietly said, 'I'll see you four at the close of class'. They protested, she tactically ignored. She kept them back and discussed their flatulence, future consequences and said 'Okay, what are you going to do about it?'. The problem diminished.

When confronted with a problem like this, consider this approach:
- Give options within class rules.
- Follow up with students later.
- Minimise grandiloquence.
- Remember that the regular context of the teacher's respectful consistency will make dealing with such incidents much easier.

Arguing with students

Arguing with students in front of their peers:
- wastes time
- heats up a conflict
- leads to irrational exchanges
- often forces either side into a win/lose position

By reasserting, giving a choice, taking the student aside, even apologising where necessary, we 'save maximum face'.

A new rule about *Walkman* radios had been in place only a day. David, complete with army jacket sporting a raving 'heavy metal' rock logo, was jigging in his seat and wearing a rather expensive, headphone tape set. Establishing eye contact, I asked him to put the headset away. He couldn't hear so he took them off. 'Dave, put the *Walkman* away. Thanks, you know the rule.' (Simple direction with rule reminder.) 'No, why should I? Not doing anything wrong!' 'You know the rule, put it away now thanks.' I know I can't make him. I can only request, direct, remind of the rule, reassert or give a choice.

'Gees! I can work with it on!'. 'You know the rule.' (Reassert.) 'I'm still doing my work.' 'It's your choice Dave. Off now, in your bag, or I'll have to follow it up later.' (Reassertion and simple choice.) He slammed it down (scene time) and said 'f ____!' to no one in particular and I moved off. Later, when he had settled, I came back to have a chat about his maths.

If a student argues back (and the audience is listening and watching), remain calm but be firm and reassert. Respond to 'You can't tell me what to do!' with 'I'm not telling you, I'm asking you to return to your seat'. If we resort to preaching, yelling or reverse telling ('I won't tell you again.'), we will often end up in pointless, fruitless arguing and even if we 'win', the behaviour we have employed is bad modelling.

Answering back or defiance

When a student answers back or makes a smart or challenging comment, many teachers will say, 'How dare you answer me back! Apologise now!' 'No way . . .!' will often come the reply. Later, the teacher may say, 'He shouldn't have answered back' or universalise it as, 'No student should answer back to their teacher'. But he did! 'But he shouldn't have.' But he *did*. That's the reality, isn't it?

Of course it's nice, preferable, better, when students are amenable but if they aren't our demands will rarely *make* them more compliant. The demand, 'Things must be this way or I can't stand it!' will certainly cause us to be unnecessarily stressed. It will further decrease the possibility of effective, long-term resolution.

If a student continues to bait or speak aggressively, the teacher can:
- restate the clear rules briefly
- call the student aside
- give a clear choice to remain in the class and work by the fair rules or leave.

Give him full attention and a clear, firm choice. 'David, you can stand here swearing all day and it won't upset me but I have a job to do. I can't do it with your constant interruption. Either work by the rules or we'll have to ask you to leave.'

Dividing our attention: 'overlapping' behaviour

Mr O. is sitting next to Paula trying to teach her how to calculate the long side of a right-angle triangle. He doesn't crowd or tower from behind but sits next to or alongside, or sometimes kneels to get to the student's level, because it brings the power-relationship down to a more 'human' level. While he is teaching Paula, he hears Daniel and Dimi talking really loudly. He turns his head and firmly asks, not aggressively or with hostility, 'What are you doing Daniel?'. Daniel replies, 'Nothing!'. 'Actually, you're talking really loudly to Dimi. What should you be doing?' 'My work.' 'Okay, would you get back to work, thanks.' He gives his attention back to Paula.

Mr O. has done two things while working with one student. He has divided his attention briefly, firmly and decisively to discipline (question and guide) the two noisy students. This is preferable to a teacher running from one mini-crisis to another. Jacob Kounin (1977) called this teacher strategy 'overlapping'. It is used by effective primary school teachers all the time. Keeping a regular eye-sweep, a teacher is able to 'overlap' his discipline with his teaching.

Overlapping behaviour enables a teacher to be aware of several facets of the classroom dynamic at the same time. How does overlapping behaviour work? It works when teachers are aware of what is happening in the room. I once worked with a teacher who, apparently, didn't hear Maria stomping under her desk during the off-task part of the lesson; another whose visual field missed the low-level play-fight on her left; another who completely missed the paper-spitters on his left. That is not 'tactical ignoring' but blind ignorance.

Ms P. is working with Mark (Year 1) at his desk. Nancy comes up. Ms P. notices Nancy waiting for five seconds, and then immediately turns and reinforces her. 'Thanks for waiting Nancy, I'm nearly finished with Mark.' She gently calls over to Paul who looks like he's about to muck around with the maths blocks and diverts a possible disruption by giving a simple direction. 'Paul, sit down, I'll be over in a minute.' She finishes with Mark and looks at Nancy's work as she walks across the room. She marks it at Nancy's desk with a 'Well done', then proceeds towards Paul noticing two girls pushing and poking in the reading corner. She quietly walks over and gives them a choice. 'You can either both read quietly here, or I'll have to ask one of you to go back to your seat.' She uses brief eye contact. They stop. She moves off as if they will act responsibly. As she walks over to Paul she reinforces Simon and Neil at their desks. 'You're working well on those problems. When you've finished you may go on with your spelling words. Okay?' They smile and nod.

She gives feedback; shows she is aware of what's going on. She doesn't let incidents get out of hand. It's pointless waiting until there's a fight in the reading corner, or until Mark gets over to his mate with the M.A.B. Timing is important in discipline.

When overlapping, keep the following in mind:
- Correctly target disruptors.
- Discipline from where you are. When working with 'x', discipline 'y' and 'z' from that position.

- Use questioning or choices. 'Excuse me Maria, you can either work by our safety rule or I'll have to ask you to leave the experiment and sit over there.'
- Be brief in the direction of the disruption, then overlap back to what you were doing. Expect compliance — act as if compliance is the most natural outcome.
- When the disruptor has settled, go over (some minutes later) and give some specific encouragement. 'I see you've worked out how to do that problem there Dimi — well done. How will you do the next one?'

Giving choices

It is important to communicate to children, especially older children (7–8 years and onwards), in the language of choice. Empty threats by teachers are quickly seen by children as meaningless: 'One more word, just one more word and it's a thousand lines for you, do you hear?' 'I'm sick and tired of you calling out. It's always you.' It is important to deal with children in their *present*, focusing on their actions and the likely consequences. One way of doing this is to present them with a choice. If we have given several directions, or warnings, or restated the rule, or used a question/feedback approach and the child is still behaving disruptively, then they need to be given a clear choice in the light of appropriate consequences.

> Two children continue to talk. They are well above the working noise rule and clearly off-task. The teacher has already spoken to them a few times (using appropriate steps) so she now gives them a choice. 'Mary and Karen, you either work quietly here, you know our rule, or I'll have to ask one of you to work over there.' (gesturing to the isolation desk). The students argue. She repeats the choice. They shut up for several minutes, but soon the noise level rises again. The teacher walks over and says, 'Mary, take your books and work over there. I gave you a choice'. She is acting on the clear understanding of the previously given choice. Mary argues. The teacher repeats assertively (as is her right). She is decisive. The student gets up, walks over and slams her books down. She is tactically ignored. The teacher will not go back to her until

she shows on-task behaviour. She will follow up with both the girls. Just before the end of the lesson she will say, 'I want to see you both when we finish'. It is important to use the 'Can I see you?' statement as late in the lesson as possible so the student doesn't stew on it during the remaining time.

Isolating students

If a child has been given a choice to work quietly or face moving to another desk and refuses to move when asked, saying, 'I'm not going to move, you can't make me!' (power-broking time), there is little point in the teacher forcing a no-win battle, or sending the child out with a yell, 'Right, out! Get out of my class!'. Agree with the child. 'That's right, I can't move you, but if you don't I'll have to ask you to stay back and explain to me why you can't work by our class rules.'

It's also worth pointing out that few can actually move a big, loud, tough Year 6 or Year 10 boy or girl. By using the language of choice rather than threat, the teacher can save face on both sides. 'I'll have to ask you to move' is better than 'I'll *make* you sit down the back' or 'I'll *send* you out of my class'. If they continue to act disruptively in a way that cannot be tactically ignored, employ the exit procedures (see Chapter 5).

If a child is persistently calling out and tactical ignoring, rule reminder or simple directions are not working, the next step would be to give a choice via the rules. 'Peter, you know the rule for asking questions (or communication or whatever the stated class rule is). If you continue to call out we will have to ask you to leave our discussion.' With smaller children, a time-out area in the classroom can be used; with older children, who are persistently rude, brash and aggressive, direct them to sit away from the group or to leave the room.

Most children will stop if the teacher decisively communicates the fair rule in a non-aggressive way. If persistent students do stop calling out through any steps a teacher uses, it may still be important to follow up later to remind them of the rule (see Chapter 4). Find out why they are so persistently rude in class (probably attention-seeking) and what they intend to do about it.

Isolation as a consequence

If isolation is used, it is important to distinguish, in the child's under-standing, between isolation from the group (time-out) and isolation to work away from the group (logical consequence).

'Denise, you can work quietly here or I'll have to ask you to sit over there and work.' If Denise cannot work next to Pauline without being overly loud (she knows the fair 'learning and working noise' rule), she is given a simple choice to work quietly at her desk or to move away and work somewhere else. She starts the argument routine but the teacher blocks her by reasserting. 'But it's not just me, others are talk-ing loudly too!' 'You know the fair rule for working noise.' 'Yeah, but . . .' 'You know the fair rule for working noise, Denise.' 'Yeah, but . . .' 'You know the fair rule for working noise, Denise.'

Use the same words. Don't give her an audience for an open dis-cussion on 'justice'. She knows the fair rules. Stay calm and be decis-ive. Act as if she'll respond. Don't shout at her. Keep some distance away and reassert the direction. If she still barrages then give a simple choice, 'You can either move now, or we'll need to discuss it later'. Don't try pushing, grabbing, or starting the big power game. You won't win. And, anyway, winning's not what it's about. If she settles down, all is well and good. Most students do (some will try the arguing game) as long as we are not hostile or threatening. If they stand their ground and refuse to move, simply leave the choice with them.

Most children give up after two or three reassertions, if they are delivered firmly, without hostility. If they don't, it is pointless staying and forcing. Leave the final choice with them or, if they are too dis-ruptive, use the exit policy and follow up later.

Reasserting: dealing with procrastination

Michael has got out of his seat for the third time. His teacher ignored the first two excursions, then asked him a question. She calls (not shout-ing) across to him and, using eye contact, asks clearly, 'What are you doing?'. Her voice tone is not hostile just clear and firm. 'What are you doing, Michael?' 'Nothing.' 'Actually you're out of your seat. What should you be doing?' If he says, 'In my seat' then the teacher would simply respond with, 'Okay, would you get back now' and then, later, when the child is on-task, go up and ask him how his work is going.

But not Michael, he is resolute. 'I was just getting a rubber from Sean!' He says it as if the teacher is an advance scout for the inquisition. If she responds with 'But you know you should be in your seat.' then Michael will drag her off into a neat little argument. 'But it's not fair, you never pick on the others.' This teacher is too experienced for that. She knows that if she falls for his attention/avoidance behaviour she only accedes to it and gives him an audience to boot. She reasserts the direction or appropriate rule. Turning to face him, a couple of metres distance, she reasserts, 'You know the fair rule for movement in our room.' 'But I was just . . .' She calmly repeats, reasserts. 'You know the fair rule for movement.' She turns, as if he'll respond to the direction. It is important for the teacher's non-verbal behaviour to model assertion and show that she knows what she is about.

Michael's determined, we'll give him that. 'Gees, I'm only getting a rubber . . .' The teacher gives a final assertive direction, coupled with a choice. 'Michael, you know the fair rule for movement. You can either work by the fair rule or we'll need to discuss it later in your time.' He stomps back to his seat and sulks. She leaves him quickly and attends to the other children. She knows sulking is another form of acting out attention-seeking. Not drawn by it, she waits until he's cooled off. When she notices Michael creep back into his work, she simply walks over and says, 'How's that problem there? Do you understand it?'. In other words, she treats him respectfully when he's back on-task. She doesn't berate him with, 'About time!', 'Sulking like a baby!', 'Gee, you annoy me Michael!', or get into a discussion about his sulking and why she had to move him.

The quicker we can enable the student to get back on-task, to get some success out of learning and social interaction the better for all. Later, the teacher may have a quiet word with Michael about his behaviour but in the group, at the point of disruption, she minimises his audience-seeking by using decisive discipline that is non-hostile but firm.

Reassertion is a useful stance to take when a student is plainly out to argue, procrastinate, confute and confound you. It is simply the restatement of an eminently fair rule, process or decision.

I had asked Darren (Year 3) on two occasions to remember his bathers if he wanted to go swimming. If he forgot them again, he had been told he would not be allowed to go swimming. Despite this, the bathers were forgotten again. Thus, swimming was out. Marshalling his obdurate little nature against this grossly unfair adult, he started his whine, 'But I want to go swimming, it's not fair!' (even though he had been clearly and fairly warned). He got a brief, firm explanation and 'You won't be going swimming because you forgot your bathers'.

'It's not fair!' I repeated the same words and then turned to give attention to other class members. I have not got time in a busy class to sit and *discuss* with a frustrated child. I have to decide what I will do in the best interests of Darren and the class. He tried once more with a well articulated and acted 'sob'. 'But I like swimming and I want to go!' He stamped his foot. 'You won't be going swimming Darren because you forgot your bathers' (reassertion). 'Gee, my teacher's like a brick wall' he thought. Yes, I was and will be a fair, brick wall with procrastination. Later I gave him a chance to talk. He slunk off and humped his way to his seat and sat with arms folded. Next week he brought his bathers.

Reassertion with extended 'I' message

Sometimes it is appropriate (especially with older students) to extend the assertion by tuning in to the students' secondary behaviour before reasserting.

Lisa is busily into heavy-weather 'bubble-gumming'. 'Lisa, you know our rule for chewing gum — in the bin thanks.' 'Gee I'm not doing anything wrong!' (Sulk, pout, arms folded — secondary behaviour.) 'I'm asking you to put the gum in the bin, you know our rule.' 'It's a dumb rule!' 'Maybe you think it's a dumb rule, but I'm asking you to put the gum in the bin.'

Lisa marches off, makes a scene by throwing it in the bin; a scene the teacher chooses to give no direct eye contact to. If Lisa had refused to put the chewing gum in the bin, the teacher would have left the choice with her: to put it in now or follow up with her later. The teacher would then move off to let Lisa 'own' her decision.

Some other examples of extended reassertions which may be useful follow. Tune in quickly with an 'I' message, then reassert the appropriate direction, rule, or choice.

'I hate this class!' 'Maybe you do, but I'm asking you to . . .' 'You never listen to me!' 'Maybe you think I don't listen to you, but I'm asking you to . . .' 'I don't want to do this dumb work anyway.' 'Perhaps you don't, but I'm asking you to do it.'

Reasserting is our message to the child and the group that there is a time for discussion and it is not 'now'. Now is when you work by the fair rules of our group, and respond to the fair treatment of the teacher or face the fair consequences (a choice to be isolated, stay back or, in extreme cases, leave).

It is a waste of time arguing with children such as Darren. Act.

Reassertion is best used:
- when a child is clearly seeking to argue
- when you are decisive in your body language

Be firm without yelling or humiliating. Your verbal repertoire should state the case *as it is*. Normally two or three reassertions are enough. Most students comply even if sulkily or moodily. Repeat the same form of words. This gives the clear impression you are decisive. 'Dianne, you know the fair rule for . . .'

Challenging the work

'This work's boring, isn't it?' When a student dishes this one up many teachers see it as an affront to their position and effort in preparation of curriculum when, in effect, the student may be quite right. It may well be boring or apparently irrelevant. He or she may be exercising his/her right to question the curriculum. How this is handled is very important.

A reaction such as 'Listen, smart alec, just do it, okay?' or overly discursive approaches like 'Look, I spend a long time preparing this . . . it's an important part of the curriculum . . . be fair!' only prolong hostility or procrastination. A teacher is better served by using deflection or a combination of reassertion and simple direction.

> 'This is boring! We're not going to use this so why bother?' 'Probably it is boring Michelle, but it's the work we're doing *now*.' 'Yeah but . . .' 'Michelle, you know the way we work. We can discuss this later if you want to.' The teacher is not about to discuss the merits of the curriculum *now*; neither is she affronted. She acknowledges the student but reasserts a fair position. Work now, discuss later. 'Yeah but . . .' 'It's your choice Michelle . . .' The teacher could alternatively give a simple direction. 'Would you get back to it now. If you want to follow it up later we can at a class discussion.'

Issues like relevance in curriculum can be explored at separate, designated class discussion times. In this way the students' rights and obligations are both given due weight. There are also other ways of dealing with students who challenge the work the teacher has proposed. 'What do I have to do this for? I'm never going to use it!' 'You will if you become a teacher.' (defusion, don't take the bait). Alternatively, 'Well you've got a test on it. The name of the game is passing the test. Come on I'll give you a hand.' (distraction/diversion).

Task refusal

This is any behaviour which indicates the student is unwilling to understand or perform a task or activity. Care must be taken to separate *unwillingness* from *inability* to undertake the task. Out of sheer humiliation at not being able to succeed, many students reject a task rather than expose their failure or weaknesses to the class and the teacher. Task refusal is often a mask for inadequacy and fear of failure and can even be a form of attention-seeking.

Avoiding the task	*Setting*
Forgetting the necessary equipment: physical education gear, pens, books, locker keys. Lateness to class. Truancy or school refusal.	Usually outside the class. The object is to make it difficult to participate.

Rejecting and demanding the task	*Setting*
Destroying instruction sheets or throwing away textbook. Verbally passing opinion on the usefulness of the task: 'This work sucks!'; 'Bloody rubbish'.	Usually at the commencement of the activity.

Procrastinating the commencement of the task	*Setting*
Continually seeking further instructions about one task. Taking excessive time in preparation: sharpening pencils, borrowing equipment from others.	Inside the class. The student can be trying to remain as unobtrusive as possible. Sometimes it is used as a form of attention-seeking (keeping the teacher busy by constantly coming back to the student).

Passive resistance / withdrawal	*Setting*
Accepting instruction sheets and going through the motions but not actually doing the task. Taking the whole period to copy out the questions.	Inside the class.

Remember to investigate outside causes for task refusal as well as using consistent approaches in the classroom.

Strategies for task refusal

STAGE ONE

The student has announced that she doesn't intend to do the work which has been set. 'If you don't do it now, we'll have to follow it up later. It's your choice.' 'You can't make me do it.' 'That's right. It's your choice, but we will be following that up later.' Teacher walks away.

Deflective statements using humour are good for this type of behaviour also. 'Gees, this work's boring, sir.' Teacher picks up the work, has a look, puts on a studied expression and says, 'You're right!' and walks off. He'll come back later to see how things are, but at the point of 'heat', he uses repartee. The main thing is not to get into pointless arguments. If necessary reassert or give a choice.

STAGE TWO

Where any disruption makes it impossible for you to teach and others to learn, give a choice to settle down or move to another desk. There is a distinction between the blatant task refuser who tears up work, and the passive task refuser who doesn't do work due to imagined or real inadequacy. One helpful method is to include the passive task refuser in group activities which are *not* task oriented such as self-esteem games or cooperative group activities. Introduce these activities on a monthly basis. Build up self-esteem by encouraging every small step a child makes so you are encouraging *effort*. Don't over concentrate on failure. Failure crushes every small effort in students with low self-esteem. Provide learning tasks where the child can achieve some level of competence. Such children find it extremely difficult to build on failure; we need to enable them to build from failure to experience some success. Short work or task contracts are one way to cater for mixed-ability problems; another is cooperative-learning contracts (see Glasser 1985, Dalton 1985).

Beyond the classroom steps

Because disruptive behaviour by students cannot always be settled, in the short-term, at the classroom level, teachers will (with collegiate support) need to have a longer-term supportive discipline policy in place.

- Conferencing and contracting approaches (see Chapter 5).
- Notifying parents although this depends on the circumstances.

   David's parents were told about his aggressive behaviour when they came to pick him up one Friday afternoon. The teacher thought it was about time they knew and had asked that they come to the school to pick him up and have a talk. David's father immediately yelled at the child in front of the teacher and carted him off to the car. As the teacher watched through the window she saw David get a belting as he was pushed into the back seat. Teachers and senior staff need to think carefully when and how they will contact *some* parents. Normally the school will have a clear policy on this.

Giving students the right of reply

We all like to feel we've been given a chance to tell our side of the story. If a student is arguing that, 'It's not fair, you never listen to me!', he may be right. Obviously we can't have lengthy discussions in the classroom, we rarely have the time. We can, however, accord right-of-reply in one of two ways.

- Take the student aside during the lesson and have a brief chat to find out what is going on.
- Refer the matter to a later time, after class or at recess.

Taking the student aside

David comes in late. The teacher minimises fuss by simply saying 'Please sit down Dave, I'll be with you in a minute'. She senses, however, that he's got a problem. When the class is working, Dave sits moodily, refusing to do his work. He's also started to flick elastic bands at Michael. The teacher uses a question and feedback approach. 'What's going on?' 'Nothing!' She reminds him about settling down to work but he starts his disruptive, attention-seeking behaviour again, this time with loud talking to Michael. His behaviour is clearly affecting others' right to work. The teacher moves alongside, and with a quiet but firm voice says, 'David, I want to see you over here please' gesturing towards the area near her desk. Taking the student aside minimises embarrassment and hostility; it also minimises peer audience.

She will say something like, 'Looks like you're upset Dave. What's the problem?' or 'What's going on Dave?' or 'We can't go on like this — what's happening?' or 'You know the fair rules Dave'. She speaks clearly, firmly but without rancour or hostility. If the student's behaviour has been particularly problematic she may remind him of the rules and get his commitment to work within the class's fair rules. If the student is really upset she may take him just outside the door to quickly re-establish with him what the reasonable expected behaviour is.

By taking the student aside we minimise embarrassment to him and his peers; we also afford the opportunity to be a little more discursive.

Taking aside is a form of brief, private conference. 'Hey Maria, what's up? You're not normally like this.' If the student refuses to respond to being taken aside, let them know they have a choice of now or later.

Take the student aside

- 'Dave, it can't go on like this.'
- 'What's the problem? Perhaps you're trying to show me I can't make you do the work. You're right. I can't make you, it's your choice.'
- 'So, what are you going to do about it?' (putting responsibility on the student).
- 'How can I help?'

It may well be, of course, that the student does have a problem he's dragged with him to school. The immediate purpose of taking the student aside is to get some immediate feedback, re-establish a rules focus and, if necessary, assure him you'll follow up with him later. It is not a 'hammer the kid' time or preaching time or talk-down time.

Taking aside can also be used to remind students about consequences should they continue with their present, disruptive behaviour. Assure them you know they can work by the fair rules, send them back to their desk, and briefly encourage any on-task behaviour from then on.

Following up later

Let the student know at some point in the lesson that if they cannot settle down then you'll have to ask them to stay back and explain (right of reply) later. Again this will involve low-key questioning.

- 'David, we need to discuss this problem of calling out in class.'
- 'Things are not working out between us. What's the problem?'

Employ some reflective listening.

- 'It sounds like you're saying you're frustrated by the work. Is that right?'

- 'Okay. What's a better way of working out the frustration?'
- 'Could it be that your regular calling out, ten times Dave, is just to keep getting my attention? Okay, what are we going to do about it?'

If follow-up is proving ineffective, then employ more formal contracting and conferencing procedures involving another teacher.

Exit from classroom

This presumes the school has a uniform exit policy for seriously disruptive behaviour.

The exit procedure needs to be non-humiliating to all. This procedure is best carried out by another person quickly, non-threateningly, in a face-saving fashion and quietly, by an independent person, without fuss. The child would then negotiate with a third party to re-enter the class and follow up with consequences/contracting. This is discussed at some length in Chapter 5.

How assertive?

Assertion is best seen in contrast with aggression. When a teacher is acting aggressively, he is only concerned with his needs and beliefs (I must win; she must do as she's told, the little b____!). Behaviour expressed is hostile, often demeaning and embarrassing. Voice and gestures often portray aggressive power.

When a teacher is acting submissively or non-assertively, they often allow the other party to dominate the transaction. The beliefs of non-assertion often carry within the fear of rejection or of having to face conflict and 'losing'. Indecisive, non-assertive, management over-accedes to the other party, allowing the student to decide the agenda, and the objectives of self-discipline and responsibility to rules are often bypassed. Non-assertive teachers often start off trying to be fair, 'nice' and reasonable, but when pushed to the limit, by trying children, will resort to pleading and shouting.

- Act from a position of one's rights without riding roughshod over the other person's rights.
- Speak decisively, firmly, clearly, expressing the requirements at hand or, when angry, one's own feelings. Speaking assertively means trying to separate the child from his action. 'David, I am

angry about the way you're speaking to Maria. Stop it now. You know our rule.' The teacher follows up later. If communicating to the whole class, eye sweep the whole class and speak firmly, clearly about that which upsets you. It saves the angry yelling and humiliating 'you' messages. 'You make me sick 8D, it's always the same isn't it! You're like a pack of animals. I've had it with you.'

- If we're too angry to speak rationally, it is better to cool off by explaining we're too uptight and follow up later. When children are too angry or uptight, use time-out as a means to cool off and follow up at a later time (see Chapter 5).
- Speak within a *rules, rights, responsibility* framework rather than from mere status. The issue at stake is generally one relating to rights. It is often helpful to speak from a rules focus because rules focus on due rights. With older students (Years 10–12) it is often helpful to use simple directions that convey where our rights are infringed.

  A rude student continues to butt in. 'Excuse me John! (Focus.) You can see I'm trying to speak. I can't with that noise level. I expect your cooperation. Thank you.' 'Excuse me Simone. You want to talk to Maria, I need to teach. You know our rules. Use them. Thanks.' While such an approach gives significant attention to the student we, at least, assert our due rights.

- Be aware of the students' feelings. Sometimes it may be appropriate to take a child aside (lateness, crying, worry, no equipment etc).
- Observe the protocols of positive discipline.
- Work hard at building a positive class climate. The essence of good discipline is creating a social learning environment where correction is seen for what it is — the clear reminder to act responsibly and respect rights. Even the recidivist will more likely take the 'hard work' and the necessary consequences when the class 'tone' and climate is positive.

Planning steps and negotiating disruptions

Levels of teacher action should become increasingly more decisive according to the level of disruption and the context of the disruption. In the course of any lesson there are three general phases that establish the context:

- the establishment phase
- the on-task phase
- the relinquishing phase

It is worth noting these as our discipline plan needs to be modified depending whether we are 'up-front' or moving round the room when students are on-task.

The establishment phase

This is the beginning of the lesson when students are filing in, settling down and we are trying to establish initial attention. Primary school teachers, at least in elementary grades, use all sorts of listening games to get children seated and attentive. The older children get the less novelty we can apply. We do, however, need to establish initial attention quickly so that we can focus in on the learning activities.

We can do this by:

- signalling quieter members
- waiting for a minute or two and giving a general direction ('Okay, time to settle down. Good morning all.')
- simply setting up the work and waiting.

It is very important to greet the students, have a brief chat and clearly focus where the lesson will be going that session. If we are indecisive and uncertain here, it will affect all that happens from then on.

The sorts of disruptions that occur at the beginning of the lesson are:

- shufflers, whisperers
- general noise level
- calling out and/or butting in
- silly noises
- clowning
- late arrivals

When disciplining 'up-front', when we are the primary (although perhaps not the only) focus of attention, it is better to use:

- brief, simple directions
- clear rule reminders
- straight tactical ignoring
- diversions and distractions
- light humour

When giving a direction as corrective discipline 'up-front', it is important not to over-attend by walking across to a student and getting into a long discussion. This only gives more attention than is due. Keep it brief and redirect attention quickly to the lesson.

It is the Year 7 science class. Dorothy, the wearisome class clown, has her bag on the table and is playing a nice attention-seeking game of hide-and-seek from behind her bag. Regressive? Of course. The question is do we give her more attention or what? We could try a spell of tactical ignoring. We could give a brief, simple direction and leave it at that: 'Dorothy, put the bag on the floor now thanks. Good on you.' and quickly carry on, expecting compliance. We could use counter-humour or repartee. Grin back with a little giggle (focus the attention she wants). 'You do it well, Dorothy, thank you for the laugh. Bag on floor. Ta.'

Repartee, not malicious humour, is never sadistic. In the hands of those using it skilfully, it is a powerful ally in defusing conflict. If disruptions are persistent, give a clear choice within the class. Avoid arguing, threatening, discussing or procrastinating. They are all counter-productive.

The on-task phase

At this stage, the teacher is moving around the room while the students are supposed to be on-task. During this time there is an initial settling down during which some students will:
- not have pens, pencils, books or equipment
- say, 'What do we have to do again, Miss?'
- stare idly out of the window
- be out of their seat for reasons best known to them
- clearly not have understood what you meant when you said . . .

As the on-task phase continues some students will:
- call out across the room
- wander
- sit next to other students
- task-refuse
- talk constantly to a friend
- clown around

During this phase of the lesson, a teacher can use a wide repertoire as she divides her attention across the group; from least intrusive approaches like tactical ignoring and non-verbal messages, simple directions, rule restatements and reminders or casual statements, to the more decisive questioning approaches. Where students are upset, angry or quarrelsome she may take them aside or give a clear choice. Where appropriate, she will use humour (if it's an approach she's comfortable with). At all times she will be prepared to reassert a rule or direction in a fair way. She will avoid arguing, blaming or preaching, but look for ways to put the responsibility back on to the student. This is the essence of a plan, using *appropriate* steps with a decisive manner.

The relinquishing phase

This is the winding down of activity: packing up, giving any final instruction, cleaning up mess, putting chairs away, a final cheerio. The sorts of disruptions occurring here are:

- slow finishers
- uncompleted tasks
- early finishers (Have some activity they can do so they are not disturbing others: worksheets, extension activities, reading a book, library corner.)
- students who attempt to 'beat the bell'
- students calling out

Because the teacher is resuming a focus up-front, it is important to keep any discipline brief. Keep the instructions clear, establish good pack-up routines. Leave the classroom tidy, put chairs under desks (or on them), and encourage an orderly exit. Insist on this from day one by making the expectations clear. It is something that can be discussed during the rule-making phase.

The context of disruption

In all discipline transactions, the key to the teacher's behaviour is the context in which disruption occurs. If the disruption is low-level, merely walking close to the student's desk or even tactical ignoring may be sufficient. If a student hasn't got the correct uniform on the teacher would probably be best served by calling the student aside quietly (preferably near the close of the lesson) and reminding them or simply asking why. If a student is late, instead of a big discussion at the door, it is better to merely direct the student to their seat letting them know you'll talk with them later. If a student hasn't started work, if two students are merely off-task with their talking, or if a student is daydreaming, it is entirely appropriate to simply walk up and casually ask the question, 'How's it going?' or 'Where are you up to?' or 'Can I see your work?'. Casually asking a question says to the student, without a big debate, 'I'm here, you're here, you know I'm here to remind you to get back to work, or to help, or to correct'. All this can be communicated by a casual statement or question. If we sense the student is disturbed or upset, we can call the student aside, away from the others to minimise embarrassment or audience-seeking or the possibility of hostile 'one-upmanship'. If speaking from the front to a student persistently calling out, then the voice will need to be more assertive than if speaking to two talkers while doing 'the rounds' (when students are supposed to be on-task at their desks or tables).

Summary

How we combine these steps constitutes our discipline plan. The more conscious we are of what we say and do when disruptions occur, the more effective that plan will be. The more consistent we are in the practice of the plan the more likely it is that on-task learning is enhanced. Knowing what we can do and developing the skills, also minimises the degree to which frustration affects our ability to cope. A plan gives us confidence that we have chosen the better options.

The approaches outlined in this chapter have sought to classify teacher actions that consciously observe the protocols discussed earlier; they form a basis for a general discipline plan that any teacher could use with confidence. Specific discipline plans (for individual children or problem classes) or contingency plans are discussed later in this book but even those 'plans' will employ many of the approaches discussed in this chapter.

In the end, when a disruption occurs in our room, we have to do or say *something*. Planning that something, ahead of time, is what being professional is all about. When I make a good fist of that, the odds are I'll not get as upset, as often, as long.

- What are the student behaviours you currently find most disturbing, frustrating? How have you gone about establishing a positive working relationship with your students?
- Are you consciously aware of what you say and do, currently, to manage these disruptions?
- Can you list, for example, specific things you say to manage calling out, out-of-seat behaviour, task refusal etc.
- In the light of the skills mentioned in this chapter, in what ways do you believe you should modify your discipline practice?
- Where will you start?
  (See Appendix I for a personal running record.)
- What support will you need from your peers to improve your discipline practice?

CHAPTER 4

Rights and rules in the classroom

*In giving rights to others which belong
to them, we give rights to ourselves.*
John F. Kennedy

The Nobel prize-winning laureate William Golding recounts his experiences of teaching English to ten-year-olds in the 1940s. Apparently, the school's headmaster had proposed the revolutionary notion of self government. Classroom discussions were given over to student control and chairing. Mr Golding remembers with some clarity the mayhem and chaos that resulted. He had to physically intervene before physical harm ensued! Perhaps they couldn't handle student rights in the 1940s. No doubt it confirmed, as John Mortimer writes, some fundamental and dark suspicions about mankind (and 'boykind'). *Lord of the Flies*, his novel about the propensity of the 'dark soul', even in children, may have been affected by a badly handled experiment on student rights.

The problem

Whenever the issue of student rights, or democracy in the classroom, is canvassed, there are those who express the opinion that it will mean reduction in teacher authority, the 'thin end of the wedge', uncontrollable student behaviour or just 'that airy-fairy rubbish preached by the liberals'. 'We've got enough problems with students without teaching them about their rights! They won't be able to handle it.' The 1980s has seen a resurgence of discipline policy direction based around rights. What does this mean?

The moral/philosophical justification

The issue of rights is not simply one of 1980s liberationism that we must somehow adopt. The notion of rights is not a new, post-60s idea. Neither is it anarchistic or anti-authoritarian. It *is* the basis for the United Nations declaration on human rights: the fundamental application of justice and dignity to human treatment. One of the classical definitions of rights is that expression of 'something', in value, attitude or action, as fundamentally right or proper about being together and working together, as humans.

Rights

In exploring rights with students and parent groups we begin with the fundamental values we agree on as a school community. These values need to be brought out into the open by discussion and teaching. Most often these are the *assumed* values: a fair go, cooperation, the fundamental dignity of a person (despite gender, race, religion or even taste in music), honesty, mutual respect and so on. They are the basis of those 'things' we deem right or proper about social relations and groups.

Of course there will be a clash of values at times between teachers from dominant middle-class backgrounds and students from low socio-economic backgrounds. Teachers who struggle with this clash of values often concentrate on issues like disrespect, student manners, dress, standards of work and language. Teachers who work successfully with such student populations have learnt to earn rather than demand respect; expect rather than demand compliance; model fair treatment; and look beyond the window dressing of 'culture'. Many a philosophic liberal has changed their practice when forced to interact with students whose ethnicity or social background clashes markedly with theirs.

Teaching rights in the classroom

Under the aegis of rights a teacher will seek to weld a group of disparate individuals into some sort of community. In the course of that process, she will bring to the surface fundamental values by teaching, discussion, and fundamental expectations which will focus on such questions as:

- 'What do we value about others in our school community and the wider community, of which I am a member?'
- 'Is it right to put someone else down just because they are a different colour, have a different religion, speak differently, stutter, are disabled, "ugly", "not as bright as us", "poor" . . .'

A different social climate

There is no question that significant numbers of teachers disenfranchised student rights in the past through beltings, intimidation, dunces' caps for 'dummies', pushing, shoving, pulling hair, poking. The power *balance* was certainly in favour of the teacher.

Students today develop early the notion that they *have* rights. They may not articulate that notion well or clearly but their behaviour indicates that no longer will they be treated as inferior because of their status as child or minor. The days are long gone when a teacher can call on role authority to *demand* respect. These days, teachers have to earn respect by the nature of their treatment and the manner in which fundamental rights are given their due.

No automatic rights

In establishing rights, the degree of student discussion and involvement will depend upon age, situation and teacher confidence-cum-skill. In teaching rights to elementary-age students, teachers can use drama, story books, role-play or games to illustrate how we help or hurt others by how we think of and consequently treat them. Older students can easily fill a blackboard with what they believe their rights to be. Often they have the language of rights ('I got my rights') as a list of things demanded or expected. When directing classroom discussion, teachers need to guide the discussion towards responsibility. Our discipline, our treatment of students will be directed towards them taking responsibility for their behaviour. We will treat them as persons who can, and should, account for their actions and face up to the logical consequences of the effect of their actions on others.

No one enjoys his or her rights automatically as if the right to learn, for example, exists without due responsibility exercised by teacher and student alike. When discussing rights with students, we will often explore responsibility by asking, 'Well, if you have a right to learn, how is that right protected?' Just saying, 'We have a right' explains nothing about its exercise or enjoyment. Teachers can easily remove a student's right to fair treatment by put-downs, hostile, demeaning or sarcastic comments, intimidation and the like. Students can easily take away other students' rights to learn and be safe by fooling around, butting in, put-downs, and so on, just as a teacher's right can be removed by student rudeness and irresponsible behaviour.

Defining what a *right* is helps students to see that the fundamental nature of rights is concerned with relationships: justice and fair treatment. Female teachers, for example, have a right to the same basic respect as male teachers, even if some students' ethnic or cultural heritage predisposes them to see females as non-authority figures. Fundamental human rights transcend cultural differences (what was once termed the moral law). No one in our classroom will be put down simply because they are female. Sexist, jingoistic, cultural baggage is no defence against the moral law.

As Professor C. S. Lewis (1978) pointed out in 1943, behind all laws we make there is a *natural* 'moral law', a fundamental concept basic to all civilisation. Without the moral law, the essence of *rights*, actual laws (especially state laws) become a new absolute. *Your* right, is, in a very real sense, *my responsibility*. I don't actually enjoy my right (as a due) until, and unless, other members of the group allow me such enjoyment. The teacher's role is to protect rights, encourage responsibility and enforce rules.

However, a teacher is foolish to simply demand respect. If, as a teacher, I don't act and speak respectfully to my students, how can I demand it in return? There are still teachers who treat students with discourtesies that would be regarded as rank bad manners in any other social context. Teacher modelling has a powerful effect on the developing social climate of a classroom.

In pursuing the issue of rights with older students a process of listing priorities usually ends up with several rights which will include the following:

- A right to express myself.
- A right to be an individual.
- A right to learn (and at a fair, individual pace and from teachers who act in a professional manner and who prepare adequate curriculum with some attention to mixed abilities).
- A right to teacher assistance.
- A right to move around the classroom. (Should students have to put up their hand every time they want to get out of their seat?)
- A right to safety (a safe school environment free from stupid irrational bullying by teachers or students).
- A right to participate in the schooling process.
- A right to tell my side in a dispute or conflict.

In one sense, the rights of teacher and student are shared. Even the right to teach can be shared by students where appropriate though the responsibility to teach and lead the group is fundamentally the teacher's.

Values

- A value is something we consider to be very important.
- A value is something that lies behind what we actually do.
- A value is something we hold as desirable.
- A value is something we believe is worthwhile and significant about how we relate to each other.

We hold our values as a whole community of parents, teachers and children. If we value respect, then we express that as a *right*. So a right is something we ought to respect within the community, and from the community, because the community values it. In this way, because the community values these things, it also expects them and holds them as rights.

These are the fundamental values, which should be encouraged, taught and promoted within the school community.

Values	*Expressions of the values we hold*
Self-discipline Self-control Self-responsibility	Rather than merely controlling the child by using adult authority, we are seeking to promote an environment where we help children to control themselves. Obviously this will relate to the child's age and development, but at every opportunity we seek to teach the child that they are *responsible* for their own behaviour.
Self-esteem Self-respect	Self-esteem means the value we place on ourselves. It means that we distinguish between a person and their behaviour. We can value, esteem and respect the person yet still call their behaviour to account.
Equality of treatment Dignity Worth Fairness Justice	Regardless of sex, colour, background or nationality, children are treated equally and have equal access to educational opportunity within the school community. Justice in the school community depends on having clearly agreed rules — rules that uphold our values and protect our rights. Justice is the fair treatment of the children within these rules, rights and relationships.

Values	Expressions of the values we hold
Consideration for others Respect Courtesy Tolerance Team work Trust Honesty	The spirit and practice of democracy is encouraged and promoted in the social as well as learning environment. Manners are an expression of courtesy, consideration for and respect of others in the community.
Pride Effort	Pride in the school, in work, in effort as well as achievement. There is willingness to *try* rather than give up just because a task is hard.

Children's rights

1 To be able to learn in a friendly, encouraging, secure, supportive, and positive school environment.

   Responsibilities

   Children: • to be cooperative and considerate
   • to do their work on time

   Parents: • to be supportive in developing these responsibilities

   Teachers: • to work towards providing this environment by being encouraging, positive, and disciplining fairly

2 To have appropriate access to the school's facilities.

   Responsibilities

   Children: • to share equipment
   • to care for equipment

   Teachers and school:
   • to allocate use of facilities appropriately and fairly

3 To have appropriate access to the teacher's time.

Responsibilities

Children: • not to demand attention all the time
           • to try to be receptive and cooperative
Teachers: • to allocate time fairly

4 To have a safe environment.

Responsibilities

Children: • to act in a safe and responsible manner for themselves and others
Teachers: • to try to ensure that the environment is safe and that children act safely
Education system:
           • to provide a safe environment

5 To be heard and be able to express opinions.

Responsibilities

Children: • to speak out but also to listen
           • not to put others down
           • not to dominate
Teachers: • to encourage children to speak
           • to listen
           • to guide group discussions
           • to teach non-assertive students appropriate assertive behaviour

6 To know what is acceptable behaviour and the consequences of unacceptable behaviour.

Responsibilities

Children, parents and teachers:
           • to discuss this with students and make the issue clear through fair classroom rules

---

Parents' rights

To be able to participate in their children's education by having two-way communication with the school as follows:

1 To have information on school processes and curriculum.

Responsibilities

Parents:
- to ask for information if they are unsure or want to know more

Teachers and school:
- to disseminate information

2 To be able to participate in school programs and decision-making processes.

Responsibilities

Parents:
- to make the time to be involved
- to make the effort

3 To receive and offer information about their children's education and behaviour.

Responsibilities

Parents and teachers:
- to be open and encouraging and willing to listen
- to develop workable solutions to problems

4 To expect consistent approaches to codes of behaviour used by teachers throughout the school.

Responsibilities

Parents:
- to be involved in planning school policy
- to let the school know of concerns about discipline

Teachers:
- to communicate with parents and reach agreement on discipline protocols and practice

5 To expect that there will be no cultural, sexual or physical discrimination against parents or children.

Responsibilities

Children, parents, teachers and school:
- not to discriminate or to accept others doing it

Teachers' rights

1 To work in a pleasant and safe environment and to be able to achieve job satisfaction.

Responsibilities

Children: • to be considerate and provide support
Parents: • to be considerate and provide support
Teachers: • to play a part in the running of the school
            • to prepare lessons thoughtfully
            • to watch for unsafe things and practices

Education system:

            • to provide a pleasant and safe environment (watch those crook desks and old portables!)

2 To have support from within the Education system, including other members of staff if required.

Responsibilities

Teachers: • to provide that support both informally and formally (see Chapters 6 and 9).

3 To be involved in a collaborative decision-making model within the school (curriculum and organisation).

Responsibilities

Parents: • to consult with teachers and reach agreement
Teachers: • to consult with each other and reach agreement
            • to make an effort to be involved

4 To be treated with courtesy by all.

Responsibilities

Children, parents and teachers:

            • to treat others with courtesy

5 To be able to create time-out situations for children when they are disrupting other people's rights to safe movement, learning/teaching or communication.

Responsibilities

Parents: • to support this as a feature of positive discipline (see Chapter 5).

Teachers: • not to abuse this or use it to put down or ridicule children
            • to follow up time-out with conferencing and contracting procedures (see Chapter 5).

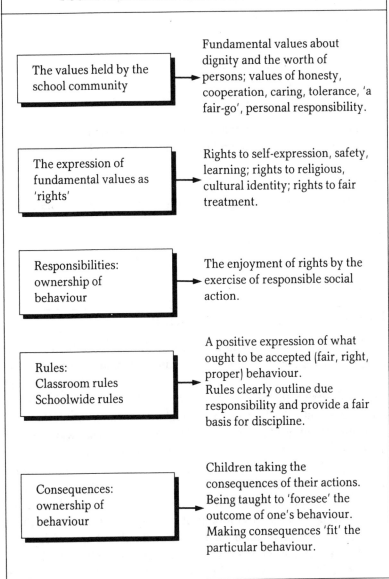

THE RIGHTS, RESPONSIBILITY, RULES FOCUS: A BASIS FOR POSITIVE STUDENT-TEACHER INTERACTION

The values held by the school community → Fundamental values about dignity and the worth of persons; values of honesty, cooperation, caring, tolerance, 'a fair-go', personal responsibility.

The expression of fundamental values as 'rights' → Rights to self-expression, safety, learning; rights to religious, cultural identity; rights to fair treatment.

Responsibilities: ownership of behaviour → The enjoyment of rights by the exercise of responsible social action.

Rules: Classroom rules Schoolwide rules → A positive expression of what ought to be accepted (fair, right, proper) behaviour. Rules clearly outline due responsibility and provide a fair basis for discipline.

Consequences: ownership of behaviour → Children taking the consequences of their actions. Being taught to 'foresee' the outcome of one's behaviour. Making consequences 'fit' the particular behaviour.

Fig 4

6 To contact, and have backup and cooperation from, parents and to
   be informed of family situations and home problems where they
   may affect behaviour and attitudes at school.

   Responsibilities
   Parents: • to let the teacher know about relevant problems
                 • to provide support for the teacher
   Teachers: • to contact the parents if there is a problem
                 • to be approachable, to listen, to make the time, to
                   act on information

7 To be seen as an individual by children and parents and be able to
   express a point of view without 'indoctrinating' children on social
   issues.

   Responsibilities
   Teachers: • not to inflict unasked-for opinions on children

The substance of the section above is based on the discipline/welfare
policy of Moonee Ponds West Primary School, Victoria.

Developing rules with students

'I think that the rules should be made by the kids and the teacher. It
would be fairer and then the kids couldn't complain about the rules.'

Year 7 student

I was discussing the need for classroom rules with a robust Year 7
class. As a visitor to their room I thought it pertinent to ask the basic
question, 'What are the rules in your classroom?'. One wag down in
the back row yelled out, 'We're not supposed to call out, we put our
hands up!'. I imagine he thought that because he had his hand up *while*
he called out that his behaviour was okay. I ignored him (tactically)
and asked the question again until somebody put their hand up. Obviously, *having* a rule and enforcing it are two different things. Rules
don't guarantee compliant behaviour, they simply set an agenda for it.
It is the teacher's duty to develop, make clear, and enforce such rules.

   For rules to be effective, they need to be linked to a process of
discussion with students during the establishment phase of the year.
This is when we need to make clear our leadership style and establish

our credibility to teach, guide and direct the group. Good rules are the *preventative* side of discipline. It will be quite normal that the rules, even when made by the students, will enjoy some testing to establish their credibility even when the students have participated in rule making. For younger students, teachers need to concentrate on the *rule* side of rights (We will not speak when someone else is.); for older students we would include rights as a feature of rule-making (We will respect the right of everyone to speak without interruption). Behind the rule for communication, for example, is the right to have our say, share our opinions, talk (at times) while we work. The rule side of the right enshrines the responsibility of speaking respectfully in ways which don't hurt, demean or put others down or limit them having a fair go. It teaches that freedoms for oneself are only reasonable when they do not deny others their freedoms. In general, rules should be:

1 *Positive in intent*

   'In our classroom we put up our hands to ask a question,' is obviously better than, 'Don't call out'. 'Walk quietly' is better than, 'Don't run'.

2 *Few in number*

We need to avoid the farcical situation of a long list of rules that even the teacher cannot remember. (No running; no throwing blocks; no fighting; no jumping on anyone's back; no shouting; no scissor fights; no climbing on tables; no hitting . . . were only a few of a list I saw in a Year 2 class!)

3 *Clear and specific*

A rule should outline what is and is not acceptable. 'We walk quietly in the classroom; we do not run.' 'In our classroom we put up our hands to ask a question without calling out. At our desks we talk quietly so others can work as well.' Rules ought to specify what is and isn't the accepted behaviour. Simply saying we should all be cooperative is not very helpful as a rule (although a desirable aim). 'Do unto others . . .' is an excellent (perhaps even the best) philosophy but it hardly clarifies the 'what' and 'when'. Make the rule clear and specific, make the general consequences clear as well. Keep away from tacit assumptions.

4 *Taught* (with younger students)

Rules should be regularly referred to and enforced. A good deal of discipline will often include quiet rule reminders. Obviously, if such rules have been made with the students, compliance is more likely to occur. The rules, rather than merely teacher authority, become the basis for arbitration.

Ownership of the rules

It is important to discuss the rules with the students. With younger students, the rules can be discussed through stories, role-plays, portrayed in picture rule cards. With older students (Years 3–6), the rules can be discussed through small groups and even written up by the children on cards to be displayed around the classroom. When setting down the final form of a rule, it is generally better to have a key descriptor such as 'Talking rule', 'Our communication rule', 'Our safety rule', 'Our movement rule', or 'Moving around the room rule'. With post-primary students, it is important that rules not be seen as mere teacher imposition ('These are my rules!'). Students are more likely to 'own' rules if they feel they have had some part to play in their formation.

Exploring rules through the notion of rights is also important. Children these days are aware of their rights though they often communicate such awareness without a due respect for responsibilities. This aspect of rule-making is essential for older students in Years 5–12.

Specialist teachers (Phys. Ed., Library, relieving teachers, Art, Home Economics etc.) will not have the luxury of time to negotiate their rules but are well served, nonetheless, by discussing the rules 'up-front'; why they are needed, what purpose they serve, and what the general consequences will be for outright disruptive behaviour. With younger students the discussion can be aided by having the rules written up on cards, briefly and positively stated. Another way of presenting them is to use overhead transparencies and a hand-out sheet. The main point is to facilitate the discussion process.

Discussion groups

One way to develop rules is through a whole class discussion on the meaning of rights. Focus on a *right* as a privilege or an entitlement which we enjoy in relation to others whose responsibility enables our entitlement. Emphasise that rights in the classroom, on the freeway, in a family, in society are not merely automatic expectations.

Where do we see rules? Who is responsible for making rules? Who is responsible for enforcing rules? What are some of the places you go to that have rules (clubs, shops, libraries, the beach)? How are rules made known? Who is responsible when rules are broken? Brainstorming helps children to see the fundamental and necessary places of rules in society. Our classrooms, too, are part of society; we too need to make *our* rules.

If I am an abusive, arrogant, hostile, demeaning teacher, what happens to the students' right to respectful discipline, or even just respectful treatment? If 'x', 'y' and 'z' students continually call out, where are the other students' rights to communicate, listen and learn? If 'x' and 'y' persistently turn around to annoy 'z', where is 'z's right to learn?

Everyone has a right to their say providing that they have their say fairly; speak at appropriate times; and give the same courtesy to others as they expect for themselves. Students quickly see the logic in this and benefit from seeing rules as 'mechanisms' that seek to protect individual rights (my right as teacher to teach, students' rights to learn, be safe, settle conflicts peacefully, to ask questions, get help with their learning, learn without interruption and so on).

Forming the rules

In making the rules, teachers can wind up the classroom discussion and move on to one of the following approaches:

1 'Well we can see, as always, we need rules. I've set up the rules we'll be using together in 8D this year. Let me share them with you and get your response.'

2 'What I'm going to ask you to do is split up into four or five groups and come up with several rules essential for our class.' After 20-25 minutes get the feedback and isolate the common, essential rules.

3 A variation of this is the 2, 4, 6 discussion groups approach. The class is divided into pairs for 10 minutes and asked to come up with several rules we'll need if we are to work well as a class. After 10 minutes, the pairs join up with another pair to share and reach common agreement. After another 10 minutes, 3 pairs join for a final sharing. In this way, there are several clarifications with each pair testing out their ideas and beliefs. The teacher will then receive feedback from the groups of 6 on their common, agreed rules. These become the class rules. (Generally they come up with much the same as what a teacher would want or expect.) The final stage is to write up the rules in some way, either to be displayed on cards on the wall, or written up as the 'Rules for *Our* Room'.

The language of rules

It is important that teachers develop with the students, their own language for expressing the classroom rules. Students, from Year 3-4 upwards, can be encouraged to write the rules in their own words. Generally speaking, there are several rules that can be culled from classroom discussions. These need to be expressed appropriately for the particular age level.

COMMUNICATION (for younger students the term 'talking rule' is sufficient)

This rule would cover: hands-up for questions and discussion; working noise at desks; use of hurtful language (swearing, put-down or racist language, teasing). Another way to cover the use of language is to make a 'positive language rule'.

Of course, working noise in an art room or trade area will be different (generally speaking) from in a maths class. Working noise may also be different when working in small groups or during set times. This needs to be made clear with the students.

CONFLICT-SETTLING (for younger students problem-fix-it-up rule)

There are any number of disputes occurring in the life of a class. 'He's got my rubber!', 'She's nicked my pen sir!', 'He hit me again, sir!', 'She's not my friend any more Miss. I hate her'. It is important to have a basic rule governing peaceful dispute settling because we don't have time to sit and negotiate each problem in the space of a lesson. Settling of disputes should stress negotiation, with the teacher's help if necessary.

MOVEMENT

This rule is difficult to specify because of teachers' different views regarding acceptable movement. The rule, however, should specify the amount and kind of movement acceptable in our room. If you believe children should only get out of their seats with permission, say so in your rule. Added to the movement rule may be the 'coming-in' and 'going-out' movement rule to be applied when lining up, sitting on the mat or moving seats. Appropriate permission for leaving the class can also be covered by this rule.

SAFETY-SECURITY

This covers use of equipment, protection of property, safe behaviour in certain classes (art, trades, science, home economics etc.) as well as in the non-specialist classroom. The safety rule may also note the wearing of unsafe clothing and jewellery or possession of any toys which are unacceptable and/or inappropriate to school.

LEARNING

This rule covers the students' learning climate. It should cover at-seat learning, procedures to get teacher assistance during on-task time, routines for work stations, early finishing, and bringing of appropriate equipment to classes.

TREATMENT (of each other)

It is important that everyone in the classroom is treated fairly. This means not putting people down because they look different from us, have different backgrounds or come from different countries. It will also address issues like protecting the right to personal space, and sexism and racism where necessary.

Consequences

These rules are only suggestions and more decisive consequences can be written in. The fundamental point about consequences, however, is to make the 'if—then' nature of the rules clear to the students. One way of doing this is to ask the students what consequences ought apply for 'x' behaviours. Often they will be quite Draconian and we will need to push their thinking back to the issue. 'How does that (stated consequence) help to fix up the behaviour?' The consequences need to be clear in advance. Here are some 'if — then' examples.

1 Calling out
   - If you continue to call out you will be warned.
   - You may be asked to stay back and explain your behaviour.
   - You may be excluded from class discussions for a time.
2 Fighting in the classroom
   - Immediate separation.
   - Working separately when 'cooled off'.
   - Staying back to 'settle-up'.
3 If you damage others' work or property, you will replace it in some way.

We can't, of course, have a consequence for every contingency but we can discuss the nature of consequences so students are clear about their responsibility.

Rules and younger students (Kinder to Year 1)

Small children live in a world where much of their social movement and play begins to interface with rules by the time they reach school age. Piaget (1932) has suggested that 'all morality consists in a system of rules, and the essence of all morality is to be sought in the respect which the individual acquires for these rules' (p 13). Piaget may not be highly regarded in educational thinking these days but he raises an

important point. Rules give some shape, dimension and limi
and moral activity. They help define the acceptable and unac
For smaller children, clear rules are part of the general teaching and
training for reasonable socialisation. As such, they assist the smooth
running of a classroom by minimising the need to be overly discursive
each time disruptive behaviour has to be addressed and corrected. 'But
I didn't know' should not be an excuse.

Rules help define 'the good' and, of course, small children need
appropriate limits; it gives them security on the one hand and confidence (if the rules are fairly enforced) in classroom leadership on the
other. Rules assist the process of self-discipline, so the means of
enforcement are as important as the rules themselves. When we
enforce the rules (bring moral force to bear) we will do it in a way that
draws attention to the students' responsibilities.

On day one, Mrs D. has set up the Prep class for maximum involvement, comfort, and learning. The room is bright, tables are well
grouped, cupboards clearly labelled with bright signs for scissors, clag
etc. She has name tags for everyone. Later she will help them illustrate
the big name tags for their 'lockers' — the plastic bins holding all their
gear.

She knows the importance of rules for young children and has
already illustrated five cards that depict aspects of desirable social
behaviour in the classroom. (If the teacher is not the 'best' artist, she
can employ a grade 5 or 6 student who can also assist in sharing the
rule ideas.) She holds up each card and discusses the behaviours
depicted as 'our rules'. She discusses why rules are important. 'Ever
tried to play a game without rules?' 'What sort of rules do you have at
home?' 'Why are rules important? How do they help us?' 'What do
these cards say about our rules?'

The pictures illustrate the main aspects of the rules:
- the fair limits to talking and asking questions
- movement around the room
- safety (use of equipment such as scissors)
- manners and cooperation

When discussing the 'helping rule' (manners, treatment, respect,
cooperation — words she will emphasise in the language/literature program), Mrs D. discusses and role-plays helpful words for asking and
borrowing. Calling up two students she asks, 'How can I borrow a
rubber from Michelle? Show me'. 'Sometimes people will snatch' (she

will model). 'What is a better way?' She discusses words and expressions like please, thank you, 'Can I help you?', 'Can I borrow', 'Will you help me?'. Mrs D. will regularly and firmly appeal to these rules by reminder or restatement. If two students are arguing over a rubber, she will gently direct their attention to the 'problem-fixing' rule or the 'helping rule' pinned up on the wall.

Knowing full well that children will test the rules, she will be prepared to enforce them by firm direction. 'Amy you know the rule for asking questions. Hands up, please.' She will rely on a firm rule-reminder (or restatement to all if necessary) to establish social harmony and teach responsibility. Much of the discipline in K–2 is 'training'; rules are a useful vehicle for such training. If students argue ('I was in the library corner first'), the teacher will resist counter-argument and re-assert the rule, several times if necessary. 'But, Amy, you know the rule for the library corner.'

As part of the discipline plan, rules form the fundamental focus backed up by positive teacher direction and a time-out corner for on-going disruptive behaviour. The class will know that the time-out corner is there for students who refuse (in effect choose) not to work by the fair class rules. It is the cool-off or settle-down place where they go until they are ready to work by the fair rules.

Some examples of visually represented rules

Our Talking Rule	*The card symbolises:* • hands up • talking noise level
Our Moving Rule	*The card symbolises:* • walk don't run • sitting on the mat • lining up
Our Manners Rule	*The card symbolises:* • helping • please and thank you • cooperation

Our Safety Rule	*The card symbolises:* • care for the classroom • using equipment properly
Our Problem-Fixing Rule	*The card symbolises:* • arguments and problems should be talked about • asking for the teacher's help

Yard behaviour

The bane of our week as teachers is often the 'patrol' time. The older the age group of children, the more difficult the time spent outside. Many secondary school teachers will report the 'blind-eye syndrome' — they don't want to *see* what is happening out there. They just want to finish the rounds as quickly as possible. When students answer back or refuse to pick up litter or argue defiantly or come up with the 101 issues they want resolved, many teachers feel the effort of 'yard discipline' is just not worth it.

Blind-eye syndrome

Is there a better way?

Solving the problem of yard behaviour is threefold:
• Adequate, reasonable, enforceable rules.
• Making sure those rules are clearly understood, by students, teachers and parents alike.
• Ensuring that such rules are enforced, and relevant consequences are consistently applied.

The yard problems basically revolve around:
• litter
• unsafe areas, out-of-bounds areas, non-ball-play areas, designated areas such as small children's play areas
• swearing (including defiance directed *at* teachers)
• fighting, over-aggressive play or unsafe play
• smoking
• 'dobbing', 'tattling', 'dispute-settling' and 'teasing'

What often creates problems is that rules for these behaviours are often unclear, uncertain or inconsistently enforced.

> Miss P. sees a Year 6 boy kicking his footy in a no-ball area. She asks him what he's doing and he replies sarcastically. (The territory of the yard is very different regarding respect, basic courtesy etc.) 'I'm not doing anything wrong!' 'This is a no-ball area. Take your footy and play down there (gestures to the ball area) please.' He replies with the standard procrastinating line, 'But Miss Davies says I can play here', and so it goes on. Playing one teacher off against another.

Making the rules clear

The focus of a better yard-behaviour policy is reasonable, just rules that protect the rights of all members of the school community. Discuss the yard rules with the students; make them a focus across the whole school. It may be possible with older students to negotiate some of the rules, although some will be non-negotiable (leaving the yard, smoking, aggressive behaviour).

It is important to make sure yard rules and their purpose are clearly understood by all students at assemblies, in the classroom and at home-group level. A clear rule is one that specifies expected and acceptable behaviour, boundaries for such behaviour and consequences for flagrant rule breaking.

Agreed plans for enforcement

Rules are one thing; the certainty of them being tested, resisted, spat at and broken is another. One way of better enforcing the rules is for all teachers to have a consistent plan for dealing with common disruptions.

We know we are daily going to face behaviours within the range from littering to fighting. It makes sense then to work together on a more uniform approach that enables us to answer these questions.

- Faced with 'x' behaviour, what is the best thing to do first, second, third and so on?
- What back-up can we organise if we meet flagrant defiance or hostility? (Staff support, time-out areas in the yard with primary age students, follow through, consequences.) Look at the following examples.

A child is clearly seen dropping litter.

Step 1
Direct the child, in a non-aggressive way, to pick it up (simple direction) or use question and feedback. 'What's going on?' or 'What are you doing?'. 'You know the rule for litter, pick it up and put it in the bin, thanks.' Expect the student to do it. If he refuses or says, 'Can't make me!' or worse go to Step 2.

Step 2
Remind him of the rule and that if he doesn't do as you ask, you'll have to see it will be followed up (litter patrol in his own time during detention). There is a sense that we can't make him pick it up, certainly not there and then, if he is audience seeking with his mates.

It is important to remain calm but assertive. There is no point in aggressive verbals in the yard.

Two children are engaged in a genuine fight.

Step 1
Firmly direct the audience to 'hop it'. This is one occasion to speak loudly and assertively!

Step 2
Firmly direct the head bangers to stop and move apart.

Step 3

If they don't, get help. Don't separate unless you are really confident about physical intervention. If it looks like a bad fight, send for help at Step 1.

Step 4

Have some cool-off place for fighters where they can go immediately. With younger children, a designated area for time-out is normally quite successful (an outside seat near the administration area).

Yard environment

It is also important to enhance the yard environment so that it contributes to positive behaviour.

- Ensure that there are plenty of decent rubbish bins with small openings so the paper cannot fly out!
- Beautify the grounds where possible; even concrete play grounds can be attractively set out with potted shrubs and trees.
- Provide ample and reasonable seating for students, preferably with some shaded areas for those hot days.
- Have some well-marked areas for ball games.
- Improve the play equipment (ask students for ideas within reason, and budget!).
- Teachers enjoying games or activities with the students at recess can really enhance the tone of play time.
- Stagger play times in larger schools.
- Stagger canteen times to avoid the rush when the bell goes.

Follow-up

As with all enforcement, if the consequences are not consistently applied, the students see little point in making the effort to work within the rules. A positive yard discipline policy needs to be:

- discussed with students where appropriate
- communicated to students and parents alike
- the subject of consistent enforcement

Reinforce positive yard behaviour where observed and make sure a plan has strong support from staff and parents. A yard policy needs tailoring to age, school setting and resources. Its ultimate success will depend on the degree to which staff and students have decided the best possible actions and follow-up they can employ.

Summary

- All levels of students in groups need rules to govern the way they work together; to protect the due rights of all.
- Rules ought at least to be discussed with the class and preferably worked out together with the teacher.
- Rules should be clear, as situation specific as possible, and with general, understood consequences for significant infringement of rights.
- Clear rules (up to Year 7 or 8) can be displayed around the room, or inserted in students' books as a reminder.
- It is easier to discipline when rules are clear. A teacher can more easily discipline by referring back to *our* rules for 'safety', or 'settling problems' or 'movement' . . .
- It is expected that the basic rules would be fundamentally the same for all teachers across the school.
- Rules need to be taught. Part of positive rule enforcement is the training/enforcement cycle; regularly, quietly, referring and reminding the students when they are off-task and reinforcing when they are on-task with the rules.

Rights as a feature of rule-making guide children towards collaborative democracy. There is no guarantee they'll follow such a process but the 3Rs focus (rights, rules, responsibilities) gives a just and reasonable basis for membership of, participation in and enjoyment of the benefits of a social group.

CHAPTER 5

Supports to classroom discipline

*We are conscious of what we do to
the extent that we are conscious also of
what we do not do — of what we might
have done. The notion of choice is
thus central.*
Margaret Donaldson, 1978

Logical behavioural consequences

Andrew sports a crew-cut and a pinched, drawn facial expression; he
seems perpetually sullen and annoyed with the world. Although only
in Year 3 he already has a well-developed battery of task-avoidance and
attention-seeking strategies. The late Rudolf Dreikurs would argue that
by these strategies (frustrating to teacher and students alike), he is seeking to belong. No doubt that is true. It is also true that Andrew's home
environment includes doses of bashings and emotional harangues. Do
we blame society for his behaviour? Do we blame Andrew? Do we
blame the lousy parents? Do we avoid blame altogether?

During process writing Andrew spits on Frousoula's work. She calls
out to the teacher. 'Miss, Miss.' She waves her hand in the air — finally
the teacher comes over. 'He spat on my writing Miss!' Andrew immediately says, 'Well she . . . anyway she said I couldn't have a rubber!'. The
teacher is faced with the question 'What will I do?'. She doesn't waste
time in sorting out who started it — she'll do that later. Now she says
to Andrew, 'Get a Kleenex and wipe the spit up now thank you'. She

is firm but not aggressive. He refuses, 'No!'. She thought he might have said 'No!' so she doesn't waste time arguing. She directs Frousoula to a spare desk or to work with a friend. She ignores the sullen Andrew, she'll follow him up later. She gently tears off the spit page and leaves it on her desk.

After ten minutes, she gives Andrew a choice, 'You can either rewrite that page now or I'll have to ask you to stay back and write it at your playtime'. No comment. She moves off. He sulks. She tactically ignores this attention-seeking ploy.

Just before recess bell she reminds him, 'Andrew, stay back. I want to talk to you'. When the class has gone, she directs him to rewrite the spit-work; not because Frousoula wants Andrew's copy but because Andrew needs to see some form of logical outcome to his anti-social behaviour. She did the same when he used the scissors to scratch the desk. He stayed back and sanded it. His teacher, rather than just punish him, has used logical or behavioural consequences.

Andrew, despite his home background, is responsible for his present behaviour. While the teacher is sympathetic to Andrew's plight she doesn't blame that chimera, society. She believes that the child should be held accountable in some way in the short-term, and assisted with behaviour-change strategies in the longer term.

Logical consequences are essentially the connecting of a responsible outcome to the social disruption. They can be decided by the adult, with the child, or with the class group. The whole class will have discussed the nature of consequences/responsibility along with the fair class rules. The teacher will have discussed the general nature of consequences with the class during the establishment phase of the year. We will not be able to supply a list of *logical* consequences for every situation, but we can discuss the nature of 'if — then' relationships in social behaviour. Behind logical consequences is the fundamental notion of respect for others' rights and accountability for one's own behaviour.

In whatever form they are used, however, the child needs to understand that behaviour is related to outcome. Desirable/undesirable consequences ought to be seen by the child as an outcome of their choice. By logical we mean there is a connection between behaviour and outcome that is as fair and sensible as natural justice can make it. By consequence we mean that one thing ought to follow another.

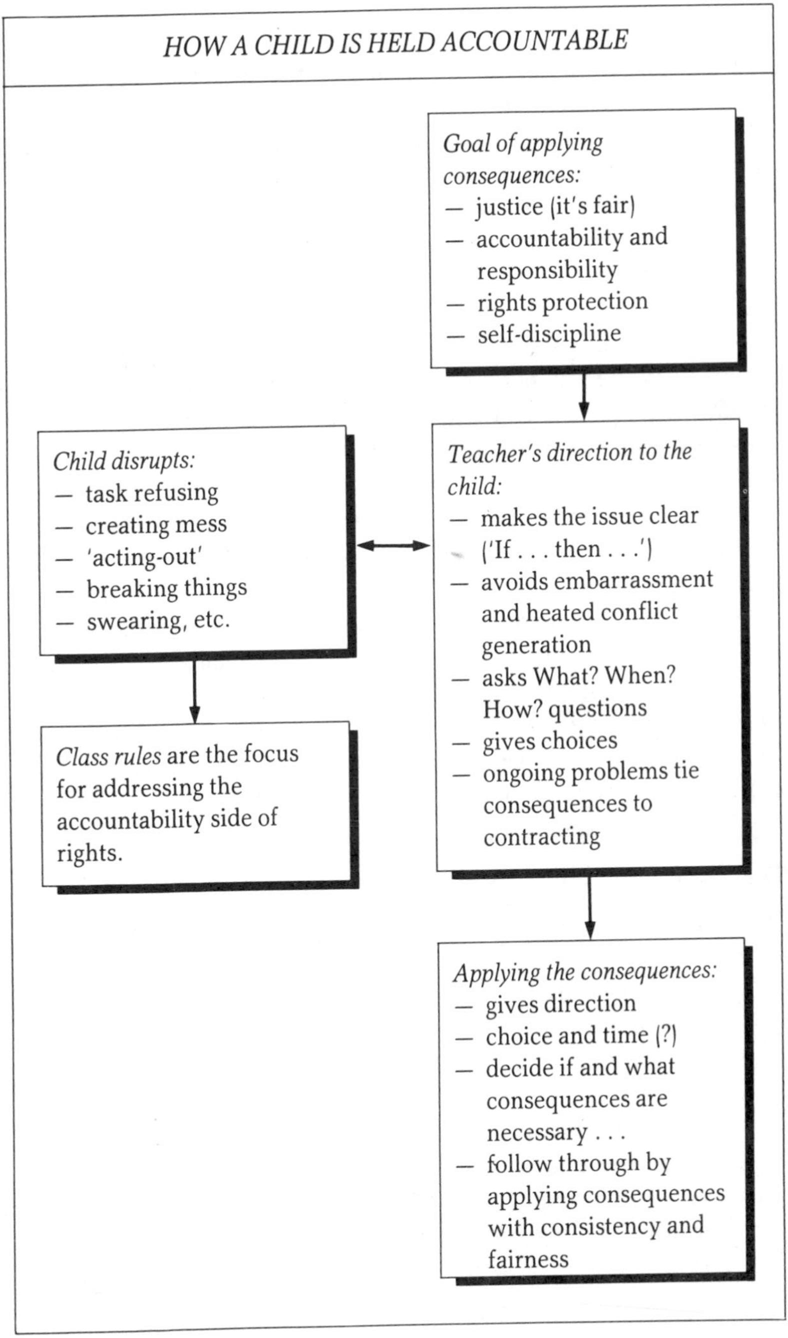

HOW A CHILD IS HELD ACCOUNTABLE

Goal of applying consequences:
— justice (it's fair)
— accountability and responsibility
— rights protection
— self-discipline

Child disrupts:
— task refusing
— creating mess
— 'acting-out'
— breaking things
— swearing, etc.

Teacher's direction to the child:
— makes the issue clear ('If . . . then . . .')
— avoids embarrassment and heated conflict generation
— asks What? When? How? questions
— gives choices
— ongoing problems tie consequences to contracting

Class rules are the focus for addressing the accountability side of rights.

Applying the consequences:
— gives direction
— choice and time (?)
— decide if and what consequences are necessary . . .
— follow through by applying consequences with consistency and fairness

Fig 5

Students have to accept the outcome of the way they act towards others and the classroom environment.

To make consequences work, a teacher needs a positive relationship with the class; a climate built on cooperation, respect, clear rights/rules understanding and one where the teacher seeks to model reasonable and fair behaviour. Because consistency is important to an ongoing relationship in a class, a teacher will uniformly apply the consequences; not giving up or in because of mood or circumstance. Try not to be distracted by excuses or special pleading or the 'It's not my fault' argument. While it is not advisable to be inflexible, it is important to consistently apply the consequence. There are rare children who will refuse all responsibility and accountability. With these children we still treat them respectfully and follow through with contracting/problem-solving strategies. We will need to apply consequences uniformly to the 'nice' student who leaves a mess as well as the 'not-so-nice' student.

It is also advisable to decide, beforehand, to what sort of behaviours you will seek to apply consequences. If Nicky hands in dirty work because she is a characteristically 'messy hands' child, will you decide that she needs to do it again? Are you going to correct it or discuss how she can improve on the general presentation of her work and that you will expect better next time?

The illusion of choice

In the normal verbal direction to the child, a teacher will better develop a sense of self-control by giving the child the illusion of choice. (I say illusion because 'totally free' choices are not really possible.)

'Tim, you may do the process writing now, as we all are, or you will be asked to stay back and do it at playtime.' 'Your mess can be cleaned up now Franca, before recess, or during recess.' 'You know the fair rule for communication in our room Simone.' (As a warning this throws up a choice to the child.) 'Adrian, if you choose not to work quietly here, I'll have to ask you to work over there.' Even a knowing glance or firm, brief eye-contact is a message to the child about choice. Even a short ignoring of low-level attention seeking can be a 'chance to choose' for the attention-seeking child (see Chapter 3).

When to enforce?

Consequences should not be forced where there is high-level antagonism or safety concerns. To force or demand Con to apologise on the spot for calling the teacher a f____ bitch is fruitless when Con is clearly after power-provocation or teacher-baiting. Positive discipline techniques use defusing/deflecting, rule restatements or choices as processes for handling high-level conflict, always leaving a choice with the student. Later, the teacher will follow through with consequences such as fix up, replace, work for, apologise, write out, re-do. At the time of the disruption, the teacher acts in a way that ensures the student doesn't have an audience.

With low-level disruptions such as leaving a mess, throwing things, ripping a page, scribbling on another's work or low-level attention-seeking, the teacher can make the issue clear but indicate that the student will be asked to stay back and fix things up later (or at a specified time). 'That language is unacceptable and against our rule — we'll discuss that later.' When following up, ask the questions, 'What were you doing, Maria, that was against our class rules? How are you going to fix it up?'.

The climate of application is important. It's not mere punishment; it is fair accountability.

How does that help?

When I speak to children about fixing up certain behaviour, I often hear them suggest: 'Give some lines', 'Pick up papers', 'Stay back', 'Tell his mum'. The question the teacher needs to respond with is: 'How will *that* fix up the broken desk, the busted racquet, the writing on the wall, the hurt child, the spit on the floor, the clay balls on the cupboard?'.

Providing the teacher is not sarcastic, cruel, authoritarian or revengeful, most children respond with an understanding of accountability and sense of justice. It is useful to ask them 'What will you do about x . . .?' It is an attempt to foster some connection in their thinking and future action. Behavioural or logical consequences can start as early as four years of age. With most children, logical consequences are not applied to accidents or forgetfulness. In these cases, we simply encourage the student to clean up, repair or fix things up with an apology as is necessary.

Ibrahim, aged 9 has gained a sense of belonging in the yard by belting others; a yard basher. Some teachers had nagged, others yelled, others had pleaded, all unsuccessfully. After some staff discussion, it was decided to use logical–behavioural consequences. He was told, 'Ibrahim, because you are unable to play in the playground without hurting other children, you will have to play by yourself'. He whined that it wasn't fair. The teacher didn't engage Ibrahim in a discussion but repeated the consequence, 'Because you keep hurting others in the playground you'll have to play by yourself'.

At lunch, Ibrahim was kept in and he looked through the window at the other children enjoying their 'freedom'. He had his playtime later with a minder (rotated staff member). No one to punch, hit or strike, except the trees and asphalt!. In this case he needed to 'feel' the consequences of his behaviour.

In one week he was craving to be 'given another go'. 'Sure Ibrahim — as long as you play by the fair rules for playtime.' This approach was applied calmly, fairly, consistently and expectantly.

Ibrahim — all by himself

Sally, in a fit of anger, busted a school tennis racquet on the school fence. What will the class teacher do? Her mum is virtually impossible to contact, the third live-in-person at the caravan park where she lives couldn't care at all. Is it worth contacting the guardians? Not really. We don't want to see Sally belted up. (There is a time and process for parental contact; it's not now.) When her high-level expression of anger cools down, 'Sally, you've busted the school racquet, it cost forty dollars, it needs to be fixed up. What are you going to do?' The teacher doesn't waste time asking Sally why she broke the class racquet. Neither is it worth getting into over-pitying because of the emotional dehumanising of her life at the caravan park.

'What are you going to do to fix it up Sally?' 'Dunno.' 'Well, you think about what you've done — it's your responsibility to fix it up. You've got a choice, you can pay for it in the next week, or we'll give you jobs to pay for it.' 'I ain't gonna buy one!' 'See this card, Sally. I'm going to write four weeks down on it. You will be asked to do jobs each day to help pay for the racquet. This is the way you'll earn the money . . .' (or, really, learn about logical accountability).

She swept, washed, tidied and so on for four weeks. The teacher signed it at the end. She was not demeaned, or screamed at — just held accountable. Firmly, determinedly.

Three boys let Mr S.'s tyres down. The V.P. firmly employs logical consequences. The boys pump it up in their own time. Tom smashed a window in room 17 ('fit of anger' during Art). His mother didn't smash the window so the principal uses a logical consequences approach and the child cleans out the glass, sweeps it up and prepares the window for the glazier. He's then 'on-contract' for two weeks doing jobs around the school as an illusion that he's 'paying' for the new glass. The contract is written up to give it an air of authority.

Many teachers let torn books, mess, unacceptable social behaviours go unaccounted for yet resort to yelling, screaming, abusing, lines or dictionary copying. All these are understandable when a teacher is frustrated but they are unacceptable. They model poor frustration tolerance and create an illogical (mere punishment) perspective on disruptive behaviours in the thinking of children.

Staying back

Mere detention, like lines, is illogical. There is no link to the behaviour except the power of the adult to coerce the child. In a sense it actually denies rational, social accountability. Mere detention or 'Write 1000 lines on . . .' is arbitrary and does not provide a logical or behavioural connection between behaviour and outcome.

If a child is asked to stay back, direction ought to occur such that explaining 'x' behaviour, fixing 'x' properly, tidying or cleaning 'x', apologising to 'x', or writing about 'x' is discussed. The 4W form is useful in this situation.

- What I did ....
- Why I think I did it ....
- What rule was I breaking? ....
- What I could have done instead ....

A copy of this form for your use can be found in Appendix II.

Behavioural/logical consequences are also very useful training *and* teaching processes for all children. A teacher will, from time to time engage the class in a general discussion about consequences and responsibility. This can also be a focus of, or theme in, a piece of literature or drama or self-esteem game. This approach, of course, is a part of the whole rights-rules-responsibility dynamic; it is not a new 'whipping-boy'.

Logical consequences enable students to think through the consequences of their own actions. Consequential and causal thinking (cause and effect) are important learnings for children, enabling a more responsible approach to social relationships.

When a child is being questioned about what consequences ought to apply, this too is a learning situation. Skilful teachers can do this with individuals (or groups) thus enabling students to see things from another's perspective ('How would 'x' feel if . . .?', 'How would you feel if you had that problem?') and to see alternative solutions ('What else could you have done when you got angry?'). The attention, through such teacher-student interaction, is on how a person is thinking out his or her problem and consequences. The helper is there to guide that process, which is one reason why effective teachers use discursive approaches even when dealing with disruptive students.

Paul threw a piece of wood at his textile teacher during class. Evidently she'd called the Year 7s, 'a pack of animals'. Acting as the advance scout for the Year 7 social justice unit, Paul threw the bit of wood in anger, and (fortunately) missed! Quite apart from the teacher's behaviour and Paul's rampant low frustration-tolerance, what consequences for his wrong action can be applied? Deprive him of textile lessons? Get him to produce a written and verbal apology? Contact his parents? Deprive him of sport?

He said he had not intended to actually hit his teacher but he agreed his action was wrong. He was asked, 'What else could you have done?' 'Counted to ten?' was his reply. 'Sure, that's often helpful', replied the senior teacher. 'Or I could have spoken to her after . . . or I could have stood up and said I don't agree (but she wouldn't have listened!).'

After exploring other alternatives, he agreed his action was wrong. He wrote an apology, and verbally apologised. He took responsibility for his action. Because the behaviour was dangerous, he was also deprived of Art for two sessions (it was felt this would be a salutary lesson to the others). What will affect long-term relations between Paul and his teacher, though, is how much she is prepared to establish a positive classroom climate.

Logical consequences are most effective when teachers have good working relations with their students. At one school where the staff had carefully explained and discussed logical consequences with their children, and begun to apply them, the children began to even pick up the language. One little chap presented himself at the principal's door. 'Yes, what do you want Mano?', he asked. Looking at the principal, with a dour and serious face, he said, 'I'm here for my logical consequences sir!'.

I'm here for my logical consequences

Logical consequences summary

- Logical consequences are part of group socialisation; consequences follow actions.
- Logical consequences are part of the rights, rules, and responsibilities of a classroom and school.
- Logical consequences concentrate on *present* behaviour.
- Logical consequences can enable a positive working relationship with students.
- Logical consequences emphasise:
  - self control
  - responsibility and accountability
  - choice
- Logical consequences are a labour-intensive feature of classroom management but they are worth it.

Time-out

Shane is a testy little seven-year-old. The term 'spoiled rotten' would not be unfairly (if unhelpfully) applied; his parents' break-up hasn't helped either.

In class Shane displays low tolerance to frustration in both learning tasks and social behaviour. A grand attention-seeker of the 'notice-me' variety, most primary teachers have experienced a 'Shane' at some stage in their career. He seems worse on Mondays (probably the father's access over Sunday). He arrives late, already making a scene as he enters the room. During morning talk he interrupts, makes silly noises and moves his place several times. Not only is his behaviour frustrating to the teacher, it annoys the other members of the class.

During the on-task phase of the lesson he goes 'off'; an argument over a Texta becomes a fight. He has already been warned several times — fairly, calmly, assertively. But, the 'scene' is on. He is given a choice to settle and work by the class rules or work by himself (isolated in a spare desk, or another area in the room). He argues, folds his arms and sulks, turning away from the teacher; she moves off. As the teacher turns her back he starts screaming (with a few choice four-letter words). She has to physically separate the two combatants and then Shane runs into the corner and kicks the wall. Has she a case for time-out? Does the child need to be removed from his peers to cool off and rethink his behaviour?

Using time-out

The notion and use of time-out has been a phenomenon of Australian schools for over a decade, especially so since the abolition of corporal punishment. However, time-out means different things to different people. As a practice it can be open to abuse and it certainly is no panacea in the discipline context. Like any technique it needs clear steps before and after its use to be effective. As a process, it should never stand by itself — it needs well thought out back-up and support.

What is time-out?

For some teachers time-out might mean sending the student to stand in a corner (in the old days some teachers made students stand in the corner facing the wall, sometimes with a dunce's hat on); it might mean isolating the student at a desk, away from other students; it might mean sitting him outside the principal's office or in a special time-out room. Though it has problems with legal supervision, some teachers remove a student to stand outside the class. However, if a teacher sends an attention-seeker outside the room, she'll most often use the window to get more attention. With small children, the notion of time-out might simply mean, 'hands on head' or 'all pencils down and hands flat on desks'.

The most persuasive advocate of time-out, as part of a well developed discipline program, is William Glasser. He particularly stresses that time-out is not a punishment but a time to reflect on one's *own* behaviour and to come up with some solution, or at least renegotiate entry back into the social group.

Why time-out may be necessary

Time-out is very simply time *out*, or *away from* the group. It is, essentially, an isolation process. All children want to belong to the group. In fact, if the psychologist Alfred Adler is correct, a person's central need and motivation is to belong to the group. In 'timing-out' a student from the group, what is essentially being communicated is that the student's behaviour is so disturbing to his or her peers that they cannot any longer be accepted as part of the group. The student is thus placed away from his or her immediate peers in the room, or in a place out of the room. Time-out, then, has a logical basis as well as a basis in utility. It's all very well for non-teaching people to overplay the case of the exit-student's rights; the rights of all members of the classroom (including the teacher's right to teach), need to be taken into account when disruptive behaviour persists.

What prompts time-out?

Whenever a student significantly disrupts another student's right to learn, to safety, to movement, to settle problems rationally, to self-acceptance, or significantly disrupts the teacher's right to teach and to manage the group, then the disruptive student should be 'timed-out' from the group. Examples of such behaviours would be:

- refusing to stop fighting
- racing round the room going 'bananas'
- constantly interrupting and refusing to settle down
- persistent abuse (though swearing can often be creatively dealt with in the class by the teacher)
- refusing to obey the fair rules of the room and thus infringing the teacher's/students' rights to safety, to movement, to learning and social interaction

Time-out presumes:

1 The teacher has fair, just rules that protect the rights of all class members. Such rules need to be clear, discussed with the students and reinforced with consequences where necessary.
2 The teacher has thought out their room organisation and procedures. For example, a time-out area in the room is helpful for those times when children need to be isolated for their own sake as well as their peers (i.e. if they are overly angry or uptight).
3 The teacher has a discipline plan (see Chapter 3). Nine times out of ten a teacher can handle the range of conflicts in a room with eye-messages, directive statements, defusing statements, giving choices, non-threatening questions, reinforcement techniques, rule restatements, or isolating a student away from others to work by himself. But where these do not resolve the issue, or more correctly, encourage the student to control his or her own behaviour, then time-out is necessary.

All time-out procedures should encourage responsibility over one's own behaviour.

With children up to Year 3, as well as special school settings, a time-out corner is set up. When a student is directed (or on some occasions physically removed) to the 'yellow' corner, a timer is set for, say, five minutes. The student knows when the timer rings he can return to the group, or the task.

As Glasser (1969) has pointed out, time-out is not merely another punishment, it is *time* away from the group, *time* to reflect on behaviours, the rule broken, and how to fix things up so the problem is not repeated. Its goal is to give both the group and the persistent disruptor a 'breather'. For time-out to work, whether in the classroom, time-out area, or in a room away from the class, several considerations need to be observed.

1 The student must need physical isolation.
2 The time-out area, or room, should be non-reinforcing. If a student goes to a place where there are toys or books, or the seat outside the office where he or she can 'preen' or watch the traffic of people, then the time-out situation may become reinforcing and the process will lose its effectiveness. A time-out room is not a jail (it is not solitary confinement), but neither is it a place where the disruptor can chat with a counsellor, the school secretary, students who pass by, the principal. Counselling best occurs at other times.
3 The student needs to know why he or she is sent there; why they are being isolated from *our* class. It is important the teacher communicates that it is the particular behaviour (rather than 'You make me sick with your calling out, now get out!') that is wrong and against the rules and that is why we are asking him or her to leave *our* class. We are trying to communicate separation from group because he or she is too upset, too angry or refuses to cooperate.
4 It is the last option when our discipline plan doesn't work or when the student refuses to choose to follow the fair class rules. This is the way it would be communicated to older students. It ought never to be used as the easy way out for the teacher when a child is calling out, refuses a task, does not have equipment, comes to class late, is indulging in low-level clowning and the like.
5 Exit-ing of the students for time-out needs to be clearly established as school policy. Should it be left to the teacher to send the student

to the time-out area? Should a third party come and exit the student? A clear, schoolwide policy needs to be worked out. It is preferable that the student is exited by a third party, especially with post-primary students who are aggressive, hostile and abusive in their behaviour. I've seen some very ugly scenes where teachers have tried to physically force aggressive students from their classes. The exit process is best carried out as calmly and with as much dignity as is possible so that it doesn't become reinforcing to the disruptor. In some cases, colleague-exit may be the only option (in small schools with limited staff for instance). Teachers working in class-rooms close to each other can use the exit-card system. A card with *exit* and the room number written on it is taken to a colleague's classroom by a trusted student. When the colleague receives the card, he leaves his door wide open, walks across or down the pass-age to the relevant classroom and directs the disruptive student to his classroom for time-out. He gives minimum attention to the student and sends her back when he believes she is ready.

6 It is important to make a decision on how long the student spends away from the class. The student is there because of his or her disruptive-to-rights behaviour. He or she needs time to settle down and come up with a plan. It will be someone's job (Year level co-ordinator, senior teacher, vice-principal, principal) to enable the student to renegotiate entry to the classroom. A student needs time to cool down, think, and state his or her intention. Fifteen to twenty minutes is an average time, unless the student (for some reason) is excessively angry or hostile. In the cases where the student refuses to cooperate then parents would normally be notified.

7 The student ought to be made aware that their behaviour is their responsibility. The manner in which a student is questioned should indicate this. At each point in the teacher's statements/questions to the student in the room, the student should be given the choice to manage his or her behaviour (with simple directive statements such as, 'What are you doing?', 'You know the fair rule for learning in our room.', 'David, you can do this now or later in your own time'.

When the questions, statements or choices are not picked up, the student then needs to know they cannot remain part of our group with that present behaviour. Where he or she can't, or won't, they are asked to remove themselves to the time-out corner or, in serious disruptive situations (high-level noise, on-going provocation, fighting that won't stop), the time-out room. If a child needs to leave the room, a clear exit policy for the school needs to be worked out.

If a specific room is used for time-out, then it is preferable that all teachers are rostered to staff the room. A clear policy of teacher action should be established.

- There is minimal discussion with the child (at the time of 'cooling off').
- The details of time, child's name, class etc. are recorded.
- Ask what they've been sent to time-out for.
- When the child has appeared to settle down, direct them back to their class.
- Establish a clear policy of student movement to and from the time-out room.

8 Students will need to know the purpose of the time-out corner, time-out desk area (older children), time-out room, or time-out area away from the classroom. They need to know it is part of the fair treatment in our room, and our school.

When a student is overly angry, throwing a tantrum, or very upset the student needs to be isolated to settle down before they can rejoin the group. The emphasis with all time-out is isolation from the group until the student can renegotiate their return. Where any student needs physical control, a teacher should talk firmly to the student (while the physical removing takes place), explaining that they are being removed because of their behaviour. 'David, you cannot stay in our room when you keep hurting people. You can come back to our room when you agree to work by our fair rules.' Small children can be firmly held by the hands, or picked up firmly and led off to the time-out corner. Older students should always be directed verbally. 'Your behaviour is unacceptable, we cannot tolerate your fighting (or whatever)'. Then, either send Cathy out, or get a 'safe' student to get the exit-teacher to come and effect the exit.

When your reasonable requests and steps are being ignored, then time-out is a necessary part of the process of teaching a student responsibility over their behaviour. Time-out, therefore, needs to seek a verbal or, in some cases, written 'contract' about future behaviour. Time-out, then, is backed up by all the other relationship-building steps that teaching staff engage in to enable and encourage a student to behave appropriately as a member of a social group.

Setting a time limit

The student should be aware that within 15–20 minutes they will be required to go to a designated teacher and say they are ready to go back into class and work by the fair rules.

Going back into the class is a negotiated process and will often include a verbal or written contract about the student's own behaviour.

At no point is time-out to be used as a degrading, humiliating process. A teacher will need, at times, to be firm but not humiliating or derogatory. Concentration should be on present behaviour, how such behaviour is against our class rules and fair consequences discussed with the student.

At all points in the process, the class teacher and the time-out teacher will encourage the student to make choices about their behaviour, gently, but firmly, calling the child's attention to the rule-breaking nature of the disruptive behaviour. While the teacher will help the student to come up with a plan to keep the fair class/school rules, the student is required to make their choice towards acceptable behaviour.

The most difficult usage of time-out is the staffed time-out room. Very few schools ever reach such a level of time-out, but such a room is an ideal place for children whose acting-out behaviour is so disruptive to class dynamics and learning that removal is the only option. However, whether used at a 'chair in the room' level, or in the corridor, or *other* classroom, the principal's office or a colleague's classroom, the process remains the same.

Time-out summary

- Time-out is part of an overall school policy used at class level and whole-school level.

- It is not punishment and should not be used indiscriminately or as a 'one-off' strategy.
- It needs to be part of a series of steps or procedures known to *all* members of the school community (especially parents).
- Above all, its use needs to be accepted philosophically and practically by all members of the school community.

Contracting

Contracts are an aid to a well-developed discipline plan. Essentially they are an agreement between the teacher and the individual or the teacher and the class group about desirable social behaviours or task goals. They rely on negotiation and discussion between teacher and student or a teacher and the whole class. On some occasions, contracting will involve senior administration and parents.

The form may be verbal or written; may contain short-term or long-term goals; can be modelled or rehearsed (with younger students) as a means of reinforcing the target behaviour; and, finally, ought to be evaluated by all parties as part of the process of achieving behaviour change.

The rationale

A contract assumes teacher and student/s are able to negotiate. If the relationship climate doesn't lend itself to this the teacher may need to call in a support teacher.

A contract is built on the belief and expectation that children can be helped towards better problem-solving, exploration of alternatives, making of choices, making of commitments and following-through. The teacher's task is to enable, encourage and support the student to take responsibility for their behaviour and learning. The student also needs to understand that there are consequences relative to their choices or non-fulfilment of the contract.

Students, therefore, need contracts they can cope with; not too much too soon. The fact that contracts are used often indicates that normal classroom approaches have not secured appropriate social or task behaviours. The contract should, therefore, not try to change everything overnight. Start with small, daily or weekly, achievable areas.

Types of contracts

Contracts may be written down. If they are, it's better that the student do the writing, even signing it to add verisimilitude (see Appendix III). Small children can be helped to draw a picture of the desirable behaviour, or have a chart for on-task work. If the contract involves behaviour modification, then task records or goal charts can be used. Little Boris wanders from class teacher to art to library with his little behaviour book. When he hits ten gold stars (in any day) he gets a special stamp. He has a picture for his target behaviour, he has rehearsed it and his teachers expect, encourage and reinforce it.

Contracts may be verbal. Essentially this contract is a commitment to do a certain task or follow a set of behaviours. The target behaviour is set. It may be rehearsed. The task can be modelled and rehearsed with small children particularly angry-outburst, hitting children. 'When you get angry, I want you to come over here and tell me. Then

I will suggest you go and sit in the time-out corner.' The modelling helps to specify the contract behaviour. This rehearsal approach can be applied to tasks as well as behaviour, but should be practised at behaviour-neutral times.

Starting a contract

It's best to think through, with a helpful colleague, the problem behaviour and the desirable target behaviour/s. Remember, it is better to define the target behaviour clearly and in small steps. Here are some examples:

- Sitting at their desk for five minutes during work sessions (then a follow-through to next step).
- Writing half a page in process writing.
- Putting up their hand and waiting, instead of yelling out.
- Reading 'x' pages of their reader with a friend.
- Doing a jigsaw puzzle, game, without upsetting the game.
- Asking for help from a designated person (teacher or aide).

The teacher starts the process at a neutral time by clarifying what the behaviour problem is. She best does this by discussion with the student using a problem-solving approach involving a defining of the problems, an exploring of solutions, and selecting and modelling a target-behaviour for the contract. The student needs to know and be treated (relative to age) as if they are a part of the process. Find an emotionally neutral time and start the process. 'David, we need to discuss your behaviour in class. You know the rule for asking questions — we need to discuss your calling out.'

Verbal contracts

The children are busily at work, engaged in process writing. Working noise is acceptably low. Mike, often disruptive, has a ruler in his mouth and is tapping the desk with it. What will the teacher do? The teacher could demand he stop, take it away, tell him to stop it, yell at him, humiliate him. However, the teacher uses a simple questioning process. She asks, in a non-threatening tone, 'What are you doing, Mike?'. Her eye-contact is firm, her body-language doesn't crowd, she is relaxed and controlled.

He answers, 'Tapping with the ruler'. The teacher doesn't grab it off him saying, 'Well, you should be writing, not eating rulers'. She merely says, 'What should you be doing?'. 'My writing.' 'Okay', she responds. That's all. She doesn't hang around and wait. She walks away expecting him to act appropriately, her approach has been to expect compliance rather than demand it. William Glasser (1969) argues that students should be treated as if they will and can take responsibility. The teacher therefore speaks to him *as if* he can act responsibly.

She goes back once or twice to use this approach when he is playing with his car on his desk. He stops for a while but picks it up again. Coming back to his desk she says, 'Michael you're not working by the fair learning rules'. 'What are you going to do?' 'Dunno, I'm only playing.' (Actually, the teacher had made a rule that no toys should be on the desks in the Year 4 room.) She gives him a choice to give her the toy, put it on her desk and get back to work or stay back at playtime and explain his behaviour. This is it! This is Mike's cue to throw one of his anger fits.

He throws the car at the blackboard, then picks up his book and throws it at the board. He runs up and dances on it, tearing some of the pages then slumps down on the floor folding his hands. He has his audience; what next? The teacher could yell, scream, demand, but none of these will work with this low frustration-tolerance child. The teacher already has a plan. She sends a student to the class across the passage to call in Mr B. thus executing her exit-policy plan. Past experience has taught her that Mike is too strong to carry or drag out when he's wild.

Mr B. calmly walks up to Mike while the other teacher is walking around working with, and thanking, the rest of the class for not getting upset. In this way she distracts their attention. Mr B. gives Mike a quick, firm choice. 'You can come now, with me, or I'll have to take you out.' Mike does his 'slumped-sack' routine and kicks the wall for some last-minute grandstanding. So Mr B., holding him firmly by the arm, calmly directs him from the group. He says briefly, 'Because you are breaking the fair rules of our room I'm taking you from our group'. Mike protests but is ignored. Mr B. thanks the class (thus not giving attention to Mike) for settling down while he is dragging Mike out. Even at the last, little Mike gets minimal attention. They go to the time-out room which is off the library.

One of the senior teachers takes Mr B.'s class for ten minutes while he 'time-outs' Mike. (It's about fifteen minutes to playtime.) Mr B. tells Mike he can sit and come up with a plan to fix up what he did — when he's settled down. He asks, 'What were you doing against the class rules, Mike?'. No answer. 'Okay, I'll give you a couple of minutes to settle down and think, then I want you to tell me.' 'Suppose I was wrong' Mike eventually says. 'What did you do that was against our fair class rules?' (Mr B.'s voice tone is clear, controlled but firm, though inside he's angry with Mike.) 'Yelling.' 'Yes — what else Mike?' 'Tearing the book.' 'And . . .?' 'Chucking my car!' 'Yes I know . . . Now what are you going to do to fix up this situation?' 'Dunno.' 'Well, you think Mike. I want you to come up with some things to fix up the wrong things you did.' 'You tell me' says Mike. 'No, it's your job. What are you going to do Mike?'

Mike decides to say 'Sorry', fix the book and finish his work during play. This is his contract; Mr B. will see he follows this up with his teacher. As they leave Mike puts up his chair on the table. He taps the teacher and says, 'Mr B. you forgot to put your chair up!' and smiles. 'So I did. Let's go Mike.'

Mr B. has been firm, clear and accepted no excuses. They go back to the classroom. Mike says 'Sorry', sits huffily down and begins to tape up his book (logical consequences). His class teacher ignores his huffiness. She goes up, just before the bell, and says, 'I'm pleased to see you've fixed your book. Let's see what work you need to catch up on'.

This behaviour has happened several times before. Each time the plan and the verbal contract is carried out, as calmly as possible. It's working. Neither teacher excuses Mike's behaviour because his Dad walked out, or because he has low-frustration tolerance, or because he's a latch-key kid. Sometimes they will explain their anger about his behaviour while directing him to do something about his actions. This approach has:

- reduced his acting-out behaviour
- kept class stress and teacher stress down (because both teachers have a plan and stick to it)
- shown Mike he is accountable for his behaviour and will not be treated by reactive teacher behaviour (which only tends to reinforce the child's totally inappropriate way of 'belonging')

Written contracts

Vicky was a 'problem' according to her Year 8 teacher, and was constantly being referred to the year-level coordinator. She was 'rude' in class, kept calling out, and was regularly late to classes, sometimes missing them completely. Quite apart from the need to firm up the teacher's discipline plan, it was suggested that a contract be formed. A problem-solving group was organised; it included Vicky, her parents, her year-level coordinator and a regional consultant. The process involved several stages:

- making the problem clear (Everybody is asked to contribute.)
- brainstorming possible solutions (The chairperson guides the process by reflective listening, gentle probing, clarifying questions, restating. All 'solutions' are noted down at this stage.)
- working through the solutions and deciding on the most appropriate
- making a plan to implement and meet again to evaluate whether the contract is working

It was hard work. But, with careful guiding by the group's chairperson, all sides were considered and Vicky came up with a tentative plan to deal with her behaviour. A timetable was drawn up to clarify her class times. It was decided that Vicky write the contract herself, covering calling out and handling her frustrations in class (the cause of her rudeness). The year level coordinator agreed to support her effort and we decided to meet in a week. There was a forty per cent improvement in that time which was acknowledged and affirmed. The plan was reassessed and a few changes were made. Three weeks later we had our last meeting to agree that Vicky had handled her contract well.

This problem-solving approach requires that all parties have an opportunity to contribute and work through the process. This approach needs careful guidance by the chairperson to work through each stage leading to the final expressed commitment. One of the by-products of this contracting process was a more positive effort by the teacher to assist Vicky. The teacher noted how she had begun to look for positive behaviours from Vicky, expecting them, and commenting on them. What the process had allowed, of course, was to get all parties to acknowledge the problem and commit themselves to support for change.

Behaviour rehearsals

1 *Clearly explain and describe target behaviour.*
   Make clear the target behaviour, explain why 'x' behaviour needs to happen in the group. Focus on the rules as a 'hanger' for why 'x' behaviour needs to happen. Be firm, clear, fair and avoid embarrassment. 'We need to make a plan because ...'

2 *Demonstrate.*
   Demonstrate the appropriate behaviour concretely. Role-play it. To reinforce what is appropriate and inappropriate, also role-play unacceptable behaviour. While demonstrating this, talk with the student about the key points in the target behaviour. Hinge the behaviour around two or three verbal reference points.

3 *Call the student to demonstrate.*
   Now ask the student to demonstrate (role-play) the appropriate behaviour. 'Nick, I want you to show me what you will do if you are starting to feel angry.' The teacher can add self-coping/ affirmation statements such as 'I am getting angry but I know what to do. I can handle this.' The student is asked to verbalise the affirmation aloud a few times, then sub-vocalise. 'Show me now. What are you saying inside your head David?' 'I am angry, but I am doing my plan.' 'I made a mistake but I know how to fix it.' 'I can stop getting angry when I use my plan.' 'I can use it now.'

4 *Check if the student understands.*
   'Do you understand what you have to do?' 'Say it to me please. Show me again.' 'Well done, I can see you know your plan.'

5 *Reinforce the student when they use their plan.*
   In the class, when the student is acting out the plan (see example), reinforce in a verbal or tactile way. 'I can see you have remembered your plan Paul, well done.'

In the process of contracting we are trying to enable the student to take some charge of his learning and behaviour. The descriptions for the contract should be as brief as possible, clear and achievable. If it's not achievable, the child may give up too quickly, too easily.

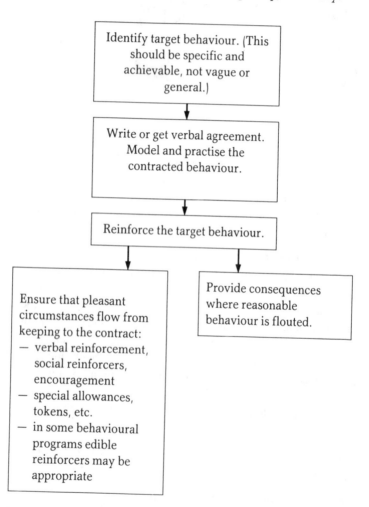

Acting out target behaviour

The student will often need help to identify the circumstances that trigger off-task behaviour. Then the student can be instructed on how he can use the same circumstance to develop self-control skills. It doesn't take long to 'act out' the contracted behaviour; it is another way of affirming the contract.

1 'When you feel frustrated (you know, when you feel really upset about your work), I want you to sit still, put your hands on your lap and count slowly to five.' The teacher can act out what is meant. 'Do it while you close your eyes. Let's practise it now. Well done.'

2 Then, 'Go back to your work and slowly start again. Say to yourself, "I am able to do my work when I try." Let's practise it now. Say it aloud. Now say it to yourself inside your head. Show me.' Self-coping statements are useful tools to build in to the student's repertoire:

- 'Shaun, what could you say to yourself that would help you to feel better when you are angry?'
- 'Shaun, I want you to try saying to yourself . . . when you feel . . .'

3 Try these steps every time you get upset about your work time. Let's practise it again.

In the on-task time, the teacher would watch the rehearsed signals and give a brief social reinforcer. 'I can see you are practising your plan', or just a slight pat on the shoulder. The point is to make the contract with the student, at their level of understanding, need and ability, have a rehearsal, then reinforce at on-task time. Re-negotiate if the program is struggling. Short steps towards the longer-term goal are better handled than trying too much too soon.

Picture contracts

Picture contracts provide a way of continuing behaviour reinforcement with kindergarten to Year 1 children. Target behaviours are illustrated on a card depicting the child performing the set task and these are rehearsed.

The card sets out a target behaviour such as 'sitting at my seat and finishing my work'. To build up a three-minute period of on-task behaviour, the teacher goes through the required behaviours with the student using the card as a cueing agent.

1 'Jason, this picture shows you sitting at your desk working. What are you doing at the desk?' Jason replies, 'I am finishing my work'. 'See the big bubble. What are you saying?' Ask the child to repeat a helpful phrase relevant to on-task behaviour such as 'I can sit here and do my work!' (or 'finish my work').

2 'See the egg timer Jason?' Explain that it will be his job to sit and write or draw or complete the set task until the sand runs out. It is a visual cue for the child's three minute on-task behaviour.

3 Go through the sequence of behaviours with the child. 'Show me how you can quietly walk over to the paper tub (or box) and pencil tin.' 'Get your paper then return to your table.' 'Sit and copy this picture Jason until the sand runs out.' 'What can you say to yourself to help you finish the picture?'

4 Rehearse the sequence with the child. Encourage him to say aloud the coping/support statement. With children who are still struggling with reading, the think bubble can have a picture showing a coping statement (such as a drawing of the successful activity). The student should then be encouraged to go through the sequence again: get materials; sit, think and say, 'I am going to finish this work'; stay sitting and working until the sand runs out; go to the teacher, quietly, and explain that you have finished.

The object of behaviour rehearsal is to give the child a simple reference and support for on-task behaviour. The picture-contract is then used in the social setting (within the normal classroom rules and discipline). For example, a star can be given for each three-minute segment of on-task behaviour and say five stars (15 minutes) can be traded for a special sticker and ten stars for three special stickers or a special pencil.

Of course, this approach presumes the teacher is using positive, social reinforcement as a normal practice. If the student is on-task, he is encouraged. If off-task, he is asked what he is doing or should be doing with reference to the picture-contract (there on the student's desk).

The contracting questions

Changing behaviour, whether social or 'learning-task' behaviour, is a big task for some students — especially when emotions of anger, self-doubt, frustration and failure are dominant. This is why it's useful to often use the What, How, When questions.

• 'What are you doing?' or 'What are you doing that is against our classroom rules?' helps the student to be specific about the actual behaviour.

- 'What should you be doing?' helps the student to be specific about acceptable behaviour.
- 'What can you do to change?' helps the student to be specific about solutions for future behaviour.
- 'How can I help?' helps the student to think of solutions and assures them of support.
- 'What can you do that is different?' helps the student to be specific about what should be possible.
- 'Let's make a plan' helps the student to be confident about future support.
- 'When will you start?' encourages the student to be committed about the plan.
- 'Which of these things are you going to choose?' helps the student to be responsible and move towards self-control.

At all times, the teacher is helping the student to take responsibility for their own behaviour. The teacher ought not get distracted or accept excuses. 'Yes I can see you were angry, but what are you going to do now?'

Contracts summary

Contracts can be drawn up through:

1 Brief verbal assurances that encompass a 'special' plan for student 'x'.
2 Behaviour rehearsals (especially with prep to Year 3 students).
3 Formal written and picture contracts where student and teacher discuss needs, rules, behaviour and responsibility. Keep the contract simple and situation-specific: 'The behaviours I need to change and agree on with my teacher'; 'How I will do it'; 'How my teacher will help me to keep my contract'; 'These are the behaviours I want to stop. These are the behaviours I want to start' (see Appendix III).

Such contracts can be designed on a one-to-one level; in a support group; or with parents.

So, the focus for the target behaviour is the current dysfunctional behaviour, not the historical antecedents over which we, as teachers, often have little or no control. We are aware of the student's emotional baggage, but contract with the student about their *current* behaviour.

We are looking for and encouraging overt behaviour and through this, attitude. We do this by stating clearly objective tasks or behaviours. In this way, both the student and teacher can measure change. We measure frequency, intensity and durability. This is why the contracts should be made small enough to be focused on by this student, and achievable enough to experience some success. Success is part of the reinforcing process. Struggling children find it very hard to build on failure, it's much easier to build on success.

Persistence and commitment characterise successful contracting. The teacher best achieves outcomes by not giving up but by encouraging, using consequences, evaluation, and allowing the working through of failure. It's easy, so easy, to reinforce failure in children, especially where they have failed regularly in the past.

Experience and research shows that contracting can be a productive adjunct to a teacher's characteristic discipline plan. It works best when the teacher has peer-support in the planning stages.

Counselling

We have to deal with many difficult children in our role as teachers, children whose emotional even physical deprivation may cause us to get frustrated, angry and depressed about their home environment. If only we could step into the child's home history . . . but we can't. The best we may be able to do, most times, is to take the route of fairness and friendliness.

Begin from the useful belief that a child is not simply a product of their past or present. It is not inevitable that they will end up 'at-risk' because of social, economic or psychological deprivation. Treat the child, therefore as if each day has within it the opportunity for change for that child and for us. This requires moral effort and will towards an expectation of change in behaviour for the child's benefit.

There will be times when we counsel to provide appropriate comfort such as when the child is clearly distressed (home break-ups; discord at home; being bashed at home; being sent to different parents at the weekend). 'Do you want to talk about it?'

Sean (aged 8) comes in late. His teacher says 'Good morning, Sean'. He mutters some words with head down, plus 'Shit!'. Many of the other children say, 'Oooh, did you hear what he said?'. The teacher quickly moves to Sean and says, 'Okay, I can see you're upset, sit over there, I'll be with you soon' (distraction and diversion) then walks back to the children she was working with before Sean came in. 'Sean's upset. Right. Now back to work. How's your process writing getting on Maria?' She continues to move around the room, leaving Sean until he has settled down.

Later, when the children are all back on task, she goes over to Sean. 'Sean, what's up?' 'My mum got me up in the night to go to my nan's place because my dad's fighting with mum!' 'Okay, Sean I can see you're upset. Let's do some writing now? (distraction) I'll talk later if you want.'

All the teacher needs to do is assure Sean that she understands. She doesn't need, in front of the class, to get into involved discussion. Later she might follow up by saying, 'How do you feel now, Sean?' She doesn't over-push Sean or demand he perform at the same level as the others. It is nearly always best to counsel students when the initial upsetting time has gone but assure them you will give them time to settle.

When you sit down with a student to counsel (listen, direct, clarify, guide) you need to observe the following.

- Make sure you're not alone. Sit near or in an office area with a door open.
- If it's a sensitive issue, invite a colleague in (especially for male–female counselling).
- Keep a record for yourself.
- Don't over-pity; show appropriate concern.
- Help the student to sort out options by getting their story first.
- Add options, action and solutions to their input: 'What do you think you need to do?', 'How can I help?', 'When will you start?', 'Who else do we need to help?'.

The use of welfare-support groups for behaviourally disruptive children

A welfare-support group is simply a means to enable all parties involved with a child's schooling welfare (as well as the child's general welfare) to be brought together to facilitate workable solutions, to minimise disruptive behaviour and maximise social and learning behaviours.

What's different about such a group?

Parents, even these days, often find school a place of authority, somewhat cut off from the world at home. Probably this has arisen from the parents' own perception of school (especially where disruptive behaviour labels tend to stick with particular families or have been experiences in the parents' own childhood). A student/welfare-support group seeks to create an environment that neither patronises or is out to demonstrate that the 'school knows best'. The concept of the group is to facilitate all parties who have a stake in the child's welfare and education towards a workable solution.

Something can be done

The notional attitude is, 'We are all barracking for this child and, while we recognise that they are a problem, or rather their behaviour is problematic to teachers, other children, even themselves, we are *all* here to try to work at a solution'. The attitude conveyed is essential. With the minimum of rationality and goodwill on all sides, and the climate to exercise it, there's a good chance of achieving some sort of mutual gain in the problem-solving process.

Of course, teachers will have tried one-to-one counselling, negotiation, perhaps some behaviour modification process or contracting before resorting to a welfare-support group. However, where a teacher has exhausted (or is exhausted by!) classroom-based strategies or year level coordinator support, then the welfare-support group can be focused to highlight the school's concern and care; demonstrating that the issue of a particular student's behaviour is serious. Such a group would be formed for all students who are suspended from school for serious disruptive behaviour and would be used prior to any formal inquiry process.

Certainly, the notion of a welfare-support group is in line with integration policy generally and positive school discipline procedures.

Procedure

The parents would be notified that John's or Tracy's behaviour has been disruptive and is an issue of concern to the school and that we need their assistance, along with the student, to try to determine a solution that is meaningful and acceptable to all parties having a stake in John's or Tracy's ongoing education. The letter need not define the problem/s specifically though the concern over the child in question and the need for all parties to come together should be clearly stated.

The parties ought to include:
- The student (where appropriate)
- Parent/s
- Parent advocate if so desired
- Classroom teacher
- Year level coordinator, senior teacher, student-welfare teacher.
- Regional support person/s if necessary (consultant, school psychologist, social worker, interpreter)

The parents and the child need to be put at ease quickly by the chairperson (preferably the senior teacher or even the regional support person if present). Parents especially need the assurance that this is not a judgement session; that we are here to try to help the student and the classroom teacher with the issue of behaviour.

Rules for the meeting

1 The purpose of the meeting is not to hurt one another, put one another down or score points; it is to find out what the problem is and come up with a workable solution. An offered cup of tea and biscuits is a helpful ice-breaker as is a comfortable room, an agreed time, time/release for the classroom teacher, and chairs arranged in a circle format to try to engender (as far as is meaningfully possible under moderately stressful conditions) a 'democratic' environment.

2 All parties are asked to explain their side of the story. Encourage definition of the problem from their perspective. 'Well Tracy how do you see it?'. Each person gives their understanding of the problem. If personal 'bitching' comes into it, the chairperson will need to firmly remind everyone of the basic procedure.

3 Generation of possible solutions is the next step. Each person generates possible ways of fixing up the particular behaviour or problem. These will involve the student's own solutions where feasible. (Get rid of that teacher, or get me away from Mrs Smith.) At all times, seek to incorporate all solutions without initial judgement. Reflective listening by the chairperson is essential. 'So what you are

saying Mrs X. is ... Is that right?' Try to clarify what the problem is. 'Is the problem just Mrs Smith's class, Tracy or what?' Do not seek to score points or argue. Be gently persistent but do not provoke confrontation as that will simply create the win-or-lose mentality we are trying to get away from. Try to concentrate on the student's *actions* as they affect the rights of others in the classroom.

4 'Which of these solutions will work out best for us all?' Communicate that this is not just a one-sided deal; we all have needs at stake in this group. There will be at least one mutually agreeable and acceptable solution. The solution may be a form of agreed contract. Stress that everyone has a part in this solution and that everyone must support each other in the agreed solution. Any solution has to maintain the due rights and responsibilities of all members of the classroom group.

5 The solution can be verbal or written (preferably by the child if possible) and clearly stated. It is best that the solution be short term in order to get some success for teacher, student and parent as soon as possible. It also ought to be achievable and have support inputs to enable its achievability. So the specific commitment is stated and, if necessary, formalised into a contract (post-meeting), written and perhaps signed by the student. The classroom and support teacher will agree to support Tracy in the process of the contract.

6 The agreed solution is trialled for one or two weeks and then the support group meets again to review the progress. If the proposed solution is not working, the process (steps 1–5) ought to be pursued again. After all, children with low self-esteem, poor self-concept and a history dotted with failure will not always succeed quickly with such a method. They may not be used to a non-blaming solution process. (Blame is often an easy cop-out for all!) So prepare for a re-evaluation. If there has been any success or improvement, give clear affirmation. Do not give in or give up after the first attempt. Students will not always keep to a commitment, but a solution-oriented approach is a far better (and in experience more effective) solution to on-going discipline and disruptive behaviour problems than mere suspension. If the process has been rigorously tried and has not been found to address the issue effectively, of course suspension and inquiry may need to be employed, but these more drastic measures ought always to include a welfare-support group process.

Support group summary

- The emphasis is on all-party resolution with two-way dialogue. All information is on the table and there are no secret meetings. Set rules for the process.
- Clarify what the problem is as meaningfully and precisely as possible for all concerned.
- Generate possible solutions.
- Select an agreed and workable solution.
- Augment the solution as quickly as possible with short-term (1–2 weeks) goals.
- Expect reasonable success and support the student and classroom teacher in that goal.
- Make a time for all parties to review the process.

The process sounds time-consuming but where on-going disruptive behaviour has not been successfully addressed at the classroom or coordinator level, the welfare-support group approach can serve to:

- demonstrate the school's active concern to students and parents
- demonstrate that we can *all* contribute to an effective solution

- demonstrate that while we do not want rights-infringing behaviour or rule-breaking behaviour in the school, nevertheless we are still 'barracking' for the student.

A student does not simply *equal* their behaviour. We are there to help them to modify their behaviour, take some responsibility for that behaviour, and get some success back into his schooling life.

Classroom meetings

It is the beginning of the school year and the teacher wants to discuss rights, rules and responsibilities with her students. She has used classroom meetings before, with other groups, so she decides to try it with her Year 9 English class.

As they file in and sit down, she writes the two words on the board and draws, underneath 'classroom meeting', four quarter circles (the seating plan). As they settle down, she introduces herself and explains that to start off the year she wants to discuss rights and rules with them. Handing out name tags (already written out from the class roll) she calls the roll. It is important to learn students' names quickly during the first few weeks of the year (establishment phase of the group).

Before she directs the class to move into a circle of seats she explains what a classroom meeting is, why it is happening, what the rules for the meeting are and what outcomes are expected. She directs the class to move their desks against the wall, bring out the chairs and stand behind them, a quarter of the class at a time. 'Okay, now move in, that group there first, into a circle. Great.'

Once the circle (amid normal chatter) is formed the teacher draws up a seat to join in. 'To start, let's try a simple little exercise.' She begins with a word game or ice-breaker. A student starts play punching his mate. How will she discipline? A plan helps. She could ask a question or direct him but she distracts and diverts. Calling across the circle to the grandiloquent, attention-seeking Bruce she says, 'Bruce, can I see you for a sec?'. Bruce swaggers over (he is the centre of attention now). She draws him down by whispering, 'Bruce (she rises up out of her seat), I'm swapping places.' Before he has a chance to think, she quickly takes Bruce's place and distracts the group's attention by beginning the ice-breaker. There will be several disruptions during the discussion; she will have prepared for these, at all times bringing the focus of attention back to the purpose of the discussion — *rights*.

'We haven't got any rights anyway', says Michelle, and so it goes. Bobbing and weaving her way through a lively discussion, the teacher gradually draws out some recommendations which are recorded by a volunteer student recorder. The class establishes, under her direction, some basic understanding of rights and what rules are needed to protect those rights. It is not easy, but it is worth the effort.

Setting up a classroom meeting

There are many approaches to discipline and classroom management. Effective teachers normally have thought through the processes that enable them to deftly weave their way through the range of disruptions that can occur in any classroom. The approach tabled here, however, is one that relies on using a class meeting which means setting aside a time when the whole class is encouraged to discuss and think through issues of concern as a group. The classroom, after all, is a social system. One child's behaviour both influences and is influenced by the other members of the class group. Discipline problems can be addressed at a group level as well as the individual level. The group can learn to make decisions about curriculum, room organisation, procedures and even socially disruptive behaviours that affect the group such as swearing, off-task behaviour, attention seeking, lateness, messy work, and high noise levels.

According to Stanford (1980), Dreikurs, Grunwald and Pepper (1982) and Glasser (1969), teachers who implement group approaches in their classes often find the incidences of misbehaviour and disruption receding. Reason? Both the teacher and the group go through changes because a group approach forces, by its very nature, a different way of focusing on concerns and problems. A group meeting is a way of saying, 'This issue affects us all, we need to share responsibility and this is a forum for such sharing'.

This activity is not one where a teacher merely stands in the traditional up-front role to field questions (valid as such a stance is); it is rather, a structured meeting where teacher and students have clear norms for the group, where cooperation is taught, expected and encouraged, where problems are confronted, and, it is hoped, democratic decision-making the outcome! Such group meetings may appear impossible. Having worked with many teachers who have recalled

failure in 'discussions' with classes, the reasons are due to:
- lack of careful planning
- poor understanding of group dynamics
- expectation of failure
- lack of persistence during the first few meetings. It's easy to give in when a discussion ends up in mayhem and silliness.

Children need to be taught how to behave in a group. The 'lateral tyranny' of the peer-group has put many a discussion goal into an early grave. Like all learning, cooperative discussion needs clear guidance from a democratic leader. Students need to experience the nature of democracy through testing their views, gaining feedback from peers, learning to participate in decisions and shouldering the responsibility flowing from decision-making processes.

The benefits

There are many positive outcomes arising from class meetings.
- Active student involvement and interaction.
- A sense of openness to the needs of others.
- Learning to listen to others.
- Reducing the level of 'threat' of sharing by providing a climate where students can be more comfortable with one another's ideas and opinions and, consequently, less defensive.
- A climate where people's views and ideas are taken seriously.
- Cooperation.
- Confrontation of mutual problems such as discussions about social behaviours, problems in learning, problems in social organisation.

Of course there are benefits for the teacher as well: taking risks; getting to know what and how the class thinks about 'x'; providing a forum for decision-making (even about an individual's behaviour). Group meetings can be organised at any age level with appropriate modifications. I've worked with teachers who have run class meetings with children as young as five or six.

Running a classroom meeting

1 *Inform the class.*
   'We will be having a special class discussion on Thursday (whatever) and will be discussing . . .'

2 *Organise seating arrangements.*
   Seats are best organised in a circle. Plan for the meeting to be about twenty minutes (build up to 30 later), at a set time in the lesson, preferably towards the end. Friday afternoons are often a good time. By arranging the chairs in a circle, the members of the group, including the teacher, are more 'open' to each other. The sense of territory changes when people are facing each other. When people start communicating, they can see each other, hear and focus on each other more easily in a circle. Members of the group (especially the teacher) can observe the non-verbal signals that play a very important part in feedback and communication. Tuning into non-verbal signals aids a teacher's insight, sense of timing, and control.

3 *Establish clear rules and norms.*
   Share what the expectations of the members of the group should be. For example:

* To cooperate.
* Share concerns and problems as we feel comfortable.
* Be responsible to others.
* Give each member of the group a fair go.
* Not criticise another's ideas or put others down, yet be allowed to share our concerns.
* All take a turn to speak (raising hands may be appropriate).
  (One school I worked in, in East London, had a 'speaking pillow'! The Year 4 students could only speak when holding the speaking pillow. Students would not interrupt the speaker, unless the pillow was passed to a new speaker.)
* Stay on the subject.
* Listen to each other.

The rules for the meeting are there to protect each member's right to contribute and be part of the group.

The teacher's job is to make these rules clear and enforce them. This requires firmness, warmth, sensitivity, determination and some judicious humour. My first few class meetings tested all these qualities to the limit, especially the warmth and sensitivity side. Like all growth, there are stages of development, the most important being risk-taking and willingness to grow. I learned that leaders only get better and the process only gets easier with practice.

4 *Reinforce the rules.*

This is an important part of the group process. If one or two members of the group call out instead of using the fair rule, the teacher can ignore them (not even look in the direction of the students calling out) but give firm eye-contact and verbal reinforcement to on-task members. 'Thanks for putting up your hand Frousoula, it makes the group work so much better.' 'What's your question Nick? Thanks for putting up your hand by the way.'

If certain members continue to call out, the teacher can use a rule restatement: brief, firm eye-contact and restate the rule. 'Jane, you know the fair rule for making a point or asking a question. Use it thanks.' That's all, then give attention back to the on-task members. This can be applied to other behaviours such as put-downs and annoying, pestering behaviour. The teacher could use a brief question like 'What are you doing, Jane?' (being firm, not sarcastic or hostile). 'Asking a question!' may come the reply. 'You were calling out, use the rule thanks.' Alternatively, the teacher could follow with a secondary question (especially with students up to Year 7). 'What should you be doing?' The teacher doesn't add anything else. Make the assumption she will respond on-task next time the question is asked. If the student continues to call out, put down, tap her feet or disrupt in some other way, give a choice to remain in the group or stay back and explain her behaviour at recess. When maintaining discipline, be as natural as possible in speech. Even when speaking assertively with hostile students use a firm, calm tone. If they resist, remind them that they can either work with our fair rules or we'll have to ask them to stay back and explain why they can't — later. Shift attention quickly back to the on-task members of the group. Even in a group setting, the normal protocols and practice of discipline are observed (see Chapter 3).

5 *Be a democratic leader.*

In running a class meeting, it is important that the teacher take the role of democratic leader.

- Keep the students on the subject or question. Watch the issue doesn't wander.
- Draw shy and quiet members out, slowing down abusive, detracting members.

- Use reflective listening and responding.
- Watch the louder, overly assertive members of the group.
- Keep to the fair, clear rules for the meeting.
- Enable the group to move towards a conclusion through maximum contribution, being fair to all sides, sticking to the point of the discussion/meeting, checking with the group and summing up towards a solution.

Our own modelling and reinforcing of others, gives a lead and a training ground for their discussion skills.

'What's wrong Paul, you seem annoyed about something.' 'What do you think Dimitra?' 'How do you feel when . . .?' 'Jodie, have you anything to say?' 'What if someone said that to you, how would you feel?' 'Frousoula has suggested "x". Does anyone else want to add to that?' 'Well, would that fix the problem? What do you think?' 'I see that you think we should punish Jo. How will that fix the broken chair?' 'You sound angry. I can understand we can feel angry about this, but what can we suggest to fix it up?' 'We're talking about swearing today. We can discuss stealing property at another time.' 'David, you've made your point. I'm sure there are others here who would like to add something.'

It's really important when emotions start to run high that the teacher take a democratic but firm lead.

- Protect the weaker members of the group.
- Restrain the more assertive or aggressive members; use blocking statements if necessary (see Chapter 3).
- Model and invite cooperation and listening using firm eye-contact, reflective listening, providing feedback to the student and the group.
- Draw the threads of opinion and ideas together. 'It seems that the group is saying . . .' or 'From what you've said, the group seems to agree that . . .'.
- Encourage quieter members. 'Kim, would you like to say something?' 'Does anybody want to add anything more to that?' 'It looks like there are several possibilities here. Which of these should we follow?'

So the role of the teacher is to lead, guide and provoke discussion. What, When, How, and Who questions are generally more helpful than closed questions. Sometimes the questions can be planned ahead, depending on the topic or issue.

An educational focus

Groups such as these have been used with an educational focus for maths, science and humanities, as well as for issues affecting the social life of the classroom. The broad goals are always the same: cooperating, exploring issues, learning to take risks in expression of one's ideas.

In maths groups a student will often make a mistake as a result of taking a risk. The leader can invite the group to affirm that member. 'Give him a clap.' 'Why did you clap him?' Some members may reply, 'Because you said so!'. 'No, because Jack took a risk. Good on you Jack. That's how we learn, by trying and testing our ideas. Well done.' Jack's self-esteem goes up.

Note: If the group is obviously flagging or getting unwieldy despite firm control, don't hesitate to call the meeting to an early close. Students are often not used to group discussion and it may take a few meetings to get them used to the experience of cooperation, sharing, taking turns, expressing ideas etc. Our persistence and modelling is often the best means to such an end.

Choosing the issues

If the group meeting is planned to deal with a class problem, the teacher ought to define it clearly at the outset, then keep the group on-task. For example, 'I've called this meeting to discuss a problem we've got in our class with swearing. You know the rules. I'd like to start the discussion by letting you know how I feel'. Then, 'Who'd like to speak next? Yes Jenny'.

Keep the meeting moving by asking, directing, restating, inviting, challenging, at times provoking the members to participate. Use divergent questioning as much as possible.

Where classroom meetings (even short ones) are a regular feature of classroom life, teachers can use an agenda board where students can list agenda items for the next meeting.

A warm-up activity

This is a useful way to 'unlock' the initial hesitation and unusualness of being in an 'unprotected' circle. The teacher could start with a brief turn-taking game. 'My name is Bill (or Mr Rogers). Two things I like to do are tea-drinking and reading novels.' He then turns to Mark. Mark says, 'This is Mr Rogers, he likes tea, I mean, he likes *drinking* tea and eating (laugh), sorry, reading novels. My name is Mark. I like footy and skateboarding'. Mark turns to Barbara. To make the game a little easier, actions can be added. So it's a game of identifying and remembering names and persons. Barbara then, a bit concerned, says. 'There's Mr Rogers (points), he likes ... This is Mark ... and I'm Barbara and I like ...' and so on. It can get confusing but it's a good example of a warm-up. It opens the vocal cords and helps to free things up with a few laughs and with a bit of help from the chair.

Another useful activity is the quick unfinished sentence game. Begin with 'Finish this sentence Andrea, "One thing that really makes me laugh is ... " '. If Andrea can't come up with something, move on and come back to her. Then go round, in turn, with each member completing the sentence. Gene Stanford (1980) has a range of games for groups. See also *100 Ways to Enhance Self-Concept in the Classroom* by Cranfield and Wells.

If you decide you want to run a group, but feel apprehensive, try it out with a small group first, or invite a trusted colleague to assist you. We can best minimise uncertainty (we can never eliminate it completely), by thoughtful planning.

One Year 3 group I worked with had a class meeting to discuss swearing in class. Sitting in a circle, we used De Bono's P.M.I. approach (plus or good points, minus or bad points and interesting suggestions, neither good or bad). 'All right, who wants to start? David, you've got your hand up.' 'Denise should get a battery and some wires (ha, ha, ha!) and tie it on her tongue (ha, ha!) and she will get a shock!' 'Interesting, but minus I think.' (Don't waste time on class wags. Briefly acknowledge, give a wry smile and move on.) 'Paul, you've had your hand up.' 'Make her run around the playground till she is sorry!' 'But, Paul, how does that help her swearing?' 'Michelle?' 'Get her mum down, she will smack her.' 'But who was swearing? Was mum?' After several more non-logical (minus) suggestions, Veronica said, 'Couldn't you say, say, say — something will happen to her?'. 'What will happen, Veronica?' 'I don't know, but something will happen.' 'Are you saying that we should warn the person who swears?' (and we modelled it). 'Yes, that's it!' 'What sort of warning?'

Finally, we all agreed a fair, clear reminder from our class rule on hurtful language would be the warning (a form of rule restatement). If the swearing was hurtful, the student would have to stay back, apologise, and explain their behaviour. We would only contact the parent if the student continually refused to use the class rule about good communication. We would (and did) help the student to use better words when frustrated, and positively reinforce him when he did.

WHAT WE THINK

Plus	Minus	Interesting	We decide
talk to her say sorry	battery smack	send a note home	1 Reminder of the rule. 2 Stay back and explain. 3 Use better words instead of swear words.

Classroom meetings summary

- Decide what the topic for discussion is *or* decide whether you want to use the group for a role-playing exercise, a self-esteem activity, a discussion on behaviour concerns within the class, or whether you want to use sub-groups (small groups of five who all discuss the same theme with the teacher moving round to assist, then back to a large discussion format).
- Decide on the time for the meeting. A vote can sometimes be used as a way of getting an agreed time.
- Decide how you get the chairs and desks moved into a circle. Let the children know beforehand that we'll be forming a discussion group at such and such a time. Often it's easier to just get the children to organise the furniture.
- Establish the rules quickly and enforce them.
- Define the topic clearly. Perhaps begin with a warm-up activity, then get into it with as much divergent questioning as possible.
- Keep the group meeting on-task. Draw the threads towards a decision. Encourage a positive decision that reflects the fair rights,

rules and responsibility focus. The essence of a classroom meeting is to open up and guide discussion towards responsible choices within the fair rules. A group secretary or recorder can be used to minute the proceedings and outcomes.

Similar models are found in Gordon (1974) and De Bono (1986). Gordon's steps are oriented to problem-solving by exploring several stages. Each stage is given a fair go before moving on to the next.

- Define the problem clearly with all parties contributing.
- Generate as many solutions as possible.
- Select an appropriate solution and process; one that is workable and achievable.
- Make a time for review.

De Bono's process is similar. He calls it P.M.I. The leader asks the group to look first in the plus direction (all the good points), then in the minus direction and, finally, in the interesting direction; one phase at a time. If a thorough job is carried out a 'simple map' or 'possible map' will emerge.

CHAPTER 6

Building a positive classroom climate

A good self-image is the most valuable psychological possession of a human being.
John Powell, 1976

Class tone

The time is 8.50 a.m. She's late (she's been late on many occasions this term) and she catches the principal's glare as she belts into Room 12. She's prepared some work for numeracy this morning (she planned this as she drove to school), but hasn't had time to write it up. Several children plague her about swimming money. 'Look, I'm busy now, can't you see! Give it to me after the bell.' David comes over to show her his new robot game and she says, 'Yes, nice David', but keeps writing the swimming numbers down so she won't be embarrassed when someone from the office announces on the internal speakers, 'Will Room 12 please send the swimming numbers to the office immediately!'.

The rest of the children file in after the bell. She says good morning as if she was pronouncing an oration over a dead cat. She finds it difficult to scan her eyes across the Year 3 faces. She's thinking of what she needs to teach in the next five minutes. 'Okay, morning talk. Who wants to say something?'

There are few smiles on the children's faces. David puts his hand up and calls out, 'Can I show my robot game?'. 'David, I've told you not to call out, haven't I?' The rest of the class looks at David quietly, thankful it's him not them. 'You can't come up now. Someone else?' 'Yes, Paula.'

Nick's playing with a matchbox car, driving it across his leg. Ms P. stares at him (as does the rest of the class) and reaches over to grab it off him. 'You're supposed to be listening Nick! Look up here, we don't play with toys during classtime.' Her voice tone is sharp, some would say caustic. She's already getting edgy, annoyed, frustrated; she decides to tell them she's annoyed. That's okay except for the way she does it. 'Look, I hope you're not going to be ratty like you were yesterday. I was very annoyed with most of you yesterday, especially you, yes you Nick, you know who I'm talking about. And you Cathy, don't you hide your head pretending you don't know what I'm talking about.'

After morning talk she moves through several examples of pattern and order on the board. She calls out to half a dozen children not to fidget or call out answers. 'I won't tell you again!' 'If you move one more time Paul!' Her disciplinary style is largely reactive. A child disrupts, Ms P. feels threatened, frustrated, even angry, and she acts from such feelings.

Inside, she's angry at herself for getting overly caustic and hostile. She doesn't apologise to the children however. She largely disciplines from the belief that she is the teacher, therefore she controls the students and they should do what she says. 'It's not fair,' she says to herself, 'why is my class so noisy, so messy, so stupid? Why did I become a teacher?'.

Positive classroom tone

Positive classroom tone is largely linked to the teacher and the way she organises her class so that the self-esteem of its members is maximised and effective learning can take place. We've all sat in lectures, as students, and said afterwards, 'That was so boring I couldn't wait to get out, it was so irrelevant. He went on and on' or 'I wish it was more relevant' or 'The atmosphere in there! It's so stuffy, if only we had a tea break' and so on. Classroom tone can be affected by anything from the lecturer's tone of voice, to the way feedback and questions are dealt with, to spacing and organisation of the curriculum.

When we remember the better lecturers or teachers we had, we invariably think of the positive class tone engendered by a teacher who:

- was fair
- had a judicious sense of humour
- was humane and treated you as an individual, not just a 'student'
- made learning tasks as clear as possible
- rarely, if ever, embarrassed you in front of your peers
- invited your cooperation
- offered to help
- gave you a sense of belonging to the class (whether you were popular, bright or whatever) and protected your rights to fair treatment

REDECORATE !

Class climate

Class climate is the tone the class experiences in its normal daily life. Because a class is, fundamentally, a group of people, the relational dynamic is central to how positive the class is, how positive each of its members feels about belonging to *this* group. Because the class is a group engaged in learning, growing up in social direction, building a sense of identity and purpose, it is important that the teacher seek out ways in which the class can enjoy a more positive learning and social environment.

Factors which influence class tone

Obviously there are many, from the kind of lesson the teacher prepares right through to how she feels on a given morning when she has that ghastly headache. Several factors, however, clearly stand out when exploring the issue of class climate. We, teachers, create the environment as much as anyone, especially through our verbal and non-verbal behaviour. A number of questions need to be asked.

- Do we speak hastily? calmly? clearly? Do we nag? How would our children describe us most of the time?
- Do we have clear rules and procedures that are known and reinforced?
- Are we aware of what our children are doing? Do we encourage them, listen to them, notice their positive cooperative behaviours as well as their off-task disruptive behaviours?
- Do we plan to cater for mixed abilities with a bit of variety in our approach?
- Do we ever use small groups to encourage cooperative learning?
- Do we evidence some humour from time to time?
- How positive is our discipline style? Do we plan ahead for possible or likely disruptions?
- Can we respect students even when we dislike them? How often do we evidence consistency in the way we discipline?
- Do we follow up disruptive students?

Children are very forgiving when we fail, when we have a bad day, providing there's a basic consistency to our teaching. Establishing positive discipline and building positive class tone is one way of achieving that consistency.

Organising a healthier tone

Look at the environment. Make life together just that little bit more bearable. Primary teachers have long practised aesthetics. Secondary teachers, too, are beginning to value classroom ownership either through the adoption of a classroom or by using a home room project to create a more worthwhile learning and social environment.

One teacher I worked with in a rather demanding secondary school decided that a drab, boring classroom with chipped desks, bare floors, dreary walls, a broken overhead projector screen, walls with graffiti, and no curtains was simply not on. She was also fed up with only having the class for a couple of sessions in that room so asked those responsible for the timetable to reschedule the room to get maximum time there. She pestered the administration for paint money, varnish for the floor, beading, sandpaper, a new overhead projector screen etc. A colleague (textile teacher) helped her to make curtains, the students helped paint the walls a relaxing light blue. The room smelt of paint and varnish for two weeks but the kids loved it. It was the one room that had no graffiti. It sported pot plants, colourful posters and clean desks.

It can be done. We may get stuck with a rotten portable or classroom; it doesn't mean it has to stay that way. Pot plants, pictures, posters, thoughtful arrangement of seats, a plan for easy moving around the room (especially 'work stations'), clearly marked cupboards, curtains, bookshelves, special activity corners, organised display boards, all help to create a positive learning environment. At my last school we had our class photos arranged on a poster (with names, including the teacher's) fixed on the outside of the door. It added to our 'specialness': The famous Year 5! There are a great many things that you can do to create that 'specialness' in the classroom.

1 Pester the administration for what you need. Scrounge, bring in some odds and ends. If you can't get a whiteboard for extra board space, repaint the lousy chalkboards. Use large sheets of paper for work prepared before class and pin these to the wall.

2 Try to develop an environment that *enhances* learning with special activity centres and sharing of facilities with other teachers.

3 Watch height access to cupboards especially for smaller children. If equipment is squeaky or faulty, get it replaced as quickly as possible. Don't put up with a flickering fluorescent, cupboards that jam, sliding doors that don't slide. It's your working environment. It's part of preventative discipline.

4 Have a painting spree if necessary (those ancient desks). Our Year

5's had a choice of three colours. Sand and paint — it increases ownership.

5 Check before putting up hooks, shelves, etc. Make an environment plan. Ask a colleague to help, look for ideas, then seek administration support; your classroom space is *your* working environment too.

6 Neatness is very important. If Ms P. has all the readers chucked in the bottom shelf, what does that say to her students? What about thick dust covering the chalk rail and the desk. There is a real problem if all the children's work lockers are crammed into one corner and all the desk lids jam and when there are ten different places to put scissors, pencils, science equipment, finished work etc. Neatness and organisation enhance efficiency and learning.

7 Is there a place for everything? Children learn by the example we set, by the consistent and clear processes we set up to enhance the learning flow. Ms P. has the process writing folders in a cupboard whose metal door has jammed. It's a great disruptor when some clown wrestles with it and is joined by someone who says, 'I know how to open it! Let me try Miss'.

Mrs D. has a quiet reading area. Some cushions, a chess table, a sign saying 'Our quiet reading corner' with a picture of a child reading. Her room is not messy or too busy, but attractive. Some desks are against the wall, some in a rectangle arrangement. She's tried to arrange the children's seating relative to size. Books are neatly stowed (she does not allow sloppiness). She is firm on this. Books are special. Her class rules are phrased as Our Class Rules and are pinned up around the room. (This can be done up to Year 8. See Chapter 4.) Early finishers have a range of things they can do, from chess to reading, to special projects to worksheets.

Mrs D.'s room is colourful, with curtains, bright display boards, mobiles of work and of ideas, a photo montage showing children going through the writing process. There are six steps, with photos. When children ask 'What do we do again?' she simply says 'Check the chart'.

Mrs D.'s students know how to come in and out of the room. Respect means that rights are respected. We don't all charge in and out to prove Darwin's theorem! There is a movement rule.

There are set routines for lunch money and a master list of the canteen offerings to stop the 'What's it cost for a pie, Miss?'. This also encourages independence.

Respect works two ways. We are the primary model. Our 3Rs program is designed to enforce, encourage and stimulate positive attitudes and manners. When David says 'Can I have the book?', say 'Pardon?'. 'Can I have the book?' 'Pardon?' He finally gets the point. 'Oh, please.' He doesn't need 'What!', or 'Don't you speak like that without any manners!'.

Encourage cooperation through self-esteem games and cooperative learning. I have used cooperative groups in every area of the curriculum where children share their learning in small groups. Work is set up on a poster to encourage as much independence in the group activity as is possible.

Special times

Foster the special feeling of 'our room' by having a coffee morning or afternoon (smaller children can have cordial). My Year 6s had coffee and maths each Friday. Two waiters, two coffee makers. It was our special morning. We sometimes had a meal together (Chinese rice we cooked ourselves, Dim Sims and Chinese vegetables) or a barbecue. 'But they'll make a mess!' I hear you say. If we go in half-hearted expecting them to, then maybe. We often get what we expect.

With the Year 3s we made our butter and served up bread and jam and cordial. With older children have coffee and cakes and science, or humanities and Italian cheeses and biscuits.

The need for support

Doesn't all this mean work? Yes. Shouldn't children just come to school to work? Yes and no. We all work better when the environment is conducive to learning — not harsh, restrictive, cluttered, dirty, demeaning and embarrassing. Do you remember some of the places you've worked? Apart from the money, what made them *worth* working in? It's good for us too — not just the students. The benefits are both an increase in positive, effective socialising and, therefore, a more positive learning environment. Remember, a classroom is a group of people, not just a work station.

Of course the creation of a positive class climate depends on the goodwill of the teacher: time in planning and preparation; seeking collegiate support and creativity; sharing ideas and concerns with the children; and taking risks (ever tried putting a suggestion box in the classroom?). But isn't that what learning is all about anyway? Don't try to do it all by yourself. Share your ideas, ask for help from colleagues you feel comfortable with. Check out the school routines first, scrounge around, visit the art teacher and librarian for ideas. Ask to look at other classrooms. Invite class discussions on how to make 'our' classroom a better place to be in, then make a plan.

Try to create an environment that says, 'I care about you/us/this place'. Think about your morning greeting; the use of personal names; greetings outside the class; birthday specials; inquiring about pets and hobbies. Try to end the day on a positive note. I have worked with many secondary teachers who never greet their students with a 'good morning' or 'good afternoon' or even a mere 'hi' or 'goodbye'. Before we focus on our learning tasks it's worth personalising the time we're going to spend together.

Our job is as much about human relations as it is literacy, numeracy, science and so on and *we*, largely, set the tone.

Self-esteem in the classroom

If a child could tell us:

When you make me feel smaller than I am, I get angry, especially when you do it in front of other people. I often try to get back at you, by being a 'pest'.

When you correct me or put me down in front of others it doesn't work. Inside, I'm angry at you and I say all kinds of things that will show in my behaviour. I'll take much more notice if you talk quietly with me away from others.

When you try to get me to apologise, or ask me 'Why?' when I'm in conflict with others (or you) you'll see I'm not very cooperative; it will look like I'm not listening. I don't mind you taking action but can you find a way to 'turn the heat down' and provide a face-saving way out of it? After all, your social skills are better than mine. You're more effective, you know, when you stay calm.

When you apologise, you show me you, too, are human, that it's not beneath your dignity to say 'I'm sorry'. Your honesty helps me feel warm towards you, it also reminds me that to be human is to be fallible. I can live up to that.

When you preach to me (or, more often, *at* me) you forget I already know what's right and wrong. If you nag at me I might appear deaf (this is a way of protecting myself). If we have clear rules, expectations and consequences of behaviour, preaching won't change me.

I already know what's right or wrong. If you nag at me I might appear deaf (this is a way of protecting myself)

When you go on about my mistakes, especially in front of others, I feel rotten, like I'm really no good. Sometimes I would like to learn to make mistakes without feeling I am no good. It's hard to build on failure.

When you're firm with me, I don't really mind. At least I know where I stand. All I ask is that you do it without making me feel stupid,

hopeless and worthless. When you're inconsistent I just get confused. I even try to get away with anything I can. When your expectations are clear and your treatment fair and calm, I know where I stand.

When you're inconsistent I just get confused. I even try to get away with anything I can.

When you demand reasons — you know, full explanations for my behaviour — I often don't really know *why* I did it. If you ask *what* I did and suggest alternatives, that might be different.

When you do things for me that I can do for myself, I feel like a baby — like I can't do it. If you keep doing that I might end up always relying on you and putting you in my service. You may end up labelling me as a 'learning failure', or a 'hopeless case'. When you go on at me about playing and not concentrating, remember I sometimes learn by experimenting.

When I don't get a chance to tell my side of the story, when you try to force or frighten me into telling the truth, I often tell lies or, like you, 'bend' the truth.

When you remember the most important thing I'm most happy. You know — I can't really thrive without understanding and encouragement.

You are able to help me feel and believe I'm okay but I don't really need to tell you that ... do I?

THE RELATIONSHIP BETWEEN SELF-CONCEPT, SELF-ESTEEM AND BEHAVIOUR
(adapted from Bernard and Joyce, 1984).

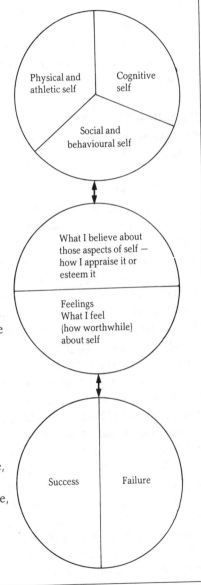

SELF-CONCEPT

The picture I build about myself — what I conceive (concept) myself to be.

Physical and athletic self

Cognitive self

Social and behavioural self

SELF-ESTEEM

How I esteem or value that picture of self. I feel then appraise or believe certain things about my 'self'. I do this largely from messages I receive from others.

What I believe about those aspects of self — how I appraise it or esteem it

Feelings
What I feel
(how worthwhile)
about self

MY BEHAVIOUR

How I perform in the cognitive, social, emotional dynamics of home, school setting. How I see, and others see, my behaviour.

Success

Failure

Fig 6

The basis of a positive classroom climate

Self-esteem is the *value* or esteem we put on what we perceive about our abilities, our body, our feelings, our social interaction. The trouble is that many children (and adults) process critical comments about *self* in critical ways. These external messages may unfortunately become internalised as internal beliefs being reprocessed as 'I *am* a failure' (rather than, 'I sometimes fail'); 'I *cannot* succeed at this' (low tolerance to frustration); 'I'll *never* manage, I *always* fail'; '*Nobody* cares'.

Building a self-concept

As children develop, they begin to build a mental picture or concept of themselves; an emerging 'I-am-ness', a perception and conception of themselves as *selves*. This picture or concept of self, as a self, is built largely by others. As a child interacts with parent/s, teachers, other significant adults and peers, he or she forms a concept of self in the intellectual, physical, social-emotional and spiritual realms.

The who-I-am and who-am-I(?) process arises from the way a child processes information from 'outside'. The way a child is spoken to and treated is processed through his feelings. Children don't reason things out like adults (and many adults don't reason things out!). If a child hears regular critical comments about his abilities or disabilities he will *feel* unsuccessful and may come to rate himself as unsuccessful (stupid, fat, ugly, useless, a failure).

Take a child who is trying to cut out a picture of a dog during a cut and paste activity. She obviously has poor fine-motor ability, low concentration, and low tolerance to frustration, all of which makes the dog look like a map of Brazil. In seeking to help, a teacher might say, 'Look Sandra, you should be able to cut that shape by now. Haven't I told you before how to use those scissors! All you need to do is follow the lines. Come on, I'll show you. You don't want to be a messy worker do you?'. Sandra may end up feeling, 'What's the use?' or 'I'm hopeless' or in some cases 'I can't do this — why not agree with that adult judgement?'. Children, like many adults, often rate themselves globally on a small aspect of performance.

Self-appraisal is powerfully related to how we feel. A child (and many adults) find it hard to build on failure. If a child feels failure strongly (via the messages from others) he may well begin to believe he is a failure.

Disciplining from emotion

In classroom management, it is so easy to discipline from emotion. The trouble is, much of the emotion is self indulgent. Teachers sometimes say that their students infuriate them; they (the teachers) say the first thing that comes into their heads when really they say the first thing that comes into their guts. If it did come into the head, perhaps they would be able to redirect their frustration to say what needs to be said more productively instead of: 'If I have to tell you once, it's a thousand times.'; 'Gee, you're thick as a brick!'; 'Can't you listen?'; 'When will you ever learn?'; 'What's wrong with you? — It's always you!'; 'You never listen, are you deaf?'; 'Yes you, you with the cotton wool in your ears!'; 'Were you brought up or dragged up?'; 'Where were you when they handed the brains out?'; 'You idiot!'; 'Fair dinkum, you're stupid!'.

Indulgence emotions are tempting but unhelpful.

- They damage the student's self-esteem.
- They limit any long-term change in the student's behaviour.
- Relationship building is central to effective discipline. Indulgence emotions, while giving some teachers short-term gratification, work against a relationship-building climate and breed resentment.
- There are better ways to handle our emotions.

Being firm and concentrating on wrong actions, trying to bring some separation between the child and the action by not totally equating the two is not a weak approach. When we're angry, it's better to use 'I' messages, 'I am very angry about what you have done . . .' rather than easy 'you' messages, 'You blasted idiot, I'm sick and tired of . . .'.

The power of the tongue

'Can't you understand that by now?'; 'You always . . .'; 'You never . . .'; 'I'm sick of reminding you'; 'You'll send me to an early grave!'; 'Others can do it properly, why can't you?'; 'You stupid boy, you . . .'. Global terms like this (sometimes just a slip of the tongue) are often interpreted by children as ratings of them *as persons*. Having worked with many children with very low self-esteem, it seems to me that the common thread is the message received from teachers or peers such as 'That's not right, you dummy!'. Teachers who poke at a child's work, screw it up ('What rotten messy work!') and throw it in the bin, or demean it in front of others, demonstrate more than rotten manners.

The teacher who yells at the Year 1 student about the scissors, 'Hey, are you stupid or something? Didn't I just tell you to put those scissors away?' may get the scissors back in the scissors' tray but he has said something to *all* the students. The 'ripple-effect' (Kounin, 1977) of a teacher's verbal discipline affects more than the target audience. The adult tongue is a powerful weapon. Some teachers use it intentionally to exercise power-dominance and cope with internal frustration or anger about intransigent and disruptive behaviour. Others use it unintentionally because the emotion of frustration takes over.

A teacher's voice is their dominant working tool. Words strung out in sentences employ tone, strength, pitch and emotion. Words are things. They *do* something — they are instrumental. As far as possible, we should seek to develop an interactive style that is more reflective, more conscious of the effect of our verbal presence in the room. We need to think about:

• what we say (especially when we are frustrated or angry)
• how we say it
• when we say it

Developing a more positive verbal style is something to be worked at. It is a skill. It rarely comes naturally.

The way a child is spoken to and treated is processed by the child largely through their feelings. The message, 'Look, what's wrong with you, I've told you a hundred times how to do that!' is not processed as 'You have made a mistake', but 'Gees, you're hopeless, you always muck up!' often leading to 'I'm no good at this'. If a child hears regular put-downs, global messages of 'You never . . .', 'You always . . . leave a mess, do untidy work, are always late', 'I'm always telling you!', how do we imagine they process it? As helpful reminders? How do we feel with similar teacher-learner messages?

External devaluing may often lead to internal devaluing. Erik Erikson (1960, 1968) relates self-esteem to the long-term reflected appraisal we pick up from significant others (parents, siblings, teachers). Healthy self-esteem is related to how we internalise those external appraisals. As teachers, we may not be able to influence the home messages; we can do a lot about the messages *we* give and how we give them.

Many teenagers negotiate the world through poor, low pictures of themselves, especially their physical selves. Through the way they're spoken to, the images they see in the media, watching their peers, they feel, believe and rate their concept of their bodies: too fat, too ugly, nose too big, ugly freckles, funny-shaped legs, slobby-looking etc. Human nature has a proclivity towards neat, global labelling. It's convenient, easy, simplistic, and even satisfies our desire to hurt, 'get-back at' or 'teach so-and-so'. Such labels are the soil in which poor self-esteem is nourished; as encouragement, appropriate praise, trust and respect are the soil for healthier self-esteem building.

A child is more likely to build a stronger, healthier, self-concept and value himself or herself more positively when:

1 He is achieving in some successful way, when he feels that he is able to accomplish *something*. Encouragement for specific improvement is one way a person can feel better about their progress. One of the harder tasks of teaching is enabling a sense of accomplishment by the way we organise curriculum for mixed abilities, learning outcomes geared to even small successes, and group activities that can give 'social strength' to the less successful classroom members.

2 She feels that the teacher cares for and respects her *as a person*. One of the more profound statements I have heard many students say of their teacher is 'He (or she) treats me as a human being!'.

Emotional baggage

Simone struggles, deciding whether or not to get out of her warm bed. The first voice she hears: 'Get up, come on, I said it's time to get up, I'll be late!' 'Look if you don't, I'll come in and get you out myself!' 'Damn it Simone, get up!'.

Simone starts to put on her cold clothes. Dressed, she moves off to negotiate another lousy breakfast. She'll probably have to make it herself and her hastily organised lunch won't be much better. 'Look, what are you wearing that blouse for Simone? It's filthy. What's wrong with you? If you'd put it in the wash like I told you . . .' Simone is awake enough to argue back now. 'Don't argue with me! Gee you really know how to upset me, don't you! All you think of is yourself . . .'

Simone finally makes a rough sandwich for lunch and walks to school. It's not always as stressful as this. It's been worse since dad left two weeks ago.

Simone is in Year 3. Each day she carries a weight of emotional baggage into the classroom. She has little to be hopeful or happy about — yet. School could help, for a short while, to change that. What she doesn't need is a teacher who replicates mum (at least mum on these days).

All students bring their emotional baggage into the classroom group. So, too, does the teacher. The on-task and relational dynamics, therefore, need to consider that reality. This does not mean we can over-compensate for a child's difficult home life; it does mean that we treat our students with respect within a discipline framework that includes self-esteem as one of its goals.

Children learn best when:
- they feel confident, secure and happy
- they are affirmed and encouraged
- the focus of learning is made clear
- learning tasks and experiences give opportunity for some success. (It is pointless having the one algebra lesson in Year 7 for all students when it is manifestly clear that only half-a-dozen can cope with it.)
- the learning program caters for mixed abilities
- our dialogue with students is positive, and careful to concentrate on their *present* ability and present behaviour
- learning includes group tasks as well as individual learning tasks

In short, children learn more effectively when they feel better about being in *this* group and coping with *this* work. Students' preference for a subject is often linked to their liking of a particular teacher. If I have a teacher carping on at me about what I can't do in maths, who refers constantly to my wrong answers, ('What sort of work do you call this?'), who tears out a page (in front of the class) from my maths book because I was drawing in the margin and then proceeds to humiliate me in front of the class, my effective learning is linked to how I feel about those messages. When we enhance self-esteem, we enhance the capacity for learning.

Unseen baggage

Respect: at the heart of self-esteem

Peter is sitting outside the Principal's office, waiting. Peter is a child who has been labelled socio-emotionally disturbed (SED). He presents as a scruffy, jaded-looking chap. His jeans are filthy, his sneakers ragged, his black dracula windcheater seems somehow appropriate. At seven years of age he's experienced much emotional and physical 'bruising' from home. He swears easily and loudly when frustrated. He finds it difficult to sit still on his chair in Miss S.'s class. He has been described as a 'pain', an 'A-grade attention-seeker', a 'shifty-eyed little bugger', 'a failure', 'a dummy'.

Today, he's been exit-ed from Room 10 because he threw his books on the floor in a fit of low frustration-tolerance. Built-up emotion from home? Who knows? His teacher is not a psychotherapist. He finds himself waiting for Mr D. to return to his office and deal with him.

Mr D. is a 'tough' principal. He certainly does not like children like Peter. Eyeing him sitting there, morose and sullen, he yells, 'You, you again! It's always you. What are you here for today? No, don't tell me, it's probably another lie. I'm sick and tired of seeing you at my office!'. 'You're nothing but a nuisance Peter Makin, a damned nuisance!'

Perhaps Mr D. is having a bad day. Perhaps he doesn't like this child. Perhaps he even hates him. Of course, Peter's behaviour is a 'pain'. This child has taken several years to learn a range of attention-seeking behaviours. It's got him where he is now. He's getting enormous attention, from a male, right at this moment.

Can one respect a child like Peter? One of the confounding problems when dealing with such children is our spontaneous like or dislike of them. The trouble with this is that we may often be relying on our feelings to dictate our actions.

We often feel we should react angrily when we're angry — that's certainly what our feelings are telling us so why shouldn't we? But, of course, our feelings are not, prima facie, proof of anything. It's like instinct. Many a teacher and principal believes that their instinct for discipline is right. The trouble with impulse, instinct and feelings as guides for what to do is that they are devoid of guidance. As C. S. Lewis (1978) observed in 1943, 'Each instinct, if you listen to it, will claim to be gratified at the expense of all the rest'.

Because discipline is more than mere punishment or control, it is helpful to superintend our so-called 'natural' reactions (being natural does not make them automatically right). We best superintend our discipline by bringing some consistency to the treatment variable. In this way we are still able to be decisive and firm without simply reacting. I believe this is called respect.

When dealing with Peter, the principal could have:
- counted to ten (it often helps)
- minimised embarrassment by keeping his voice firm, but down

- sat next to, instead of towering over, the child
- had some sort of plan for handling such children such as using 'what' questions; using 'I' messages ('I am unhappy about 'x' behaviour'); referring to the rules relevant to the problems; using logical/behavioural consequences; developing a contract; using a time-out process; having a teacher-student conference
- not taken the child's behaviour as a carte-blanche invitation to prove his manly power either over the child or the passing audience ('Toughness' in discipline is more to do with applied actions than an acerbic tongue!)

These children are not easy to deal with. They've clocked up several years habituation. Teachers who are in any way effective with such children are those who don't give up or accept excuses, don't resort to simple labels (he's a 'pain') and take a concentrated team approach.

The treatment variable

Ms S. is the humanities teacher. It is a 'sort-of' drama lesson. They're going to be reading a play — soon. 'Any questions?', she asks. Sean, a large boy with a very loud, annoying voice yells out, *without putting his hand up*, 'Which book do we have to get miss?'. 'Look, I've told you not to call out, haven't I. The books are down the back, you know where they are! What's wrong with you?'

About five minutes later, Michelle, not a trouble maker, quietly calls out *without putting up her hand*. 'Miss, is it the same book we used last time?' (The teacher hadn't really made this clear.) 'Yes Michelle, the blue books, down the back in the white locker.)

Both students called out, breaking the fair class rule, but each received different teacher treatment. And don't the class know it.

The only variable we can really manipulate day after frustrating day, is our treatment of 'x', 'y' and 'z'. Even if (when) we dislike 'x', it is important to treat him as we would treat those we do like. Michelle and Sean both deserve reminders of the clear rule, or to be questioned about the rule, or given a choice to work by the rule. The treatment variable means, further, that when the student is back on-task, we will spend some positive time with him even though we may not like 'x'. I can't do much, necessarily, about my feelings of like or dislike, but I am able to do something about actions towards 'x' even when 'x' is rude, irritating, off-task.

Liking or respecting: the professional difference

It is not a matter of forcing ourselves to like 'x', this disruptive person (damn those stupid earrings, that ridiculous haircut, that whining nasal voice). To psych ourselves into such a feeling is psychologically unhelpful to say the least. Showing respect for a child even when their behaviour is rude, arrogant and rule-breaking is a different matter. It is about speaking to and with them, acting towards them in such a way as to acknowledge that it is their *actions* that are wrong. Condemnatory, rude, sarcastic, caustic language is, therefore, unnecessary.

It is not a matter of pretending we like 'x' either, it is commitment to an action, a treatment variable. We cannot say truthfully, 'I like Maria' because we know we don't — especially when she swears at us and wears us down with her attention-seeking behaviour. So, what do we do? Well we certainly don't waste time bothering about trying to like her; we're on a safer course when we try to treat Maria with respect.

Respect is to do with *how* we treat 'x' and we can do something about that. Feelings will come and go. They are dependent, too often, on mood, digestion, amount of sleep, vagaries of time and circumstance. It is helpful, when our feelings trigger hate, rejection, 'she deserves to be punished', frustration, animosity, to remember the treatment variable — respect; even in extreme crisis-discipline settings. If we just give in to our feelings, we will lose out on long-term discipline aims and tend to perpetuate unhelpful, even stressful, teacher behaviour. Even our intense anger can be communicated respectfully.

The rights focus in discipline argues that in a community of mutual rights and responsibilities, respect is the 'oil' that develops, maintains and sustains cooperative learning. Teachers develop such respect through:

- modelling it to their students with their own verbal behaviour and body language
- encouraging it in children where it occurs in group behaviour (Part of the child's 'push for rights' is the cry for a right to equal treatment.)
- developing a rights/responsibility focus that encourages mutual respect. (Cooperation and commitment to fair responsibilities protect and develop those rights.)

- self-esteem activities (cooperative groupings and learning)
- accepting students as they are (but not their disruptive behaviour)

A teacher can develop attitudes and learn techniques that enable a just handling of disruption yet still discipline with dignity. Professional teaching eschews the foolish argument, 'I've got a right to scream, yell, abuse and let him know!'. Ask yourself, 'If I really respected "x" what would I do, how would I speak to him?'. Then go ahead and try it.

Labelling and the expectancy effect

'Labels are great for jars, not so helpful for people.' It's easy to resort to labelling of others; a kind of shorthand description of another's social or intellectual traits. 'He's slow', 'She's always messy', 'She's a real idiot', and, a commonly heard one in staff rooms, 'He's a real shit'.

The big problem with labels is that they're so often attached to definite beliefs. The user is reluctant to alter judgements so that when George is on-task or behaves in a socially acceptable way, it's an exception. Once we perceive via a label, actions by George can be open to a range of interpretations. The more firmly we believe George is a shit, the easier it is to feel and act as if he will be what we think he is. Perception powerfully affects our behaviour.

Rating others through our perception and self-talk affects the dynamic of discipline and teaching. I've worked with many teachers

Labelling is more suitable for jam jars

who ritualistically label disruptors as shits, bastards, turds, no-hopers, drongos, idiots, hopeless cases. While not unsympathetic to how a disruptor normally engenders feelings of frustration or hostility, I believe it's a most disturbing step to then use such feelings as proof positive that one must label 'x' in a derogatory way. It's far healthier to label the actions of 'x' rather than the 'x' herself; children know the difference. We communicate our beliefs more powerfully than we realise. 'But I'd never call him a shit!' That's not the real problem as Robert Rosenthal observed.

In 1963 Rosenthal and his colleagues developed experiments to test 'self-fulfilling prophecy' or the expectancy effect. Randomly assigned rats were divided into two groups and labelled 'maze-bright' and 'maze-dull'. College undergraduates who tested the rats only knew their rat sample as 'bright' or 'dull'. Ten trials later, the results showed the 'bright' rats nearly doubled the 'dull' rats in maze performance tests. Rosenthal concluded that rather than any real 'intelligence' differences raising the score of the 'bright' rats, it was the expectations of those working with them communicated through tactile and kinetic cues that had an effect on the rat performance.

This 'effect' has been widely studied with child-teacher relationships in classroom settings. 'You've got those terrors in Year 10! They'll drive you round the bend', may well affect how a teacher operates with the group. When we label a child as a shit, a turd, hopeless, useless, an idiot, or dumb, we may find our relational behaviour affected by that expectation and fulfilling the prophecy.

In building a positive climate, much will depend on what a teacher expects; not in a demanding way, 'I expect thus and so!', but in the normal treatment the teacher will apply. There *is* a difference between a teacher who expects children can and will do well, can achieve, can cooperate, will respond to the rule environment, and a teacher who communicates the expectation of (and may say it) 'I knew you'd blow it.', 'You always . . .', 'Can't you ever . . .', 'Oh! When will you . . .'. Again this largely occurs through the kind of verbal and non-verbal interactions a teacher will characteristically exercise.

We can communicate frustration, hopelessness, failure, by the perception/action process. It begins by rating and labelling (that is believing), that 'x' is a . . . The next step of acting (or reacting) to 'x' as if he or she is a . . . is often unconscious. To change the cycle means a change of thinking: 'I don't like what "x" does' is different from 'she is a real little so-and-so'.

All the discipline approaches discussed in this book are firm and clear but reduce hostile interventions of speech. They also treat children as if they are able to make better choices and are able to work cooperatively. Even if they don't, we will still treat them, not as if they are little animals, but with dignity. Even if we have to be decisive, we can still do so with dignified treatment. (See Chapters 2 and 3.)

Praise or encouragement

One way that teachers (and parents) seek to strengthen self-esteem is through the use of encouragement. Encouragement can be distinguished from unhelpful praise to the extent that encouragement concentrates on the student's effort or action rather than their person. Rather than say to a Year 3 child, 'You're a good boy for working quietly . . .', simply acknowledge it, 'You're working quietly today', smile and move off to work with someone else. When a student gives a helpful, correct or thoughtful answer to a teacher's question, rather than reply with 'Good girl' or even, 'What a good answer', simply acknowledge it; 'Yes Cassie, that's right', 'That's one way of looking at it', 'Correct', 'Sure'. Giving an incorrect answer or not knowing, doesn't *make* a student stupid or bad. It simply means he, as yet, doesn't know, or may not understand or even be shy.

Global terms (good/bad) or praise evaluate a student's *person* whereas encouragement gives the focus of attention to *effort*. Praise will often be seen by knowing students as manipulative or even insincere, rather than a supporting of the student's trying to have a go. Where a student's work is incorrect or messy, it is better to note what they have done correctly and concentrate on the effort made, then ask if they understand subtraction or suggest they have another go at spelling 'because', or say 'Let's try that again' or 'Show me, have you got that answer?'.

During silent reading with Year 3, one of my students, who had severe learning difficulties, chose an encyclopaedia to read. Rather than say, perhaps well meaningly, 'No James, that's too hard. Let me get you another book', I encouraged him to tell me why he chose it. 'See these pictures, Mr Rogers, they're about road-digging machines.' We had a discussion about machines and used the experience during process writing.

Encouragement

Avoid global praise such as 'You're a good boy because you put your hand up' or 'You're a naughty girl to do that!'. Provide encouragement, as distinct from *just* praise. Encouragement builds upon a student's strengths and assets. This is as true of academic on-task activity, as of social cooperative activity. It works at crediting effort rather than merely praising the end result. This communicates to the student that you believe in them.

- They can do 'it' and helping others in the class reinforces that. (Group activity is especially useful to that end.)
- Failure is not the issue. Encourage the trying, the effort. Verbalise the encouragement. 'Come on Dave, keep trying. I see you're thinking hard, that's it.' 'Good on you, you've finished that part, now let's work on the next bit.'
- They are not to be over-pitied when they fail. 'Perhaps you're feeling it's tough, but I'm sure that you can do this. We (not just I) can help.' Look for effort, improvement, evidence of trying. Seek, as in all social behaviour-management, to assist them to take responsibility for their own feelings, emotions and behaviour.

Encouragement comes not just from the words *per se*, but also from tone of voice, body language etc. Ineptness can be communicated to a student whether our actual words are encouraging or not. This is especially true if the *belief* behind our verbal direction does not separate deed from doer. To communicate, 'I like you, but I dislike what you did' (actions that hurt others and infringe their rights) is not easy. The balance between either overprotecting a student in her social and emotional development or punishing her with discouraging comment is the tension of creative teaching. What we are learning to ask ourselves as we manage children in groups, or as individuals in groups, is how does what I'm doing and saying affect a student's self-concept and encourage self-esteem.

Acknowledging even the smallest effort, accomplishment or contribution often requires us to reorient the way we look at our students, how we reinforce (positively and negatively) their attention-seeking or power-provocation or inadequate behaviours. The way we *use* questioning is also significant. Do we restrict the student by closed questioning? We may simply set them up for failure. Open, exploring, discursive questioning ought to be practised alongside the closed approach. If a student is set up with a closed question (only one right answer is possible), we may set them up for a chain of small, unnecessary failures. Open questioning at least gives a student a chance for a valid contribution towards the answer.

When encouraging use phrases like 'I noticed ...'; 'I saw ...'; 'I heard ...'; 'I can see you are enjoying that Paul'; 'I saw you helping Kerri, well done'; 'David, it'll make it easier if you hold your ruler like this'. Even the non-verbal approach where we rule an index finger down the left-hand margin, with a wink, is a much better reminder than the nagging, 'How many times have I told you ...'. Encouragement says, in effect, 'I'm barracking for you', 'I believe you can do better'.

Two kinds of teachers

When I first learned to sail, my daughter (then aged 10) and I arrived, nervously, at a narrow jetty at a lake to be met by a tough-looking female yachting instructor. With a bare hint of a smile she gave us her name and asked us to get into the sailing dinghy. 'Don't!', she said as I reached for a halyard to step into the boat. 'Don't you know how to get into a boat ... goodness, you step into it like this.' She showed me as she brushed past. I raised my eyes to the sky as I looked at my daughter. I was hoping it would get better — it didn't.

In the next hour, she whinged, criticised, grabbed at ropes, was sarcastic, 'humphed' and 'ummed' her way through a semblance of being a sailing instructor. Early in the 'lesson' she asked me to hold the mainsheet. I looked up at the sail (a sail is a sheet, isn't it?). Seeing my 'stupidity' she remarked, 'You were supposed to read the homework notes, weren't you. A mainsheet is the main *rope* for guiding the sail', and gave me one of those 'don't say I have to put up with another dope' looks.

At one point, when I was trying to steer the dinghy towards a fixed 'something' on the horizon, she said, 'Now keep it straight with the tiller!'. I saw the bank loom close and I registered my concern. 'Don't you worry about that!' she snapped, 'I'm in control'. Bravely I replied, 'Actually I thought I was steering. That's why I was worried'. 'Look, do you think I'd allow that ... Concentrate!' she said as I turned my

The sailing lesson

eyes away from looking ahead and turned to face her. 'Watch where you're going — goodness!'

As we steered away from the bank under her control (my daughter sitting, worried, opposite me) Ms Napoleon remarked, 'How old are you?'. 'Thirty-eight', I replied. (What's she on about?) 'Can you drive a car?' 'Yes, of course.' 'And you can't understand the simple connection of rudder, steerage way and wind direction.' She droned on with frustrating sarcasm. As we moved off on port tack she added a 'Concentrate!' and 'Watch the sail, watch the sail! Don't waggle the tiller!'. 'Look,' I said (I was getting quite annoyed). 'This is my first time in a sailing boat of any kind. Now, as a teacher, I've found that the beginning of *any* new activity is helped by a bit of encouragement and understanding, however old one is.' I was amazed how controlled I was as I gave her 'Credo One' of my philosophy on learning and teaching method. Water off a duck's back. 'I don't muck around', she said, 'you're in a boat, no time to muck around'.

For the rest of the hour she regaled us with seemingly a hundred and one bits of information, generally treated me as a child, huffed and haaed and, as we stepped ashore, said, 'Now make sure you do some reading by next week'. As my daughter and I walked to the car I felt like giving up. My self-esteem (our self-esteem) had been battered. But we laughed it off and I said, 'Will we try her once more?' (we'd booked two lessons). 'Yeah, but isn't she a pain Dad!' I could only agree but said, 'We'd better get our money's worth'.

Next week was worse. We almost felt like we'd never learn to sail. Ms Napoleon projected failure and even stupidity on to us. (Maybe she didn't mean to, but her whole tone in the boat was, 'You should know. Why can't you understand? What's wrong with you?')

Well, our self-esteem was stronger than her lousy teaching. We decided to try another teacher and signed up for a course (fairly cheap) with another group. We arrived, on a bleak, windy, showery day at a small bay near Geelong. There were six boats on a trailer. Sixteen people (including myself) unloaded the boats and placed them near the water. We stood shivering, facing the weather-beaten instructor and a vile, choppy sea behind him.

He smiled at us and called us over to a boat. He introduced himself and assured us all that we'd have a great day's sailing. Then he calmly and carefully explained each part of the boat we'd need to know about and how we'd need to mast it, put in the rudder, set up the sails, etc. Then we set it up on the beach, each crew with its own boat. He then showed us how to sit in the boat, how to tack, how to pull in the mainsheet and so on. All on dry land. We practised.

We *felt* reasonably confident (so far) under his clear instructions. 'The next step', he said, 'is the most important. What will probably happen is that the boat will tip over — no worries. All beginners experience it, we even practise it. I'll explain and show you how to get your boat back up should it tip you in the drink'. He calmly explained what to do, showed us how to right the boat and reminded us he'd be out there to help in his little motorised rubber duck (dinghy). 'Okay, off you go! Have a great time.'

With two others I managed to get our boat out and off. We steered it into the wind and were staggered at its power. In a few minutes we were soaked by the water sluicing up from the sides of the boat. Green as we all were, we tried valiantly to keep the boat on a reasonably even keel. Our 'green-ness' was obvious though. I couldn't seem to stop the boat keeling over, the wind seemed to push us further and further towards the drink! Surely we're not going to tip it! Maria yelled, 'I can't hold the rudder!', and my fear bore fruit as we three sank beneath the waves with the sail flat on the water. The boat then turned right over as we coughed and spluttered our way to the surface. We remembered our drill. I made my way to the front to pull the bow into the wind and Maria reached up over the upturned hull to pull down on the centre-board.

The instructor saw us and 'put-putted' over in his motorised dinghy. As we three, shivering and clinging to the now-lifeless vessel, tried to recall his drill, he very calmly said, 'Well done Bill, and you too Maria, that's it, pull the centre-board down. I knew you'd remember the drill — good on you'. He trusted us to complete the procedure and as we righted the boat and climbed in he said, 'What will you do next?'. 'Bring her round and set the sails?' 'Well done! Off you go!'

Wet as we were, we *felt*, not that we had made some great mistake but that we had passed a test! We were learning under the security of unbattered self-esteem.

Ten minutes later I put the boat in the drink again, as did the other member of our trio. Each time the instructor came over and smiled, calmly encouraged us, gave us confidence to keep on. He never took the initiative from us. Even in stressful, cold and somewhat uncertain circumstances, he gave us only as much information as we needed — trusting us to know and do what he believed we could do. His calmness and clarity of instruction were most reassuring. He'd say things like, 'I knew you'd remember', or 'What will you do next?', or 'Which direction should you head?', or 'You tacked really well that time. You're getting it Bill. Well done', or 'Don't worry, you'll get it next time'.

By the end of the session we had with him, our confidence, self-esteem and skill had all increased. Even our failures were utilised. He also taught me a great deal about how to teach or, more correctly, how to *be* a teacher. He modelled:

- consistency (in his encouragement and teaching style)
- care for the individual
- clarity of tasks
- encouragement to work cooperatively as well as learn individual skills
- the expectation that we would succeed (We did. Of course there were some students better at sailing but we all experienced success within our abilities. In this way our estimation of ourselves was positive, helpful, realistic, strengthening our belief that we could cope even in difficult situations.)

Teachers' self-esteem and welfare

Teaching is a profession with complex demands, multi-task and multi-role requirements to attend to at once — students' needs, administration demands, parental expectations, student misbehaviour. It is also a job, strangely enough, where we are 'isolated' for most of the day even though we are surrounded by children. Teachers whose self-esteem is lacking in the areas of 'belonging' (identity, acceptance, security and competence [Coopersmith, 1967]), may mask it, shrug it off, even laugh it off, but low self-esteem affects stress levels on the one hand and student-teacher relationships and learning, on the other.

Our self-esteem affects our relationship with others. It is seen in our actions. In the privacy of the classroom, it is seen in how we speak and act towards students.

If we feel insecure, unsupported, incompetent, it will show up:

- in our silence or anger at staff meetings
- in our cynicism about change, about new ideas, curriculum, joint approaches to problem solving (the 'give up' or 'why bother' mentality)
- in our cynicism about teaching as any sort of 'worthwhile' profession
- in the isolating of ourselves from our peers (This is exacerbated when the perceived or real situation is that others do not care.)
- in our refusal to share our problems over children, conditions, curriculum. (Again, this may be through fear of rejection, judgement or imputation of failure or knock backs from a recalcitrant administration.)

Cooley (1909, noted in Harter 1985) described self-esteem as a 'looking glass where the reflected appraisals of significant others' represent a 'mirror' into which we look for those aspects of information about self.

Important questions to answer

- How do I relate to others in our workplace so as to enhance our self-esteem and welfare?
- Do people generally enjoy my company or do I tend to be a loner? Have I any colleagues at school that I can share and discuss problems with?
- Do I feel I belong at this school?
- Do I feel supported?
- Do I have a significant role, or any role, in decisions that affect me?
- Do I have personal goals or merely the goals that others set for me? (The more we feel we own our goals the more committed we are to their achievement.)
- How competent do I feel in my job?
- Do I overly worry about what others think?

As we answer these questions our self-esteem comes to the surface. Can I only be significant if I'm constantly successful and approved of? Do I believe I must be able to get all my children up to a certain level or I'm a failure? Do I believe I must have a perfectly quiet class or I'm a failure as far as discipline goes?

I've seen teachers trialling cooperative learning strategies (which involve a bit of noise and discussion at the early stages) who have had to face annoying, frustrated teachers who barge in during a lesson and demand quiet! What does that do for self-esteem? Is it so difficult to draw aside a colleague at another time to discover what's going on (or conversely explain to a nearby colleague what is going on first)?

Suggestions for improving staff self-esteem and general welfare

1 Give due weight to a collaborative decision-making process in the school, especially at staff meetings. It's still a common sight to see a principal bludgeon a program or policy through at a full staff meeting. Why not break up the large group into small, facilitated groups so that people feel they own the process and the outcome.

We work better and feel better, when goals are shared goals. Where we have been able to shape the goals, we are likely to give a more significant input to their realisation. When principals and senior staff trample on suggestions and give little weight to staff input, it creates that isolation (I'll do my job and blow everyone else) so common in our profession.

2 Create a more positive working environment. Where staff rooms are dirty, there is a lousy choice of tea or coffee, dirty cracked cups, a dishwasher that doesn't work, constant mess, notice boards with last year's bits and pieces on, no filing cabinet, doors and windows that don't work properly, the working environment is negative. We feel better in a bright, attractive, clean environment; one that is cared for. A school administration can do an enormous service to teacher welfare by enhancing the school environs from classrooms (pot plants, curtains, heating, decent chalkboards etc.) to the yard (trees, benches, decent rubbish bins etc.) to the staff room. Such improvements will create good will, positive working relationships among staff, and between staff and students, and staff and parents.

The issues discussed in earlier on positive classroom environment are just as relevant for teachers as for students. The process of creating a positive environment can be established in a number of ways: circulate questionnaires; do a regular check up; personally ask teachers how things are going; give support to teachers' good will in reclaiming some of the rotten portable classrooms, or resanding of desks, or reshelving, or building new play areas. Note what other schools are doing. Pick up good ideas and translate them where possible. Have some decent school signs up for office, the toilets, classroom numbers, facility areas etc. Invite parents in to discuss their suggestions. Ask the students too. After all, it is their school as well!

A positive work environment says we care. Having visited hundreds of schools as a consultant, I've noticed a positive correlation between the school environment and the general well-being of staff and students.

3 Endorse the positive value of sharing ideas across classrooms, or visiting one another's classes. It is still a feature of many teachers' practice that they will not encourage other teachers to look at their rooms, share curriculum ideas and resources. Of course, there will be lazy teachers who may take advantage, but that's part of the risk of sharing. One school I worked in encouraged the use of a tray beside the photocopier where teachers dropped in their ideas. I've been in other schools where teachers try to photocopy in secret! It has an effect on morale. We can learn an enormous amount by visiting one another's classrooms: organisation, work-stations, curriculum ideas. (See Chapter 9.)

4 Share some difficult or demanding children across years or classes. This is one way of relieving pressure and giving structural and moral support. Teach in a colleague's grade for a change.

5 Plan lessons jointly from time-to-time. In this way we can often gain new insights and perspectives on curriculum. This is especially important when we are trialling new approaches like cooperative learning.

6 Use a wide resource base:
- Update the teacher reference library
- Print off smaller articles for staff to read. (The Australian Council for Educational Research produces an excellent range of brief articles from time-to-time. They are practical, well written, brief and topical.)
- Run mini-workshops at staff meetings using staff members themselves or teachers from neighbouring schools.
- Employ regional consultants.

- Brainstorm ideas especially when discussing discipline issues like: 'What sort of logical consequences can we use for Alice? How can we develop a joint plan for Troy?'

7 Begin to use cooperative learning strategies as a feature of the curriculum. In this way, teachers can begin to allow students some ownership over the curriculum. Goal-based learning and outcomes give students a sense of personal identity which, in turn, creates a more positive teacher-student relationship. This is something that Glasser has argued strongly for in his cooperative learning approaches to whole-school welfare (see Glasser 1985 and Dalton 1985). Where feelings of self-worth (I am engaged in something worthwhile and significant) are increased, people begin to feel better about their environment.

- How do I value myself?
- How can I effectively change my self-concept?

Feedback

If we are going to evaluate ourselves in any effective way, we need feedback. We can of course do this privately but it is helpful to pick up feedback from significant others. Not those 'chance' observations of parents, principal or senior teachers. How often have we had the experience of a principal coming in to look over the shoulder of one of our 'less successful' students only to then give the impression that he is rating *our* competence and usefulness by that isolated visit. How often do principals or senior personnel come in and give positive feedback?

> I recall a relieving principal we had who came in to my Year 3 class one day and politely waited (he didn't barge in across my teaching as some 'visitors' do) until I stopped and called him over. We were doing a theme on Beatrix Potter! We had used our process writing to create our 'own' small books of animal stories. He came during a fairly excited conferencing time (students discussing their writing with one another). He asked if he could have a look at the children's work. 'Fine, it's nice to have you.' He trundled off. I overheard his comments, none of which were negative. He gave specific encouragement, asked lots of questions (mostly discursive) and then asked if he could have a chat to everyone (it was about 15 minutes to afternoon tea). He then asked quietly if I'd like an early break — genuinely. 'Go on, have a break, you've been flat out.' I later found that this 'give-a-break' practice was something he was

doing with all the teachers. It was *ad hoc*, but it seemed to come at the right time. He also organised special morning teas from time to time (5 minutes extra play for students), handed out small, useful, articles on a range of issues, was invariably positive and, if he needed to discuss contentious issues with staff, would do so privately.

The leadership in a school can affect the well-being of its members in many ways, not least in minimising the autocratic power-status of the principal. Teachers, like their pupils, want democratic leaders not bosses. It is also important to facilitate and encourage peer-feedback (see Chapter 9) or even get feedback from our students. Ask them what they think about the class (see Chapter 5), the curriculum, the school, the rules. Feedback, where it is balanced, non-judgemental and supportive, strengthens self-concept and self-esteem.

Peer-support

On a lake, in England, I saw a bird which, I was told, was a shag; it was sitting alone on a small rock with a huge expanse of water around it. I immediately recalled the expression 'shag on a rock' and thought of the many teachers who were living daily like that: in a busy school, thronging with students, yet whose experience was very much one of isolation (me 'alone' in my room).

- Do we care when an individual is absent?
- Do we do anything about the teacher who is a perpetual isolate?
- In what way do we work as a team on any aspects of teaching or curriculum or policy?
- Are our communication processes one-way only? Merely having a faculty meeting as a small group doesn't guarantee communication.
- Do we herald 'new' ideas like cooperative learning without offering to team-teach, or model new skills?
- Do we offer help? How?

We can't make people 'belong', we can only create the environment where it is more likely they will want to. (See Chapter 9.)

Summary

How can we structure our classrooms to enhance self-esteem? Remember, self-esteem is the value a child places on their concept of themselves. What value do they hold of their intellectual, social, emotional, physical and spiritual *selves*? Their concept of self (what I am as an individual *me*) is built largely from others. Because teachers are significant others for much of a child's early development, they can encourage strong concept building by helping students to value themselves when they 'succeed', and when they 'fail' by encouraging their effort and participation.

1 Watch your own language and language models. Remember what we do in the classroom is largely a correlation of our verbal behaviour and body language. Seek never to use sarcasm, bent humour, student comparisons, over-generalising ('you always', 'you never'), humiliation, screaming and yelling. Even when we need to be firm and assertive, it can be done with dignity.

2 Be a positive model. Fallible as we are, we can still learn to model positive building-up of others. Where we are angry or unhappy, we ought to let the children know. 'I'm feeling rotten today but I'll do my best.' 'I didn't do that properly but I can fix it up.' Especially seek to model what you want from them when handling problems, displaying manners, and in treatment of others. As Joseph Joubert (*Pensees*, 1842) stated, 'Children need models more than they need critics'.

3 Look for areas where you can specifically encourage children as distinct from mere praise. 'I noticed you handled that well today, Paul.' Encouragement notices specific effort. 'You're enjoying that, I'm glad to see you coping well.'

4 Have clear, fair rules. Clear rules protect all members of the class community. Well-defined rules give security to children and enable them to move towards appropriate empowerment. Justice and fair treatment are the keys. (See Chapter 4.)

5 When you need to be firm with children, it is better that you do so with assertion rather than authoritarianism or aggression. Assertion is where we state our feelings about wrong, hurtful or disruptive behaviour and expect and encourage compliance. (See Chapter 3.)

6 Make a discipline plan which allows you to be less reactive and more responsive to disruptions and their effective resolutions. Plan ahead for the range of disruptions likely to occur in any typical range of children in a group. (See Chapter 3.)

7 Remember that our expectations affect powerfully how we treat children and, as a result, how they perceive themselves.

8 Organise your room carefully. Plan for better aesthetics, smoother procedures, quiet corners for children who are uptight or angry, quiet times as a whole group, doing things together (special treat times). Begin and end each day in a friendly manner. All this makes the time together a little more special and takes a bit of the pressure off the on-task requirements of the class.

9 Actually plan self-esteem activities within the curriculum through:
   • self-esteem games
   • self-esteem writing activities
   • cooperative groupings
   • cooperative tasks

   Do evaluation building from the children's perspective. Children, from time-to-time, share what they have learned and discuss valuable learning, problems encountered, future directions and so on.

   Provide opportunities where children have a chance to state their feelings about class concerns, problems, work. Class meetings are a useful way of doing this. Children can be taught how to discuss their feelings without putting others down (see Chapter 5).

And how is our new Miss Bates getting on then?

10 Make self-esteem building for staff and students a focus of the whole-school welfare policy. Plan together for self-concept and self-esteem building (the whole access/success debate). Staff support and encouragement is also crucial to morale. How often are classroom teachers' efforts noticed? Is support (moral and practical) a feature of school life? How are struggling teachers assisted? What help is offered to new teachers? What support processes are there when classroom management breaks down at the classroom level?

CHAPTER 7

Reinforcement in the classroom

The principle is simplicity itself, and has been understood in essence by parents and teachers since ancient times. If you want someone to do something you make it worth his while; if you want him to stop, you likewise make it worth his while, or more worth his while to do something else. Not a very noble message, but an effective one.

Biggs and Telfer, 1981

Basic reinforcement

When working with a very difficult Year 7 class, I decided to use reinforcement to slow down calling out behaviour — a predominant feature of 7C. Several of the boys and a couple of the girls consistently called out, sometimes with, sometimes without, hands up. We had made a clear communication rule: 'In our room, when we ask questions, we put up our hands — giving each class member a fair go'. The teacher I was tutoring had tried the 'Shh!' method and 'I won't tell you again' (she did — many times) and it was ineffective to say the least.

The reinforcement we planned operated on the basic notion that limited, tactical ignoring as first step might provide those calling out with a chance to stop. Their off-task behaviour would not give them what they wanted — attention.

This ignoring is sometimes called differential or negative reinforcement. When Johnny is disrupting, he draws his reinforcement from as many sources as possible. If we plead, argue, yell, threaten, or take the bait, not only do we reinforce the very behaviour we don't want but everybody else is watching too and giving the student reinforcement. Teachers work better when they use differential reinforcement to their advantage. By positively reinforcing ('Thanks for putting up your hand Anne. What's your question?'), or sometimes using negative reinforcement (tactical ignoring) we give the student a chance to be noticed for their positive behaviours.

We were working on the assumption that students who regularly disrupt do so because it provides them with some sort of reinforcement — attention from peers and/or the teacher. This reinforcement can even be teacher's anger or pleading. In line with the theory that disruption is often purposeful we planned a few steps for dealing with calling-out behaviour during the up-front phase of the lesson.

STEP ONE

Use firm tactical ignoring of calling-out for two minutes. Do not even look in the direction of the student calling out, let alone comment on their behaviour. But, at the same time as Johnny and Co. are ignored, on-task (rule-keeping) behaviour is reinforced. 'Thanks for putting up your hand Nick. What's your question?' 'Yes Maria, by the way I appreciate you putting your hand up.' 'Paul, what's your question? Thanks for putting up your hand.' In the first two to three minutes the reinforcement is positive, specific and accompanied by direct eye-contact or even a smile! Off-task behaviour is tactically, resolutely ignored. The teacher is on the look-out for the moment when Johnny does put up his hand so positive reinforcement can be applied.

STEP TWO (if necessary)

If two minutes of tactical ignoring doesn't stop them then use one of the following measures. This depends on a teacher's tolerance for frustration and how significantly calling-out affects a teacher's right to teach.

- Restate the rule. 'Johnny you know the fair rule for communication, use it please.' Don't add the rule itself (he knows it!), don't preach or add any sarcasm ('I've been waiting five minutes for you to keep the rule!'). Just give direct eye-contact and restate the rule. Add the rider of thankyou or please to communicate the expectation of compliance. This demonstrates what we call 'the expectation of compliance'. (See Chapters 2 and 3.)

- Give a simple direction (direct to the behaviour you want to see). 'Debbie if you want to ask a question, put up your hand and wait — without calling out. Ta.' Then, turn the eye-focus away to the on-task members of the class or the lesson itself as is necessary.

STEP THREE

Give direct eye-contact and a clear choice. 'Debbie, we cannot communicate fairly with that calling out. You can either work by the fair rules of our room or we will ask you to sit by yourself over there away from the group.' If she resists and keeps yelling and refuses to be isolated from the main group, go to Step Four.

STEP FOUR

She's still shouting or yelling or calling out. 'I see you've made your choice — would you leave our room now.' If she still refuses, send a student to get the teacher who is available for student exit to come and direct Debbie out of the class.

Each of these steps is
- brief
- non-hostile
- gives a choice
- fair

The first steps, consistently applied, will normally (and did) settle annoying attention-seeking like calling out.

Back to Year 7. Tactical ignoring plus reinforcement for all on-task students was working. One by one the students were getting the message: these teachers will only notice, reinforce, attend to, on-task behaviour. All but one: Dimi. He's insistent that the only way he can belong is by the teacher always, and at every point, noticing him. Why should we? He's used this gambit for years and it's often paid off, but we decided not to play his game.

Every fifteen to twenty seconds he called out. Four minutes went by. He was the only one left calling out. In desperation (he was up near the front about a metre from where I was standing) he yelled, 'I'm talking to you and you're not listening to me!'. I still firmly ignored and kept talking to the rest of the class. I was not angry. Frustrated but not angry. I was determined to stick to our plan. His mate poked him in the side and in a loud whisper said, 'He's not going to listen to you so shut up!'.

(We resisted the temptation to tell him to stop calling out, or obey the rules or whatever.) At that point I knew that negative reinforcement was working (Step One). In final frustration, half lying in his seat, he put up his hand without calling out. Quick as a flash (one needs to be on the look out for such on-task behaviour), 'Yes Dimi, what's your question? Thanks for putting up your hand'. Red-faced, he says, 'I ain't got a question now!'. 'That's okay, thanks for putting your hand up.' Then I looked straight back at the class and continued. No regaling, put downs, or 'I'm sick and tired of you'. (Tempting as these are, they don't change behaviour.)

Later, when the class was at work, he put up his hand. I winked as I walked over, 'Yes Dimi, thanks for putting up your hand'. For the rest of the lesson he sought out the winks; they had become a social reinforcer for him!

In working with teachers, I have used Steps One and Two (sometimes even Three and Four) and reduced almost all incidents of calling out providing the steps are non-confrontational, brief and within a very clear understanding of the classroom rules. The students need to discuss the fair, positive rules which protect their rights and know of the consequences where those fair rules are broken. The fair rules provide a framework and a focus for specific encouragement and reinforcement, and consequences where rules are broken. In this case, students choose their own outcomes and are held accountable in light of desirable or undesirable consequences. (See Chapter 5.)

Behaviour is affected by outcomes

The principles of reinforcement can be as basic as the previous example, or more structured as in the case of contingency or behaviour modification. This approach presupposes that a student's behaviour is effectively influenced by the circumstances following it. If Johnny keeps hearing 'Shhh!' each time he calls out, it is a form of reinforcement. He is being noticed. It doesn't matter that he's only getting a 'Shhh!' or 'I won't tell you again!' (but she will), or 'Why do you have to keep calling out?'. It is still *attention*. That's Johnny's agenda, his 'goal' if you like.

What we want to do is to structure our discipline so as to teach him that he can get significant attention — when he's on-task. We can only do that by arranging the contingencies so that they are more likely to see a repeat of the desired behaviour in Johnny. As a teacher modifies the student's environment and the kind of directions given, the student may well respond to the reinforcement process. They are not being manipulated, but simply experiencing differing rewards/contingencies which make the desirable, on-task behaviour more worthwhile in their eyes.

Punishment

Merely punishing Johnny or Debbie doesn't extinguish the disruptive pattern. Punishment, in the sense of *mere* punishment (lines, yelling, shouting, put-downs, criticisms, detention, the application of physical pain), may deter the student in the short term but the effect is rarely long-term. Mere punishment does not effectively guide or educate; it often has an inverse effect on the student chastised, and even on the group. It is important to distinguish between logical or applied consequences, and punishment based on teacher force.

Positive reinforcement

Effective teachers have long known that encouragement, specific and thoughtful praise, even short-term rewards, are far more effective than punishment. Students learn more quickly and more effectively when rewarded for on-task learning and behaviour. Interest, effort and self-esteem are obviously linked more effectively to positive reinforcement.

There are several types of reinforcement.

1 *Social reinforcement*
   This is the reinforcement noted in the calling-out example where the teacher gives attention for on-task behaviours. It can be a wink, nod or hand signal that indicates 'well done', or 'good on you'; a touch, a pat, or simply walking alongside and smiling. Often this sort of reinforcement is verbal. 'I appreciate it when . . .'; 'Thanks for . . .'; 'You set that out well'; 'Good on you'; 'I can see you've worked well here . . .'; 'You really enjoyed that didn't you'; 'That writing is really neat, especially . . .'. It is a combination of specific and general encouragement rather than global praise such as good or bad.

   It's amazing how effective social reinforcement is. Effective teachers also encourage children who are 'social reinforcers' as members of the classroom group; not necessarily in a big way but by quietly saying to a student, 'Paul, I noticed how you asked Dave, quietly, for his sharpener. Good on you'. A teacher's verbal behaviour is a powerful and primary reinforcement tool in the classroom.

2 *Symbolic reinforcement*

These include everything from stamps to symbols. Teachers have always used these, but they can be more systematically developed as part of a plan. Charts can be used with stamps to show development of successive reinforcement especially if the student can put their own stamp or sticker on their chart at the time they are 'reinforced'.

3 *Special activity reinforcement*

This is where the teacher offers special activities as a reward and reinforcement. Everything from activities such as play, reading, or free time to working with a special friend or missing homework can be used. These can be negotiated with the students on a contractual basis.

4 *Token reinforcement and edible reinforcement*

Tokens, a sticker or stamp, can be traded for a reward when an agreed number of stamps or points are reached.

> Annoying, intensely frustrating, Brett in Year 1 is classified as significantly, socio-emotionally disturbed. Many approaches have been tried with Brett with little success. Behaviour modification, however, brought some visible consistency to Brett's behaviour. In class he has a little book with several target behaviours noted. Each behaviour is on a different page (chairsitting, writing, putting his hand up, all illustrated with pictures). Initially, all on-task behaviours obtain a star on that page. He knows when he gets to ten he gets a jelly bean.

Similar 'token economies' can be used for team-work. This has been used for example, with children up to Year 8 with teams and points. All reinforcers are linked to expected target behaviours, and these behaviours are explained or discussed with the students. These tokens can be exchanged for jelly beans, raisins, textas, sharpeners, badges, rubbers, certificates, special stamps, 'free' activities etc. The token is the *primary* reinforcer, the jelly bean or pencil is the *second-*

ary reinforcer. All reinforcers ought to be linked with the verbal and social reinforcement. The reinforcement is the consequence the child experiences as a result of particular behaviour.

Reinforcement, thoughtfully applied, is not manipulation. Of course it needs to be stressed that the ultimate goal of all external reinforcement is the natural reinforcement enjoyed as a result of appropriate behaviours. The teacher's intervention may be partial, systematic and carefully targeted, charted, or merely 'catching them on-task' and verbally reinforcing. The goal is to move from teacher intervention to self-reinforcement. Initially, the reinforcement will follow as soon after the target behaviour as possible. 'Thank you for putting up your hand.' 'You're sitting quietly and working. Well done.' If using any form of 'token' reinforcement, these should always be combined with social reinforcers. Behaviour is 'strengthened' and directed if it is followed by positive reinforcement. This will mean watching for students to be on-task, to 'catch them in the act' as it were, instead of only 'catching' them when they are disruptive and off-task.

Systematic behaviour / contingency management

This is where a teacher systematically plans a reinforcement process by using the following procedure.

1 The first step is to define the target behaviour such as sitting in a seat or desk for 'x' minutes (to be increased over time); raising hand in discussion; doing a set activity; completing a set task; walking quietly around the room; working cooperatively for a set time; getting books out on time; completing a set learning goal or short-term contract. While it might be argued that children should do these things anyway, there are significant numbers of children whose social and task behaviour show they can't, or won't behave in appropriate ways. Applied reinforcement is one way of strengthening such behaviours by giving a structured framework with clear, reinforced, targets to work towards.

2 Before applying behaviour modification, the teacher accurately observes a student's typical behaviour. The data collected is the baseline from which the target behaviour can be measured. For

example, 'Adam is not sitting in his seat, he's a mobile student who calls out ten times at the beginning of class.' Observe the typical behaviour pattern for a week. Some questions to ask might be: What are the actual disruptive, off-task behaviours? (Be specific.) When do they occur? How often? With whom? (Any particular students?)

3 The third step is the reinforcement phase. This can occur through 'catching them on-task' and giving reinforcement while, at the same time, tactically ignoring low-level disruptive behaviours. More specifically, it may mean planning with the student by drawing up a chart or contract (smaller children can have a picture chart of the target behaviour). The student needs to know that they will be rewarded when they behave in a particular way. Make sure the target is achievable such as staying seated for five minutes (perhaps using a timer).

An example of planned or systematic reinforcement

If using systematic reinforcement, a teacher can chart the progress to determine how effective the reinforcement is.

For example, the reinforcement phase can be trialled against the observation phase.

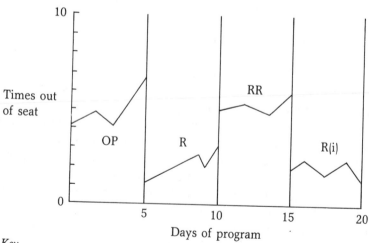

Key
OP   observation phase
R   reinforcement
RR   reinforcement removed
R(i) intermittent reinforcement

During the first five days the teacher observes the typical pattern of behaviour. In the next week he applies the reinforcement process, noticing a marked improvement in target behaviour (sitting in seat). After ten days, all reinforcement is removed and the original pattern creeps back indicating that the reinforcement process is working. The teacher then reapplies the process using intermittent reinforcement. As far as possible, low-level attention-seeking is ignored. All discipline, when using the reinforcement process, is tied into the 'steps' process (see Chapter 3).

A chart can be displayed with the child's name, days of the week, and the expected goal. Points or stars can be allocated at those times when the teacher reinforces on-task behaviour.

The basic principles of behaviour modification

BEHAVIOUR

Behaviour is shaped by the reinforcement it receives. The kind of consequences occurring after an 'act' help to determine the way in which behaviour continues.

ON-TASK BEHAVIOUR

This can be strengthened by application of reinforcement.

- Where reinforcement is systematic, it can aid the direction and maintenance of behaviour.
- Reinforcement (negative or positive) is to be distinguished from mere punishment.
- Where on-task behaviour is reinforced by teacher reward, the on-task behaviour is likely to be repeated.
- Where it is possible to ignore observed off-task behaviour and reinforce the student when on-task, the ignoring will often aid in minimising off-task behaviour.
- Where behavioural consequences are applied instead of mere punishment and combined with regular, positive reinforcement, the on-task behaviour is likely to increase.

REINFORCEMENT AND DISCIPLINE

When using reinforcement for behaviour modification several features of discipline are presumed.

- There are clear rules and an understanding of consequences. The rules are discussed with the class and are recorded on cards placed around the room. Rules are few in number and positively expressed.
- There is a plan by the teacher to use a 'steps' approach in handling classroom disruptions. Know what to do first, second and third when a student is disruptive. This should be supported by clear, in-class 'time-out' and 'exit' processes if necessary.
- There is peer-support. A teacher can be significantly assisted by having a trusted colleague observe their practice and assist in planning the reinforcement process. Support staff (psychologists and specialist teachers and consultants) can also often assist.

Summary

1 The principles of reinforcement are useful for all general classroom practice. They are tied in with respectful treatment and encouragement. Always be on the lookout for behaviour to reinforce even if by a nod or a wink. It beats nagging, slanging off and repetitious verbals like 'I'm not going to say it again'.

2 Where normal rights-rules-responsibility discipline is not working, behaviour modification can be a positive and productive means to enable a student to move towards on-task goals. I've used group reinforcement with many wild, chair-throwing classes to effectively bring the class back to some reasonable sanity and 'success' from which we can move on to less external means of classroom management.

3 The process works best when the reinforcement is partial — the student does not know when the reinforcement will come. The goal, of course, is self-reinforcement, the enjoyment of naturally occurring approval, and attention from the teacher and peers.

4 Ideally, any systematic reinforcement program should be short-term as a step to the laudable goal of self-reinforcement; no one wants to keep a student on a 'token economy'.

5 The techniques should be used with dignity. It should be explained to the student what we are doing and what we expect, what the reinforcement is and why the student is receiving it. 'Behaviour therapy does things for people, not to people.' (Ross in Poteet 1973, p. 84.)

A rights focus in education naturally abhors sub-rational group conformism (we are dealing with fellow human beings). However, where we can provide a context for students who find it difficult to behave within the agreed, fair rules, we give them an opportunity to experience success. Success reinforces success. If a student can experience a range of reinforcement (especially the verbal and non-verbal), it is likely that they will learn that they can cope successfully with the demands of learning and socialising in a classroom setting.

Behaviour modification using groups

Early in my role as a consultant in discipline and student welfare, I was asked to work with a class of Year 8 boys at a local secondary school. I didn't know what I'd let myself in for. 'Can you do something with them? They're a bit testy!', said the principal. From the raised eyebrows, and 'hang-dog' look, I had the impression that he held little hope of success.

I'd been reading up on group reinforcement and had tried it out on a few classes at other schools. With that experience in reserve, I walked down the passage towards one of the rowdiest post-primary classes I'd ever faced. You could hear their yelling from twenty metres away. Four-letter words were being hurled around along with screwed-up paper balls, half-eaten apples, and there was the 'playful punching' that seems to be a ritual with boys.

My host teacher, after being rudely addressed with nicknames, let me in. B block in the science wing was filthy. Throwing their bags across the floor and talking at a noise level akin to baboon cage number 4 at the primate compound, they began sitting down in a fashion. The talking didn't stop. Fortunately, I'd made an attempt at a plan. Mr S. lamely introduced me to 8D. The noise level didn't drop. They were completely unabashed about ignoring anybody up-front; the lateral tyranny of the peer group. I wrote my name on the board, and across the centre wrote EXPERIMENT.

GETTING THE GROUP'S ATTENTION

Facing the tumult, I drew from my bag a big pack of Twisties and a big pack of mini-chocolate bars. Don't shout bribery yet! I'll explain.

I'd read up on using edible reinforcers in groups on a points-for-reinforcement basis. The program relies on the power of one team competing against another team for points. The final *coup de grace* is a bag of Twisties for each member of the winning team. I was now going to try to explain something of this to 8D. Novelty, I hoped, would act as a kind of circuit-breaker on their ritualistic hooning. Not for this group a discussion of rights, rules and responsibilities; just knowing manipulation.

As I drew the Twisties from my bag, the chaotic noise level dropped enough for me to speak and be heard! Speaking in a loud, firm voice, and ignoring all catcalls, yells and other noises, I said, 'We're going to run an experiment this week. I'm going to split you all into four teams, and I'll need four team leaders. Each team has a chance to win a prize. These Twisties'.

CHOOSING TEAM LEADERS

Well, the calling out started. 'I'll be a captain!' 'No me!' 'I wanna be one.' 'Over here, Sir!' Not looking at any of the students I steamed on. 'Okay the way I'll choose the leaders is by giving you all a small piece of paper. Write on the paper two names of people in this room who you would like to be a leader — a leader of a team you'd like to be in. Any questions?'

Here was the next reinforcement ploy. Immediately, calling out started again. 'How many names?' 'Can I put my own name down?' Tactically ignoring the calling-out behaviour, I was expecting someone, anyone, to actually put up their hand. Someone did eventually put their hand up without calling out. 'Yes, thanks for putting your hand up by the way.' (Firm eye-contact.) 'What's your question?' 'Can we put our own names down?' As I answered, I let them know they could win points for behaviour that is fair, that keeps the fair rules. (I'd work out the actual rules with them later.)

The reinforcement began to work. I only noticed, attended and answered the on-task students with their hands up. I took a risk by not reinforcing calling-out behaviour. It worked. They smelt the game plan and saw the edibles on the lab desk. We steamed ahead. 'Okay Mark, pass out the bits of paper, please.' He swaggered off but passed them around. Amazing. There was still plenty of noisy chatter but it had dropped six decibels (or so it seemed to my ears) and they were actually writing.

CHOOSING TEAMS

'Okay, collect them please Mark. Thanks. Now I've got a list up here of all your names. What I'm going to do is sort through these names and see who have been chosen as leaders. Then we'll give each leader a chance to choose from the list of class members. First we'll find out who the leaders are. I'll need a couple of helpers.' (I ignored students who called out at this point.)

The two helpers sorted out the most recurring names into a final four. While they did this with the class teacher, I had a discussion with the class about rules.

RULES

'We'll need a few basic rules to service our class over the next few weeks while we have these teams. What sort of rules?' We had a brainstorming session where I only attended to those with hands up. 'Thanks, Frank for putting up your hand, it makes life so much easier.' 'I appreciate you waiting with your hand up.' 'Nick, what's your question?' 'Yes, down the back with your hand up. What's your question?' In the first week of this experiment, the social reinforcement was given for each occurrence of on-task behaviour. Later it was discriminate and focused on specific, rule-keeping behaviour.

We ended up, as we always do in these situations, with a communication rule, a movement rule, a learning rule, a problem-settling rule (later we added a safety rule). The key focus for each rule was the word: *communication*, *learning*, etc. To save time it can help to have several, brief rules already written up and simply stick them to the board.

By this time we had the four names for the leaders. I read them out as I wrote them up on the board, in chart form.

NICK	MARK	FRANK	CON

'Would the four leaders please come up to the front desk, thanks.' (The noise level, due to the novelty of the experiment, had dropped significantly. I was speaking at a reasonable level now.) Frank and Con swaggered up. 'On you Frank,' called out a wag from the back of the class. Mark and Nick looked bemused. Children choose leaders by two broad criteria; power brokerage and a form of 'moral' leadership. I asked the

leaders to select from the class name list (one at a time to get equal
distribution), students for their teams. No problems here. I stressed
they had to do this until each name had been chosen. I kept them
moving quickly until all names were crossed off. Collecting the four
lists of team members, I asked the leaders to go back to their seats.

'All right, we've got the teams.' I read the names as I wrote them up
on the board, reading the last name first in an attempt to give a
minuscule measure of self-esteem to the person chosen last in each
team. Frank blurted out, 'Gee, I only chose Hoong because he was last'.
I briefly reminded the class, 'We have a fair rule for treatment of
others, we'll discuss that later. Right, these are the teams'. (They were
quickly distracted to the on-task activity.)

REINFORCEMENT AND THE POINTS

'Now, — the really important part.' Rustling the bags of goodies, I said,
'Each team can earn points for keeping our fair class rules, getting on
with our work, packing up, and entering and leaving the room in a fair
way'. 'I'll put the points on the board. My job is to be the umpire. My
decision is final. If anybody makes objections about the points or makes
things tough for the group, they'll miss out on a point. The umpire's
decision, like footy, is final. Okay? But I know you'll all play fair
(wink).' 'Any questions?' Again, only on-task questions were accepted.
There were only a few calling out now. The reinforcement was working.

'In a moment, I want each leader to move with his team to some part
of the room. Move the chairs or desks any way you want, as long as
you do it quietly. I'll be giving points for fair rule-keeping. Off you go.'
Well, I expected marginal chaos. But in a few minutes they had grouped
themselves, swinging the heavy lab tables together and not kicking any
chairs around (as had happened in the first hair-raising two to three
minutes). I reinforced many movements in that short time. 'Frank! (he
turned with a worried look as he passed kids moving in the opposite
direction). Thanks for moving quietly with your group; especially the
way you got your team organised with the chairs. Well done! Point for
your team.' A smile of relief appeared on Frank's face.

GIVING THE GROUPS A TASK

There were now four teams quietly facing the class teacher and myself.
'Great, thanks for settling down so quickly.. The first job for each team
— by the way Con, your team has three points already, well done —

is to choose a name for your team. No footy names thanks. You've got two minutes. Off you go.' There was good working noise and we ended up with:

SLAGGS	DRONGOS	RAMBOS	ACES 5	
NICK	MARK	FRANK	CON	
				POINTS TALLY

For use over the next four weeks, we made up a chart with the permanent team names, captains and points.

'Con, I noticed you spoke quietly to your team members as you moved the table. Good on you — a point for your team.' His team members smiled, the other teams heard, most were spurred on. The tone of the room was positive. My job now was to quickly pick up on-task, rule-keeping behaviours, sometimes giving a point, sometimes not. The object was to move to discriminate reinforcement (sometimes a point, other times just the verbal/social reinforcement). The basic principle is that in reinforcing one team member, and giving a point (or verbal reinforcer), this acts as a visual advertisement for the other teams to observe and, hopefully, imitate.

Our second task was to give each group the job of writing one class rule. The task was:

1 Write a rough draft developed through group discussion (on, for example, a communication rule).
2 Confirm the rule with the class teacher (who may do some fine tuning).
3 Write a brief description of the rule with a bold heading such as communication or movement or learning or problem-settling, on a large piece of coloured card. (Later, we displayed these around the class at each science session with 8D.)

Each team wrote up a rule. At the end of the class session, the team with the most points (The 5 Aces) got to choose between the Twisties or the mini-chocolates. Con came up, only two minutes before the recess bell, to claim his team's prize. The three other teams looked on with moderate envy. The class was reminded that next week they could earn points by the way they entered the room and left. 'Okay, pack-up time. Desks back, chairs up, we'll see you next science session.'

As they all left, the noise level went up, and several students forgot to push in their chairs. Quickly I said, 'Mark, I noticed three of your team put the chairs away without being asked — great. Two points already for next week. Good on you'. Almost immediately several others put their chairs away. All they got was a smile and a brief, 'Thanks, see you next week'.

In the following four sessions we had our ups and downs, but the students were beginning to settle down well and were working. Normal, but improved, science lessons were planned with groups in mind and as much 'hands-on' activity as possible.

All discipline problems were settled with a focus on the rules. They were *our* rules. We only had a few major disruptions (a chair kicked, a few 'f____ing unfairs!', a bit of attention-seeking) but these were handled within our clear discipline plan. We gave clear, firm directions and asked questions. 'What are you doing?' 'What should you be doing?' We used rule restatements, gave choices and mild desists. The tone was positive. (See Chapter 3.)

In week five we had a class meeting to assess where we'd been and what we'd achieved. Seated in a circle, we began our discussion (see Chapter 5). Essentially, the students agreed that the class was much better, that they were *working* and that it really didn't matter whether they had the treats. We celebrated with a barbecue that week.

Remember, this degree of behaviour modification works best with classes who have a nasty reputation. The only time I would use group reinforcement with edible reinforcers is with groups such as 8D. Generally speaking, the novelty of such an approach wears off after Year 8. It has been used with extremely difficult groups of students aged four upwards.

The fundamental aims of the experiment (behaviour modification) were as follows.

1 Change the power-brokerage in the class membership through leadership selection.
2 Change the dynamics in the room through organising teams. The points process is a novelty to enhance the clear, fair rules.
3 Enable the class teacher to see the students in a new light, especially as the teacher needs to focus on more positive, social reinforcers and build a more positive discipline plan to make the process work.
4 Allow the students to see a change in 'climate'. They, like their teacher, experience a taste of normality through engineered reinforcers, but more importantly through social reinforcers. Both experience those small successes that make teaching a bearable, even enjoyable activity.

Variations on a theme

1 Accumulate points, session by session, and have a raffle at the end of the 'experiment'. A group reinforcement phase would normally run for four to five weeks.

Points are accumulated on the group chart, weekly. In the last week, a raffle is drawn. The team with the most points has more chances in the raffle; prizes can be individual or group. I've worked with teachers who have used elaborate raffle-wheels to clank out winning numbers.

2 Each group contributes to class rewards by having set work goals. The teacher contracts various tasks at various levels. Clear examples of required work are provided. Students move from task to task.

Points are earned for on-task and rule-keeping behaviour. All points go on a class chart that has a goal of 2000 points. When the whole class, through individual and cooperative behaviour, reaches 500, potato chips all round; 1000, a coffee break; 1500, a 'free' activity; 2000, a barbecue or special trip. Points are allocated for on-task behaviour using a timer set at random intervals. When the timer goes off, the behaviour of on-task students or groups is allocated 10 points.

The question of manipulation

Is it manipulative? Of course. I've had children say, 'You're bribing us!'. 'Yes, any other questions?' 'You're manipulating us!' 'Of course, with your knowledge. Any other questions? No, good, let's get on with it.' There is no question that group reinforcement is a marvellous group 'circuit-breaker'. Especially where long-term habituation has resulted in a class with a 'reputation'.

If a student says, 'This sucks, don't want to be in it', don't get drawn. You're the referee. 'Okay, you can sit over here Michelle, and work away from the group.' Invite her in again next week. But don't force, or coerce those *very* few who sulk or refuse.

With less difficult classes, the same process can be used without any formal reinforcers (points and edibles). Simply operating the class through a group process with chosen leadership often changes the 'climate' of power-brokerage in the room. I have done this successfully with Year 9 and 10 classes.

Like most techniques, we will get better at it with practice. One colleague, in her first session, pulled out the chips, turned her back on the class to write on the board, and a furtive Year 7 boy raced to the front, grabbed the chips, gave a victory salute and bolted down the corridor! In the second week the program was successful. Be prepared.

If you feel you would like to develop group reinforcement with 8D or their equal, but don't think you could make it work, then team up with a colleague and plan it together.

Summary

1 Clarify why you want to use group reinforcement. Be clear in your own mind that this is a short-term program.

2 Be prepared. Plan the steps well beforehand. Have the charts, paper, pencils, name list and edibles ready. Know what your opening lines will be.

3 Explain the process to the class. Explain that this is a short-term activity (and you may want to explain that it will be fun). Explain the rules. Have the rules written up in point form on cards. Express positively, or, as in the example noted earlier, employ a rule-making phase. Then explain how they can earn points for their team.

4 Organise leaders. Distribute small pieces of paper for students to write two names on. When collected, identify the most recurring names. These will be the leaders. Have work to do for students while you sort out the names.

5 Form teams. Call the leaders to the front. Ask the leaders to choose from a class list, *one at a time*, to form their teams. Have a sheet of paper for each team leader. The choosing is done up the front of the class with the teacher and four or five leaders.

6 Form the groups. Explain that the teams are to group themselves quietly in the room. Ask the teams to choose a team name (no footy names or silly names).

7 Give points regularly. Make it clear that you are the referee; no debates will be entered into. Write up points as soon as you give them. Be ready to give points especially to previously disruptive students.

8 Have a clear discipline plan. Expect cooperation and compliance. Reinforce specific behaviours that are cooperative and on-task. When using corrective discipline, be brief, clear and rule-focused. Remember to be positive.

9 Have the prizes ready. Give out the edibles to the winning group near the close of the session. In the last week, you may want to give

a small prize to each class member as well as group prizes, or have a barbecue or coffee session to celebrate.

It can be helpful to complete the experiment by holding a class meeting to see where you will go from here (see Chapter 5). By this time, the group will be amenable to a healthy discussion.

Group reinforcement with younger students (Kinder to Year 2)

With younger students, the same principles can apply. As Brown, Reschly and Sabers (1974) have observed, such a process can significantly modify even the behaviour of aggressive pre-schoolers who display kicking, fighting, biting and other anti-social behaviour.

1 Explain to the children that they are going to do something 'special' starting today (and for the next few weeks). 'We are going to work in groups. I have chosen the groups. I'll tell you what group you are in in a moment, and each group has a colour.' Put four or five (depending on the total number of students) large coloured discs, using Blu-tack, on the board. Later, attach the names of group members to those discs.

2 Bring out the edible reinforcers (for use with very difficult classes). 'Now, you can win goodies for your team by working well together in our groups — helping, sharing, working quietly, putting up your hand, sitting quietly on the mat, putting the scissors and clag away . . .'

3 Explain expected behaviours, positively, through the classroom rules. Have a large card for each rule with two or three pictures on it depicting expected behaviours (see Chapter 4). For example:
   • *Our talking rule* (hand up, not calling-out, listening to others).
   • *Our movement rule* (lining up quietly, on-the-mat behaviour, moving out-of-seat during on-task phase of the lesson).
   • *Our working rule* (helping one another, borrowing by asking, cooperation and respect).

You can model this behaviour by demonstration of manners, asking politely, walking quietly, and by little role-plays with the students. This phase of the process is reinforcing expected behaviour in a positive way. During the reinforcement phase, look for specific behaviours, within these rules, to either comment on or tangibly reinforce.

4 Organise the groups by equal distribution, or, where children can write, (Year 1, Year 2) by the name-choosing method — each child writes the name of their preferred leader and returns it to the teacher. Each team member has a small coloured badge and a designated table. Team leaders can be chosen as focal points for identifying the team.

5 Explain the points and the goal. The children can earn points for their helpful, cooperative behaviour. Each point earned by the team goes on a chart. The chart is a metre-long card with divisions to colour in the team points. The goal is to get their big coloured disc (their team) to the end of the road (the chart). Points are coloured in by a member of the team as allocated and in the team colour.

Reinforce *specifically*, 'Chris, I noticed you had your hand up and you waited. Well done. Point for your team'. 'Esta, you sat down quickly and quietly. Point for your team. Well done.' Edible reinforcers can be given each fifteen to twenty minutes for all teams who have at least one point. Towards the close of the day, as points accumulate, begin to give a running commentary. The team who reaches the goal first can choose the special prizes (a special pencil for each team member, a free activity, stickers).

6 Discipline is largely supportive. By concentrating on positive behaviours, team members start to reinforce one another (peer support). Refer to the rules where there is disruption, or simply and firmly direct the student back on-task. Where a child is significantly disrupting, direct the child to the time-out corner for two to three minutes, set a timer and expect the student to settle and return to the group. Rather than take off earned points, just don't give out the edibles to a group who have a member in time-out.

7 Assess the outcome and plan for maintenance of the improved behaviour. The aim of this exercise is to use group reinforcement, clearly expected and defined behaviours, novelty, and applied reinforcement to break the circuit of overly disruptive group behaviour. Normally a process such as this would only run for three or four weeks, then you would see if such behaviours had generalised. Of course, the process of cooperative group behaviour can continue without the organised reinforcement. An excellent book on

cooperative learning is Joan Dalton's *Adventures in Thinking*.

Variations on this approach are limited only by a teacher's ingenuity, but the fundamentals are:

- clear rules
- positive expectations
- specific encouragement and reinforcement
- building of self-reinforcement through peer-support

It is a short term, 'circuit-breaking' activity that can and does bring success back into group life for student and teacher alike, forming a basis for future growth as a classroom group.

It is not to be dismissed lightly by ideologues who are not in the front-line with an unruly bunch of four and five year olds with little, or no social skills. It is a vehicle for social reinforcement to train and guide behaviour towards that self-control which is the aim of all responsible discipline.

CHAPTER 8

Conflict resolution

It is natural that the parties involved in a conflict should settle their conflict. It is their business. Their interests are at stake. They started it anyway.
De Bono, 1986

Conflict is inevitable

If we say that conflict is inevitable, some teachers will interpret this as capitulation to the instability of the modern classroom. Not so. Whether the conflict arises out of pre-disposing factors (family modelling, place in the family, general immaturity) or classroom conditions themselves, the issues are as follows:

- How do we as classroom leaders minimise the likelihood of potential conflict?
- How do we manage conflict *at the point* where emotional heat is exchanged?
- How do we work for long-term resolution and good working relationships?

Keeping students in a small room for fifty-minute periods with a curriculum that doesn't cater for mixed abilities or take into account some of the backgrounds of our students, or the nature of social change itself, and expecting them to sit and be quiet and submissive, is a recipe for conflict and teacher stress. Conflict is, in a sense, a natural by-product of the group life. Some students will actually seek it as a form of social identity. (Dreikurs, Grunwald and Pepper, 1982)

Teachers define conflict in various ways. For some it may be a child who merely answers back. I once had a teacher say to me, 'Do you know what a Year 3 child said to me? He said, "I don't want to do this work Miss." ' For others it may be those frustrating and petty annoyances: 'No pen, Miss!', 'What do we have to do again?', late students, or the 'dropped' swear word. In this chapter, the conflicts being addressed are those more serious issues that are likely to cause significant frustration, anxiety and anger in teachers: swearing, overt defiance, aggressive behaviours (kicking, hitting, shoving, pulling, instrumental hurting), verbal aggression directed to others (including teacher).

The most common form of classroom conflict which occurs is where the nature of the transaction easily becomes a win or lose situation for both sides.

Conflict and students

Conflict is basically the presence of two (or more) competing needs or demands at the same time. Mick is frustrated and gives quick vent to his emotion, 'f____ this work!' (need met, frustration partially ameliorated). The teacher gets angry. He has a need to 'control' the outbreak of swearing and to manage his own frustration (triggered by this four-letter provocateur). The climate now exists for conflict. How the conflict proceeds will depend largely on how each party defines the ongoing transaction. Where the two activities are mutually exclusive then the environment for conflict is ripe. Weber (in Rex, 1981) describes conflict as a 'will to act' being resisted where the other party acts against the 'actor's' needs — an incompatible difference of objective. Reading (1977) has some fifty-four variations on the term 'conflict'. For the teacher it is often simply the student-teacher situation over which control is extremely difficult and stressful. By the way, if you happen to be a teacher who has not experienced high-level defiance, swearing or aggressive behaviours, spare a thought for those among us who have, and who have employed (with some success) the strategies employed in this book.

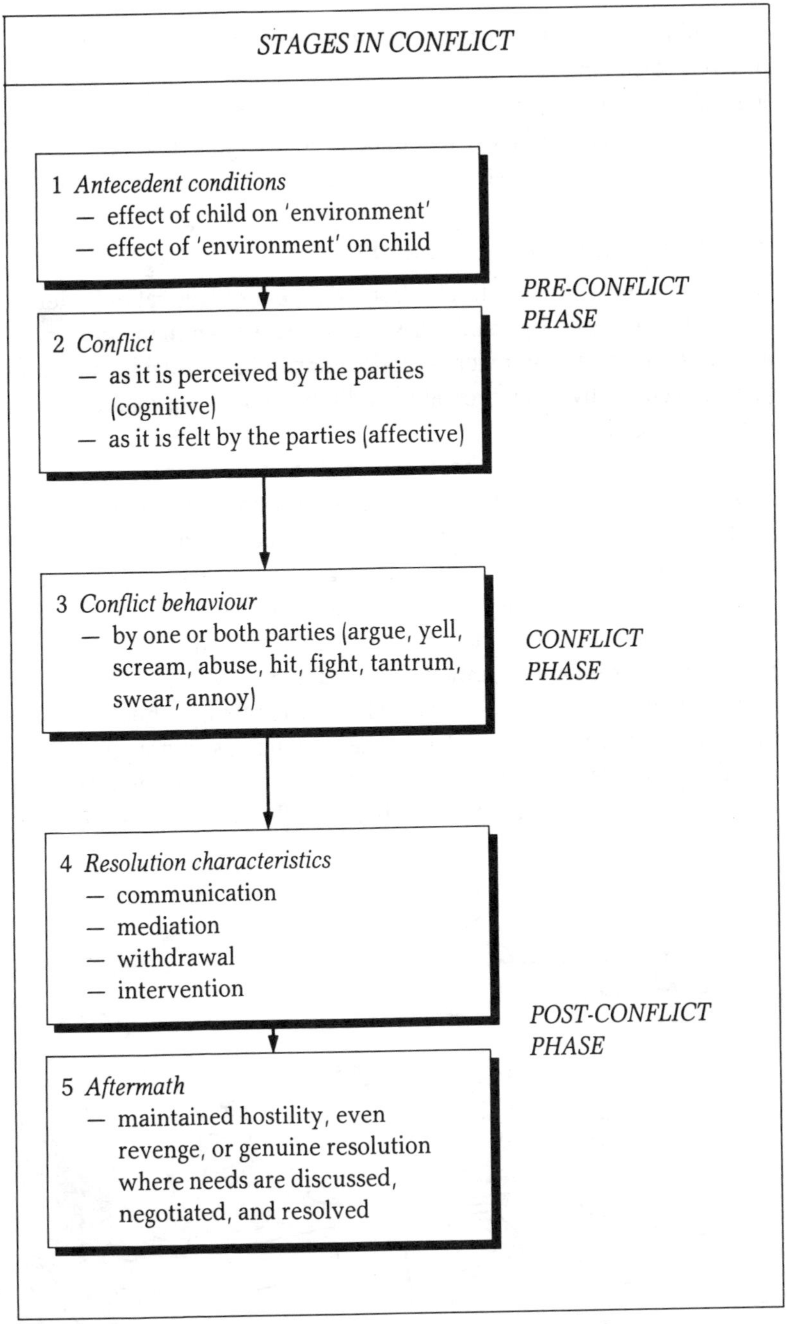

STAGES IN CONFLICT

1 *Antecedent conditions*
   — effect of child on 'environment'
   — effect of 'environment' on child

PRE-CONFLICT PHASE

2 *Conflict*
   — as it is perceived by the parties (cognitive)
   — as it is felt by the parties (affective)

3 *Conflict behaviour*
   — by one or both parties (argue, yell, scream, abuse, hit, fight, tantrum, swear, annoy)

CONFLICT PHASE

4 *Resolution characteristics*
   — communication
   — mediation
   — withdrawal
   — intervention

POST-CONFLICT PHASE

5 *Aftermath*
   — maintained hostility, even revenge, or genuine resolution where needs are discussed, negotiated, and resolved

Fig 7

Wishing and hoping for the halcyon days of 'Yes Sir!', 'No Sir!', ordered rows, and neat polite children, is professionally and psychologically stupid. Conflict, at any level, will come. How we minimise it and creatively channel it will depend to a large extent on the kind of personal and organisational planning we employ to resolve it.

Frustration and conflict in children

A good deal of conflict with children arises out of frustration; internal frustration (induced by family or social climate or an inability to manage task demands) or external frustration where outside pressures (largely actions by others) create conditions where reasonable coping seems impossible.

Younger students and those less mature tend to react to failure maladaptively (Vernon, 1969). Less able to think out an appropriate course of action, they get frustrated and will not tolerate the presence of that frustration. Much of the swearing we now hear in (some) classrooms is frustration engendered. As Milgram and Shotland (1973) noted in their research, the presence of frustration is an extremely powerful determinant of anti-social behaviour.

If Mick answers me back because he is frustrated, without excusing his behaviour, *what I do* will determine (as much as anything) how the conflict proceeds. I can increase or decrease the frustration by what I say and do. If I slam my hand on the desk (I must win, I'll show this

little shit he can't answer me back, 'Listen you, who the hell do you think you are speaking to me like that') and speak in a hostile fashion, it will have a different outcome than if I restate the rule, give a simple direction, defuse, or take the student aside (see Chapter 3). I may not be able to stop the child from *feeling* frustrated but I can do a great deal about how I respond to his acting-out behaviour.

Students who react quickly

One of the problems in dealing with such students is their failure to interpret a social situation beyond the few cues of frustration ('I'm angry!'), there's a threat ('That bastard took my rubber'), and the belief 'I must win'. Dodge (1981) describes such students (mostly boys) as 'low-searching' in their perceptual cues. They 'globalise' a threat and do not take in all the available cues (high-searching). 'He stole my rubber!' ('stole' not took without asking). 'I'll belt the bastard! How dare he!'

Teaching in a graphics class, some years ago, I watched Michael (a tough, street-wise student) wrestle with a student who had 'borrowed' his rubber. It happened so quickly. Apparently Darren, a mate, had 'borrowed' his rubber from one desk away. After Michael retaliated with a grab and, 'Give it back you f＿＿＿ing poofter!', the two fell on the floor to wrestle and to grab the rubber which had now bounced under the table. I managed to call both aside from the group and ask what they thought they were doing. As with many such students I've worked with, they saw conflict in terms of a power struggle. 'But he's your mate.' 'So what!'

Many of those 'quick-responding' students see the transaction as merely one of win or lose. Enhancement of self at the expense of others is not simply a pre-pubescent characteristic of course. Many adult males don't subjugate that win/lose predisposition (Bryant, 1977); what Bernard and Joyce (1984) call the 'undercontrolled behaviour syndrome'. In 1965 Fannin and Clinard noted that many working-class boys saw themselves as 'tough', 'powerful' and 'aggressive' and felt that such traits were not only desirable but that social placement was correlated with these traits. In a research study I conducted in 1985 with over 500 pre-adolescent students, the boys showed significantly more hostile and aggressive resolutions of conflict than girls (who indicated verbal-based resolutions to inter-personal conflict).

Gender differences

Boys are predominantly more aggressive in resolving conflict than girls. This is seen in play behaviour, in 'resolving' differences over property, opinion or friendship patterns. Girls tend to be much more verbally active in conflict-resolution, or will call on an adult to mediate. Boys are more pragmatic, more utilitarian: a punch, snatch or strike is quick and easy! Even in play settings, boys are more active and aggressive than their female counterparts — a fact borne out by study after study (Williams, Bennet, and Best, in Papalia and Wendkos Olds 1982; Rogers 1985).

Little wonder that boys see 'power' basically, as the ability to win over someone else — often by force. Talking takes time and effort.

> I recall once in a group discussion that a boy turned and referred to a female student as 'she'. 'What she said isn't right!' Annoyed, I reminded him of our rule saying 'Her name is Simone.' He continued on, 'Anyway, what she said was . . .' Interrupting I said, 'What *Simone* said'. 'Yeah what *she* said . . .' 'Simone is her name . . .' 'All right!, Simone then . . .' And we continued on. We've still got a long way to go with reasonable male-female social dynamics. (We need to do a good deal more on discussing *rights* as a feature of social behaviour.)

Where girls are aggressive, it is often verbal aggression; the mouth is used instead of the fist. The research data on male proclivity to aggression in conflict is a salutary reminder to male teachers especially about their *modelling* of conflict-resolution in their classrooms.

Classroom conflicts

In classroom conflicts, boys will evidence more negativistic behaviours: negative attention-seeking (calling out and often being re-inforced for it); anti-social aggression; physical aggression (pushing, pulling, grabbing). Even in their self-reporting, boys will nominate males (age-related) as more aggressive, more dominant, more hostile in conflict settings; as if such behaviour is the norm. Most of the complaints regarding confrontations in classrooms are noted as coming from boys. As early as pre-school age, the sex difference in conflict is clearly observed: boys retaliating more, thus more hostile encounters; girls either submitting or employing more 'devious' strategies to gain their objective. Of course, much of this pattern is to do with modelling, and social expectation through nurturing in the early years. School, especially the playground, still reinforces such pattern (Maccoby 1966, Maccoby and Jacklin 1974, 1980).

It is worth re-emphasising that with respect to calling out (with boys), if we cannot tactically ignore it and have to give any attention, give it briefly, simply and focus on the rules and then try to pick up a girl's question where possible or encourage same by calling on a female student. 'What do you think Maria?'

When it comes to the resolution of conflict, children (normally) can be expected to move through the following stages though, like some adults, they regress under stressful circumstances.

1 Physical aggression towards other children or adults (biting, hitting, kicking, pinching, punching) and towards inanimate objects (throwing, hitting something).
2 General aggression (tantrums, foot stamping, running crazily) and aggression towards self.
3 Verbal aggression towards others and towards things ('You bastard', 'You f____ing idiot', 'That bloody book!', 'That shitty hammer!'); towards self, covertly or overtly ('I'm an idiot', 'I'm useless, no good!').
4 Socially acceptable means:
   • bargaining, discussion, explaining one's feelings
   • seeking alternative goals
   • seeking third-party mediation
   • cooperative resolutions

Our goal as teachers, of course, is to enable children to work, play and socialise with others cooperatively. Developing the sustained ability for non-hostile resolution of conflict is a hard task for a teacher and is related to how a teacher seriously develops self-esteem building, a fair rights-rules-responsibilities dynamic and good communication channels for handling conflict at the point of crisis and in the long-term resolution.

Conflict resolution employed by children

Aggression: Snatching, punching, pulling (hostile mode).
Adult intervention: 'Mum!', 'Dad!', 'Teacher!'.
Threat: 'I'll dob if you don't!' 'I'll hit you if you don't give my rubber back.'

Diversions: Trying something else to divert attention.

Reasoning (basic): 'Give it back.' 'Don't do that, it's mine!' 'Why did you snatch my rubber?'.

Reasoning (mature): Talking through issues and problems to resolution.

Children employ all the characteristics that adults do when facing what they perceive as 'conflict'. Girls, generally, are more likely to use an adult mediator and to use threats, or reasoning. Certainly they show more likelihood of mature reasoning in settling disputes than boys who lean heavily on aggressive modes of resolution.

Teacher frustration, anxiety and anger

Damien doesn't like school that much. Already, in Year 6, he's scored up an impressive record of unmanageable behaviours. He comes to school dirty, has holes in his jeans, is quick to swear and is often aggressive. Many teachers are thankful that he is not in their class.

He's already butted-in several times during morning talk (to the teacher's annoyance). Now, as the on-task activity in maths begins (applied number), he starts one of his interminable conflict rounds. Of course he's got problems at home, of course he has learning difficulties and his social skills are not good. There are countless numbers of students like Damien in our schools. His teacher has been fair and reasonable in her discipline behaviour. Damien throws his books off his desk and says loudly 'What do I have to do this shit work for?'. He sits, arms folded, in 'dumb insolence mode'. It's a scene. Whatever the teacher does, there is a lot of interpersonal heat being generated.

How does the teacher feel? She probably feels *very* angry (at the very least extremely frustrated). She feels acutely threatened (what will the other children think? What will the teacher in the next room think?). What makes her feel this way? Is it just Damien's four-letter defiance? Has he some special magic to make her very upset? I've worked with many teachers who have gone right off at swearing, as if the swearer had 'lit a fuse'. The reactive behaviour of students sees many women teachers flee '8D' in tears. I've seen teachers throw kids, in a fit of anger, across a room. 'He made me so angry!' How the conflict, and the student, are defined is very important.

While not unsympathetic to teachers' feelings, it is important to identify where intense feelings of anger or powerlessness come from when faced with power-provocative children. Our feelings do not just happen. When we get frustrated, even angry, several things are happening and happening quickly. We are perceiving a child's behaviour as highly threatening, we are believing that we must do something about it. We have attitudes that quickly rise to the surface. We experience, on the one hand, emotions of anger and, on the other, physiological arousal (tense or vigilant muscle reaction, increased heart rate etc.). We also react or respond to the threat (see Fig 8).

When we get angry we tend to behave in one of three basic ways:

- with reactive anger
- with passive anger
- or by utilising anger

1 *Reactive anger*
   'No one is going to swear in my class!' 'I must not lose face!' 'I *must* win'. Belief, emotion, physiology and behaviour combine to produce shouting, yelling and rough treatment — counter power. The conflict is defined as a power struggle. The emotion of anger is seen as valid proof positive that 'I *must* act angrily', especially when dealing with high conflict. I feel I must do something, I am compelled. If my emotion is the primary motivator to action and the emotion is anger, I must act angrily. Of course *reactive anger* is often irrational, over-rates the threat and is counter-productive in the long term. ('No little shit's going to swear in my class!' 'Sorry old son, you're stuck with Sean. We can't remove every difficult student'). Such teachers tend to provoke, or feed, such behaviour by their counter power. They often don't care about their anger.

   Although emotions don't tell us *what* to do, they certainly describe (quite naturally) what we are experiencing; what we do with them will depend on how we characteristically manage that emotion rather than simply letting it manage us.

2 *Passive anger*
   We hold it in for fear of 'letting go' and acting irrationally. Non-assertive teachers often feel that anger is a bad thing especially when they've seen some models of it in other teachers. The emotion of anger is one of the most powerful of human emotions. If we internalise our anger it will be to our cost, even if we hold it back for 'high motives'. All that energy has to go *somewhere* as teacher

stress records show: days off, inability to face that class again, physical distress or sickness itself. If we restrict the emotion in the setting of the conflict, we may only release it later, at home, on some poor, unsuspecting person who has nothing to do with the original cause of the anger. If we do nothing about the anger or the conflict that precipitates the emotion, we rarely resolve it.

It is unhealthy to ignore our feelings or pretend that we are not *really* angry when our body is clearly saying 'I am twisted up, I am furious. My heart rate is up, my hands are sweating, my muscles are tense.' Behind such thinking is the irrationality that says a good teacher shouldn't get angry.

3 *Utilising anger*

There is nothing wrong with anger or emotions as such. The emotional energy is there for a reason. There is a demand on our coping ability. How do we rate it, perceive it and control it? I can't stop the ire rising when Sean says, 'Piss off!' to a reasonable request. If I plan ahead, I can do something about using the emotion assertively to both express my feelings appropriately, and manage the due rights of all.

If I just react, or sulk, or withdraw, or curse back when I'm angry I learn nothing about this useful emotion. We have a *right* to get angry on issues that count but because anger is such a stressful emotion it needs management. High emotion clouds our perception and our thinking processes and affects our actions. Planning ahead will enable us to manage emotions; not to eliminate them, but utilise them.

Perception and emotion

How I perceive the conflict will affect the degree of emotion I experience. We often forget the place of belief and perception in our behaviour. Many angry teachers I have spoken to will recount the list of conflicts which made them angry, and while they can't remember what they *said* when angry they can recall why the child shouldn't have sworn or answered back or defied them. In effect they are explaining the social reality by attributing their anger to causes outside of themselves. Behaviour doesn't just happen, it interfaces powerfully with both emotion and belief; I am not made angry just by events themselves; I contribute to the anger process too.

Take swearing as an example. Where swearing is another form of defiance (and not merely a slip of the tongue), ask yourself where your feelings are coming from when you become angry about it. Frustration and anger, powerlessness and fear? If you believe, and say to yourself 'Children must not swear! They should not use filthy language like that! They should respect me! Swearing is awful!', where does such demanding thinking get you?

Anger is, like all emotions, powerfully linked to our beliefs. One affects the other. The actual swearing does not *simply* cause the anger we feel. The cause of our feeling, and the intensity of it, comes from what we currently believe. While we may strongly dislike swearing, if we demand Frank shouldn't swear (when in fact he just has), the demand locks up our feelings and stifles productive handling of the conflict.

Of course it's preferable that students (and teachers) find appropriate avenues to handle bad feelings, but to demand they act as we say they should creates unnecessary stress especially when such demands are often refused. There is a preferable, realistic and much less stressful alternative: to say, 'Well, I dislike swearing, but it is a reality. Now, how can I better handle it in the short and long term?'.

We need to recognise that we do have some provocative children in classrooms these days whose goal is 'power'. It's unpleasant, frustrating, and annoying but it's not the end of the world. This is not excusing the swearing, it is simply distinguishing between a *demand* for desirable behaviour and a *preference* for desirable behaviour. All the demands in the world won't stop swearing. They will make us more stressed about the swearing behaviour. No student who swears or defies has inherent magic to really upset me, unless I attribute to them that they do have the power. I'll acknowledge my anger but I do not have to slip into a win-or-lose mentality. I do not have to yell, react, force, or coerce. Such behaviour is most unhelpful. There are other, productive ways to handle feelings of anger such as assertive statements, avoiding the debates and arguments of power-provocative children (an ancient ploy), not over-attending, and giving clear assertive choices rather than threats and demands (see Chapters 2 and 3). In effect it means converting one's old 'involuntary emotional habits back to their original (sic) state.' (Bernard and Joyce 1984, p. 86–87)

The issue of anger management and conflict revolves around the twin issues.

1 Emotional coping: managing the intensity of frustration or anger.
2 The practical problem of *dealing* with conflict in a way that doesn't create too much stress and doesn't wreck the inter-personal dynamic in which frustration and anger is aroused. Poorly handled anger interferes with effective management goals. Teachers who react angrily to inter-personal conflict often create longer-term conflict by demanding, blaming, and judgemental beliefs.

Physical reactions

Because the body reacts to emotions, it is important to be aware of what is happening to it. As we perceive a threat, we become emotionally involved and the emotions affect our bodily responses. The heart rate is affected and beats above the normal range, the neck muscles become tense, the face becomes red as the heart pumps the blood to the excited areas. We may grit our teeth or find our fists clenched. The body is getting busy to do something. But what? We can't hit, strike or strangle that intransigent creature! (Unless it's self defence!)

These bodily signals are important. It is the natural way our physiology prepares us for conflict. So, use the tenseness as the signal to recognise and utilise your anger. When conflict arises:

- Consciously recognise what is happening.
- Clench the fists to concentrate quickly on the body's reaction then unclench.
- Concentrate on breathing more slowly. By quickly doing this we acknowledge what is happening. The pattern of 'tense and release' emphasises and acknowledges the anger and gives us a brief breathing space; we do something about the emotional arousal. As we speak clearly and firmly we also do something about our frustration.
- Count to three, exhale and respond. Speak firmly and assertively to the student/s about your anger; the situation; the rule. Give a clear choice and avoid prolonged argument. If the conflict is low-level call the student/s aside.

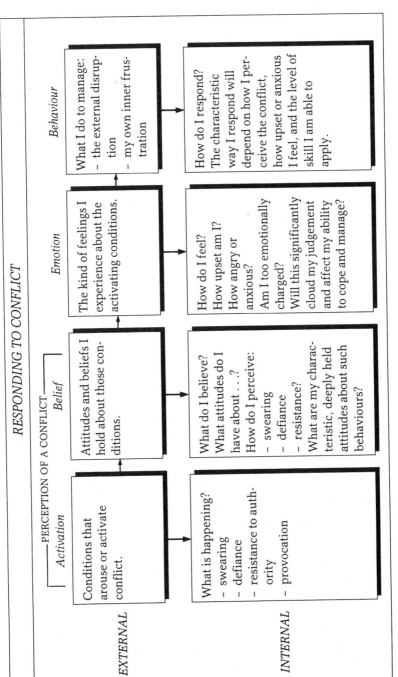

RESPONDING TO CONFLICT

PERCEPTION OF A CONFLICT

	Activation	*Belief*	*Emotion*	*Behaviour*
	Conditions that arouse or activate conflict.	Attitudes and beliefs I hold about those conditions.	The kind of feelings I experience about the activating conditions.	What I do to manage: – the external disruption – my own inner frustration
EXTERNAL	What is happening? – swearing – defiance – resistance to authority	What do I believe? What attitudes do I have about . . .? How do I perceive: – swearing – defiance – resistance? What are my characteristic, deeply held attitudes about such behaviours?	How do I feel? How upset am I? How angry or anxious? Am I too emotionally charged? Will this significantly cloud my judgement and affect my ability to cope and manage?	How do I respond? The characteristic way I respond will depend on how I perceive the conflict, how upset or anxious I feel, and the level of skill I am able to apply.
INTERNAL	– provocation			

Fig 8

How we *define* the conflict at its earliest stage will normally determine how successful or unsuccessful are the resolution and aftermath. This is why we need to make a conflict 'plan' as it were.

Basic protocols of conflict resolution

1 *Address the situation.*

Attack the problem, not each other; it's easy when the emotion of anger rises up to start giving 'you' messages. 'Listen you! I said get it out of your mouth. I'm sick and tired of telling you about your damned chewing gum!'

Whatever the situation is, chewing gum, noise, task-refusal, address *that*. Have some characteristic verbal repertoire in mind to say when precipitating ('anger-producing') student behaviour arises. 'David, if you want to ask a question put your hand up.' is much better (said assertively) than, 'You always scream at me, what's wrong with you? Can't you put your hand up or what?'. Try to stay on the issue itself, as briefly as possible. Hyperbole doesn't really help, 'I've told you a thousand times!'.

2 *Avoid put-downs and criticism of the person.*

As an adjunct to anger, it is tempting to 'get back'. But remember, we may be in the wrong too. If we are, we ought to apologise. 'Sorry Maria, it was wrong of me to scream like that. I was uptight about what you said.' Avoid comments about students' home environment (over which they have little control) or words like 'idiot', 'stupid', 'drongo' or worse. Distinguish between the person (however unlikeable) and their action: that's what we're getting angry about. When there is a fine line between the two it is even more important to concentrate on the behaviour.

3 *Acknowledge the emotional climate.*

Rather than using our feelings as *carte blanche* actions, share them. 'I am angry about . . .' is better than, 'You swine!'. 'I feel . . .' is better than 'You drive me up the wall, you stupid twit you!'. 'I feel angry about . . .' concentrates on what we are feeling about the behaviour. There is no harm at all in telling a student we are angry. There may also be some occasions (when Damien calls Maria a slut) when *acted anger* is appropriate. 'Damien! I am appalled at what you've said!' (Drop the voice now, to a firm level.) 'I expect an apology.' As Ginott

(1972) points out, anger situations are high-attention situations. We should describe what we *see* and act in a way we would want our students to act.

Gordon (1974) noted 'I' messages enable the teacher to take some responsibility for their own inner condition (their feelings of frustration or anger) while at the same time communicating the teacher's need. It is a way of taking responsibility for our emotion and is often *read* less antagonistically by the student. 'When I find the books left out, Carol, I have to waste a lot of time putting them all away' is enough for a clear 'I' message. It explains to the student what the situation is, and it implies a desired action. It can be followed, if necessary, by a simple direction. 'I'm really angry about what you've said, I expect an apology' is better than standing and demanding one. Move off if an apology doesn't come. You've said you expect one. It looks like you have saved 'face' as far as is possible in a stressful setting. You've also explained why you're angry. During the on-task phase of the lesson you can continue 'I' messages by directing a student aside. It is important to think about the sorts of 'I' messages that are appropriate when one is frustrated or angry (see Gordon, 1974).

We may not be able to do much about our feelings coming but we can learn to treat the other party more respectfully *when* those feelings are present. Respect is an attitude, feelings come and go.
Note: It is my opinion that 'I' messages, when used 'up-front' are best used with older students from Year 5 upwards. Normally, simple directions or rule-reminders are enough with younger students.

4 *Keep the heat down and avoid a power struggle.*
Conflict (sometimes high-level) is inevitable and even unavoidable at times. The potential 'struggle' often created by conflict *is* avoidable. When we use the language and action of win or lose we only *define* the conflict in the most restrictive way. If there can only be one winner, we will tend to employ any behaviours (however damaging) to reach that goal. *Aim for resolution.* There are several stages in conflict (see Fig 6). What we do at the point of conflict determines how successfully we resolve it later.

Keep the heat down, don't inflame. Watch the volume. There's little point screaming and yelling (unless a real danger can only be attended to by a raised voice). Shouting, a constant raised voice tone, an argumentative stance, or sharp caustic staccato language, only conveys that we can't communicate in a normal, firm, voice.

If you're *too* angry to really speak, explain that to the student and avoid the open-emotion slanging match. 'Look, Dave, I am too angry to discuss it with you now. I'll talk about it later. You know the rules.'

Provide a face-saving way out for both sides. A gracious route away from conflict can only occur if the teacher takes the initiative. It is unlikely the student will care enough to want to save face — especially if his agenda is 'power'.

Keep the heat down by:
- making the rules clear (without nagging)
- taking the student aside

Avoid escalation of conflict — follow up at a calmer moment

- giving choices (clear choices within the rules rather than forcing or threatening)
- remaining calm
- speaking assertively rather than aggressively (see Chapter 3)
- explaining how the conflict affects you
- following the issue through later

5 *Call in a third party.*
If the conflict is getting unmanageable, call in a third party. Have an exit plan well developed already — either a colleague working in a classroom nearby or a more formal session support process. Don't hesitate to have a student removed if the situation is *clearly* getting unmanageable and your fair steps have not achieved the desired control.

6 *Follow-up classroom conflict.*
Follow-up may also require a mediator (preferably a teacher effective in student-teacher negotiation). It may be appropriate to ask the student which teacher he'd like. The object of follow-up is to work at a mutually acceptable solution. Use a problem-solving approach. 'Linda, we need to sit down and talk about what's happening in class . . .' Explain the facts as you see them. Explain how particular behaviour affects class rights (or rules for younger students). Include the student in this. Generate solutions: the possible and the achievable. Select appropriate solution/s and necessary consequences. Contract if necessary. Use reflective listening: 'Are you saying . . .', 'As I hear it, you mean . . .', 'Let's go over that again', 'I can see you are angry Linda', 'How do you feel when . . .?', 'What will you do . . .?'. The teacher, the student, and the third party mediate and contract consequences and future behaviour.

Swearing and defiance

During a Year 7 textiles class Adam, minus a front tooth and sporting a tough jeans jacket replete with studs and swastika, was trying to stuff a piece of dowel up the back of his felt crocodile. The theme was *Crocodile Dundee*. 'F____ this dowel!' he said, loudly enough for all to hear. What is the teacher to do? Before we get angry we need to consider how swearing occurs in a classroom setting.

A lack of social skills

When we get frustrated we probably say, 'Oh bother, I've just snapped my pencil.'; 'How annoying, I've dropped my hammer on my foot'. With our well developed social skills, we work within the parameters of social convention, curb the 'shit!' and drop it elsewhere. Not so Adam and many others. I've heard muttered 'shits', 'buggers' and 'bloody' in every type of school. The social conventions in yard, street and school in terms of frustration-engendered swearing seem rather thin these days. Many of the students who drop the four-letter clangers do so out of social skill deficit or sometimes to set their teacher up.

Some students will swear *at* a teacher as a form of defiance. For many students, swearing comes easily. When the pressure is on, they rarely think about the consequences of their action or words; they react. We hear a lot of this kind of swearing these days from 'shit!' when Sean drops his pencil case to the rigorous 'f____' used by Adam. So what do we do? Ignore? Correct? Take the student aside? Yell at him? Restate the rule? We know that doesn't help. Yelling back at the student or moralising only stops it, at the most, temporarily. If swearing is an unfortunate norm in a child's language, our preaching won't change it; a power struggle only reinforces that power is the agenda.

Try a simple rule reminder delivered quietly and firmly. 'Sean, you know the rule mate' and then redirect him back to his work. If this isn't going to work, take the student aside and have a brief chat about unacceptable language. 'We all get uptight Sean, you know the rule. Next time you're frustrated, try saying sugar.' Use repartee to defuse the situation. The student says 'shit' clearly enough to be heard. Poor lad has dropped his new silver pen which has now broken and the spring has popped out. The teacher walks past and says 'Where?'. The student looks up, 'What?'. 'Where?' replies the teacher. The student gets the joke, giggles and the teacher quickly redirects. 'Okay Sean, pick it up — the pen I mean.'

Other students may laugh, if they hear, and that's the point of defusion. By using light humour, the teacher is, in effect, taking the 'heat' out of a potential conflict. She may follow up with the student later and have a chat about the four-letter word dropping. Rebecca turns to her friend, during an art class, and says (loudly enough for her audience to hear), 'F____ this useless knife'. The teacher bowls in a smart one-liner. 'I didn't know you could do that with a Stanley knife.'

REACTIVE ANGER

The teacher is a combatant, defining conflict as situations that must be defined in win or lose terms.
Reaction is the mechanism by which the emotion is ameliorated.
The other party's rights are minimal or even trampled on.

PASSIVE ANGER

The teacher is intimidated, often withdrawing from the conflict. Anger is internalised.
There is a fear of failure.
The teacher believes the situation is unavoidable.
The other party tramples on teacher's rights.

UTILISING ANGER

The anger is acknowledged.
The teacher uses the emotion to *explain* anger to the other party.
The teacher works towards non-aggressive solutions; gives choices and seeks to maximise face-saving.
The rights of both parties are considered.

Some teachers will object to the use of humour saying that it excuses the behaviour. Not so. It is a way of defusing potential conflict *at the point* where emotions are running high.

Consider the teacher who starts a big debate about swearing. 'What did you say! You know swearing is not allowed in our room!' 'Gee, I didn't mean it . . .' says Dean. (Who knows whether he did, or didn't?) Dean folds his arms and sulks as if to say, 'Don't pick on me!'. (He's not game, yet, to say that.) 'And don't you sulk at me, Dean Maxwell.

You know the rules the same as anybody else; I don't care if you swear at home. You will not swear in my room. Do you understand?' (He obviously feels compelled to preach at Dean.) 'You always pick on me — fair dinkum!' 'Listen to me, I do not pick on you . . .' — and so on. The teacher has now got another conflict on his hands beyond the initial swearing. It was a bad move to refer to Dean's home background. One of the cardinal protocols of conflict-resolution is to maximise face-saving on both sides by eliminating unnecessary embarrassment and hostility.

Of course many teachers are reactive in their behaviour because they feel angry, but behind their anger is a firm reasoning process that embodies such self-talk as, 'I must win here', 'Children shouldn't swear!', 'I must prove who is boss', 'I'm the teacher', 'I'm bigger, stronger, wiser. I can't lose face!'. The teacher's belief quickly raises the feeling of anger because reality doesn't fit the belief; stress arises as much from firm, set 'beliefs' as it does from the four-letter language of Boris or Kate.

Power struggles in conflict situations

Many teachers believe they must use counter power (more power, more force). 'It's the only message that so-and-so will understand!' They believe that they must compel the rude students of this world to submit to the rule, to their requests, demands or whatever. The trouble with pouring on more power, however, is that it never influences; it coerces or forces. Thomas Gordon (1974) points out that merely falling back on power in no way educates or persuades a student, in no way gives a choice. The student will either fight back (especially if they are after power), submit, or withdraw for a while until the pressure is off. Power *by itself* doesn't change the conflict; it is almost always counter-productive.

When we challenge students, in a heated voice, 'Who the hell . . .! You'll apologise now!', those who are after power will, most times, resort to counter power; the combatant mode of conflict resolution.

'Get knotted' says Boris in response to a teacher's direction to be quiet. 'How dare you speak to me like that! Apologise this instant do you hear!' 'I'm not gonna apologise, you always pick on me!' Boris has got his audience. All eyes are on these two protagonists. So much heat, and neither side wants to 'lose face'. 'If you don't apologise now, I'll, I'll suspend you', says the teacher. 'You can't make me!' says Boris. Who is going to back down? Who is going to win?

When we play the win or lose game we are committing ourselves to only one way out. And of course, the more credibility we give to the threat (of such power-provocative students) the more we empower the student. By giving a clear, firm choice in a situation of defiance, we put the responsibility back where it belongs. But if we demand and threaten, often there is a no-win situation established. Finally, the student will be removed or the stressed teacher will remove himself. This common conflict cycle leaves the teacher uptight emotionally, the child still hostile and an effective aftermath more difficult. As well, the teacher will not get sympathy (or support) from the rest of the class.

The win or lose approach will often escalate the conflict to unmanageable proportions simply because the teacher has to then behave as if they *must* win; hence power tactics come into play. In an emotionally charged dynamic like a classroom, it takes a significant change in thinking and belief as well as strength of will not to use coercive power. As the conflict begins to reach its peak, the issue of competing needs becomes obvious: the student's need for emotional outlet (frustration, anger, confusion) or for expression of power (defiance, humiliation of another, ridicule) and the teacher's need for self-esteem, the right to teach, the need to protect other children's rights. Some teachers invest their whole teaching in a conflict; 'My authority is at stake!', 'My power is at stake!'. Once we define the student as the enemy, we have to play war and there is no room to manoeuvre.

If we want to better manage our anger, or frustration, or fear (of not being able to handle the conflict) then we will need to examine what we are thinking. Here is an example of a different perception.

- 'Now I know Johnny's probably into power-provocation. He's defiant, rebellious. If I pour heat on, he'll only further believe he gains his goal by provoking and challenging me.'
- 'I don't *need* to yell, scream, abuse, or threaten. I don't have to be *inevitably* upset. I don't have to have my personal peace destroyed.'
- 'Okay, I don't like this, but I can stand it. It isn't the end of the world. Let's try those steps I worked out before to handle conflict. My influence will be reduced if I simply try to compel or force.

Some may object here and say, 'But why should I change? He shouldn't be swearing and that's that!'. The point is he has, does, and may swear again! How does a demanding belief possibly help to manage either our emotions or the conflict between us and the student? If we demand that reality be thus and it isn't, the fact that reality doesn't conform to our belief causes stress *as much as* the incident itself. Power-provocative children don't care a hoot about our demanding beliefs. When our angry behaviour erupts from our beliefs and enters the conflict, they will simply lock into counter-power, or submit and find other ways to retaliate later. As well as this, our yelling, screaming, humiliation, sarcasm, put-downs and so on only model that which we don't want to see in students' behaviour.

Albert Schweitzer once said: 'Children learn in three ways, the first way is by example, the second way is by example and the third way is by example'. What models of conflict-resolution do we regularly leave in the minds of our students?

Dropping standards?

Many teachers will see this approach as a dropping of standards. Not so. We can, by our example and teaching style, often reduce swearing more effectively than all the moral preaching under the sun. If we have made a clear rule about swearing, we will need to decide how best to enforce it. On some occasions (frustration) we may defuse or quietly remind; on other occasions we may assert, forcefully, our displeasure. Denunciation won't stop a student's swearing; neither will suspending every swearing student. At the end of the day, as in all discipline transactions, we'll need to decide our steps *in advance*. If we have already communicated our expectations, moralising (as distinct from a reminder or assertion) won't help.

Swearing as defiance

Students swear *at* teachers for one of three reasons.
- As a form of testing out a power relationship.
- Because the teacher has been aggressive initially. ('Where's your late notice!', 'Listen, I've told you before if you don't hand the work in you stay in after school.')
- Because they cannot handle their own emotions. (They say 'Get

f____!' or 'p____ off' as a quick solution. It's not easy for an angry student to *say*, 'Excuse me, I'm quite angry about the way you just slammed your hand down on my desk and demanded I stop talking to my friend'.

If a student does swear *at* you, or speak defiantly, it is better to either restate the rule, assertively express your anger, take the student aside or use repartee. Never ignore swearing as defiance and always follow up and discuss it with senior personnel if you are overly upset by the student behaviour.

1 Re-state the clear rule about swearing and assure that there will be follow-up. 'David, you know the rule for swearing, I expect an apology.' Speak with a clear sense of controlled anger and use decisive body language. Avoid the dropped shoulders, pained expression and pleading tone that says, 'What have I done to you that you speak to me like that. It hurts, David, when you swear at me like that'.

2 Use an assertive message. 'Excuse me, I don't *ever* speak to you like that. I don't expect you to speak to me like that.' Use direct eye contact, but keep some distance away. Make your point clearly. It is not a fight, it is an assertion. It is important not to stand there in 'fight mode' because it is not a fight until, or unless, we define it so. Move off, and expect an apology, later, when the student has cooled down. It is also important to re-appraise such insults as non-devastating. 'I don't have to be inevitably upset just because he swore at me. I can speak with assertive anger to make my point without letting it personally traumatise me.'

3 Direct the student aside, or away from the group and briefly discuss their rights-infringing behaviour and how you feel about it.

4 Defuse the heat. Use repartee or humour to deal with those students who 'set you up'. It is one of the most powerful approaches for the so-called hard-case students who swear 'to the gallery', or lay the 'bait'.

Repartee

Repartee is very effective because it defuses the inter-personal heat. I have seen many teachers effectively minimise audience-seeking, power-seeking swearing. When using repartee it is important to:

- not be malicious
- take the heat *out*, not increase it
- not comment on the student but rather on the words used
- be 'quick off the mark'

When the other students laugh along, quickly divert their attention back to the task at hand.

'I hate you!'
'Thanks for the compliment! Now get back to work thanks.'

'Get stuffed!'
'If I could find a taxidermist willing to do the job — possibly.'
'What's a taxidermist?'
'Someone who stuffs people.'

'Bull shit!'
'Where?'

'You bastard!'
'Yeah, so's my dog!'

Remember, you're trying to minimise the generation of heat (interpersonal aggression, anger, hostility, angry verbiage), provide reasonable 'face-saving' on both sides and protect the due rights of all class members.

Robert, (aged thirteen) was firmly asked to settle down by his English teacher. He replied with a 'You piss me off!'. Young Robert was definitely after power (' ''I belong'' when I'm as powerful or more powerful than that bitch!') There was not a contest — yet.

How the conflict proceeded largely depended on:
- how the teacher perceived and defined it ('Is this kid with his larder full of sexist jokes out to get me? Is this the end of the world? Has he some magic to get me totally angry? How will the other students react to what I now do?')
- past and present skills in handling conflict
- preparation for such events

This teacher was as prepared as she could be with fair, clear rules. She followed up later but for now, she recognised his little game.

Recognising his teacher-baiting game, the teacher turned, kept her distance, was direct in eye contact and voice tone, and said 'So I do, but

I want you to get back to your seat now. Thanks.' Robert's game didn't hook her in. His teacher baiting didn't work. A simple defusion. She acted as if there was no contest. She was not going to *create* a conflict. So her defusing, in effect, took the heat out of the conflict game.

On yard duty, other children from the class came up and said, 'Miss, that was great, what you did to Robert'. (They know all about group dynamics!) Later, she kept Robert back, when the audience was not around, and discussed the baiting game.

During a Year 7 class I was conducting (on rights and rules) a boy in the front row called out midway through a sentence, 'You've got a face like Frankenstein!'. I was a visitor to the room. There was silence. In the brief seconds that followed all eyes were on me and the boy. I would have liked to have said, 'How observant' or 'No, that's my brother', or 'Ten out of ten for recognition' (defusion). But I was caught off guard, so I quickly used deflection. 'I can see you're uptight, you know the fair rule for hurtful language. I'll talk to you later.' Then I got the rest of the class back to the discussion. I later found out this student was an 'integration student' and labelled as educationally disadvantaged. Having used a rule restatement, I had thankfully taken the least embarrassing approach. When in doubt, restate the rule.

Be firm, brief, decisive. If the swearing or ethnic, sexist comments are directed at others or yourself, then use assertive rule restatements. 'You know the fair rule about hurtful language, I'll see you later!' 'I never use that language with you. I don't expect you to use it with me.' This protects the aggrieved member and assures the rest of the class you'll follow up. If the disruptor keeps going on, give them a choice. 'You can either work by the fair rules of our room or I'll have to discuss it with you later.' Then quickly return to the on-task students.

Simon has a permanent scowl on his face. When his science teacher hands out some work, he says in a loud voice, 'This work sucks!'. The teacher calmly walks over, picks it up and says, 'So it does' with a lilt in his voice. The class laughs at the teacher's words and the teacher quickly gets the class back on-task. Later, when they are working, the teacher goes over and asks Simon how it is all going. Although he doesn't particularly like the scowler, he tries to speak civilly to him when he's on-task. Minimal attention when he is off-task, maximum attention when he's on-task.

Miss J. is writing algebraic formulae on the Year 9 chalkboard. She turns to face her class and one little wag calls out, 'Miss, someone just did *that* when you had your back to us!' and he demonstrates by sticking his two fingers up at her. Unfazed, and skilled in defusion and deflection, she recognises teacher baiting and with all eyes on her says firmly, but without aggression, 'Well I'm glad I didn't see it. Okay (directing attention back to the task), we were discussing algebra'. She is brief, decisive, firm in body language; and not drawn by teacher baiting.

Note:

Don't use defusion if you're tired, uptight, jaded, really frustrated or upset; use it on your good days.

If you don't like, or feel you can't use, defusion then employ the other approaches described. Defusion is a personality-based style of conflict resolution.

Always follow up later with consequences. Ask for an apology, have a conference, make a contract. Use detention, during which the swearer writes out:

- what they did or said
- why they think they did it
- what they could have done instead (if they were uptight, angry, upset, etc.)

Contact parents when constant aggressive swearing is a regular pattern.

THE DOMINO EFFECT

Of course other students will laugh when teachers defuse potential conflicts and some teachers argue that this is a bad thing; that it teaches students that we excuse swearing and only encourages it. Not so. There are few students brave enough, silly enough, arrogant or stupid enough to swear at their teacher. That is why defusion is effective. It communicates quickly that the teacher:

- knows the game
- will not put wind to the sails
- is confident about what she is doing
- has intentionally used repartee

At this point of conflict she defuses. The matter of the wrongness of swearing can be followed up later — when the audience isn't there. Don't worry, the tribal 'tom-toms' will soon pass it on that the swearer has had his consequences.

Integrating problem students

Rodney is described in various ways depending on whether you speak to his 'father', his teacher, the principal, social worker, psychologist or other poor sod whose time is eaten up by Rodney's life. Emotionally bastardised, when he arrives at school with his dirty jeans, foul mouth, face full of acne and bad diet he is sullen, remote, aggressive, disturbed. He has a well-won reputation. He is in that small percentage of socio-emotionally disturbed students (three to five per cent).

Having worked his way through a state wardship (following a home split-up and a father who couldn't handle him), many suspensions, several schools and a remand home, Rodney is, in Year 6, a child who makes life very, very difficult for his teacher.

Mr D.'s ten years experience as a teacher seem of little help with Rodney. He has baited Mr D. many times calling him a 'suck', a 'pain in the arse!', a 'shit' and has told him to 'get f____!' several times. Mr

D. yells, threatens, demands apologies, regularly 'throws' him out of class. On one occasion, he came close to punching him.

Whenever work is required Rodney refuses to do it, sometimes with arms folded, sometimes with attention-seeking stunts like, 'Ain't gonna do this shit — you can't make me'.

How do we balance the due rights of the teacher, the individual student and other students in a case like Rodney's? While not wasting time apportioning particular blame (apart from the need for formal suspension at times), a school has to come up with a supportive plan for teachers and students alike. Under the education guidelines all children are entitled to fundamental education rights in a schooling process that, in the 1980s, minimises labelling and supports, at least ideologically, full integration in mainstream schooling for all students.

With seriously and continuously disruptive students, it is important to check out all the possible circumstances which may be contributing to their anti-social behaviour. Is there a health problem or physical deficiency? Social workers or school support personnel may need to contact parents regarding problems with memory, limited attention span, withdrawal, outward fixations (nail-biting, hair-pulling or eating), constant rocking, frequent calls for the toilet or regular soiling of clothes, constant out-of-seat behaviour, regular falling asleep.

Of course we are not social workers or psychologists or psychiatrists but, as part of a professional team, we need to come up with a supportive plan that will enable the student to take some ownership over their behaviour.

Problems at home can affect a student's school life. A student's physical/emotional/socio-relational life at home may be so totally different from school that they find school a threat; a place of anxiety because they can't fit in or cope with the demands of the teacher, the system, or competing emotional stresses. Any number of socio-emotional disturbances will present themselves within a class dynamic as a student seeks to handle their own emotional baggage in the group environment: low frustration-tolerance; general laziness and sloppiness; nervousness or restlessness; timidity and shyness; listlessness; aggression; manipulation, lying and tale-telling. This emotional baggage can be a product of divorce, or family break-ups; sexual or emotional abuse; sibling rivalry; death of a close friend (even a pet), or family member; health problems of family members (as well as the child's own health problems).

Often the student's perception is one of fear of such circumstances; fear that any security they have might disappear. The student's 'acting-out' behaviour is often their way of drawing notice to the problem. That is why it is important for the teacher to always ask, 'What's wrong? Do you want to talk about it?'. Sometimes, a student may have experienced overly permissive or authoritarian styles of parenting and this may affect their ability to cope at school.

Mrs N. presented her Year 1 child, Stephen, to me on day one with the words, 'You know my son is a free spirit at home. We let him be creative and allow an open-ended approach to his development'. 'Oh, really, Mrs N. We'll do our best to accommodate your son, and as long as he works by the eminently fair rules of our class, I'm sure he'll have a marvellous year.'

It took Stephen a full term at school to realise that he couldn't manipulate his environment there as he could at home. He tried wandering out of his seat whenever he felt like it. 'I don't want to do this work.' He swore at me when I told him firmly to get back in his seat; threw tantrums if he felt he wasn't getting enough attention; stole scissors; poked children with pencils; hid under the table and refused to work. We were firm, fair, friendly and decisive with him. We tactically ignored much of his attention-seeking behaviours, but gave him appropriate verbal and social reinforcement when he was on task. He was placed, regularly, in small group tasks where he could learn from appropriate models.

When he left a mess he was consistently directed to clean it up; not by brute force, but 'If you leave a mess then you have to clean it up — even in your own time'. It took him a while to realise that school was not like home — you couldn't just expect someone else to clean it up. When he was overly aggressive in the yard, he was not allowed to play with other children at all for one week. He was begging to go out after a week of logical consequences.

Some specialists, such as school psychologists, special education teachers, even school principals have been heard to say, 'Well, Joanne is very bright, I get along with her quite well. It's hard to see why she's a problem'. Of course, such students present well with a total audience of one! Put these students in a class with others and see what happens.

It's in class, in the 'natural setting', that we need to observe such children and there, in class, help teachers to come up with strategies to cope with and assist them.

We best manage such children by having a well-developed discipline plan that involves a hierarchy of interventions that we have practised, rehearsed and have support for. Children who are regularly tagged as 'disruptive', 'nuisances', 'lazy', or 'spiteful' all present as problems through their behaviour. Indeed, for some children, actual disruptive behaviour is a way of calling attention to their needs. Such children may not show readily identifiable disabilities, but because of their social and emotional background they may experience failure in the social and educational life of the school.

Such students demonstrate difficulty or an inability to either build, or maintain, positive inter-personal relationships with peers and teachers. They display inappropriate and often extremely disruptive behaviour: spitting; chair throwing; jumping out of windows; fighting in the class; swearing at the teacher; aggressive behaviour; destroying others' work; dangerous behaviour with equipment. Such behaviour is often very difficult for the teacher to manage and, with stretched resources, puts significant stress on all the members of the classroom.

Disturbed, atypical behaviour arises from time to time in many students. However, when it is regular and on-going, it becomes a constant unsettling feature of classroom life and needs to be addressed in a structured, thoughtful way. It is important that the teacher and the administration:

- check out any causal factors
- recognise that much of a student's 'acting out' behaviour is a purposeful way of belonging to the group
- develop a consistent approach using fair, firm steps in handling disruptions when they present in a group
  The overall goal of any school strategy is to:
- enable the student to 'belong' to the school community
- enable the student to gain some success in their learning
- move the student towards active responsibility for their behaviour
- encourage the student to be accountable for behaviour that is rule-breaking and which hurts the rights of others
- teach the student to make a choice about behaviour so that they gain self-control and discipline

• challenge the student to see that everyone has rights and responsibilities

It is important that teachers work together on any strategies. Also, acknowledge the 'goals' of the student — power, attention and so on, and start each day afresh. Try not to hold grudges. We don't have to like our students but, professionally, we ought to respect them.

Encouraging long-term change

The processes take time. It is unrealistic to expect success overnight, when behaviours have been built up and practised over years, often under inconsistent adult tutelage. Students *can*, and often do, get strong reinforcement from teachers for negative behaviour. (Hostile attention, nagging or rough treatment by an adult is still a form of attention which some children actively seek.) It will take significant resolve, good will and support to make any impact with such students.

1 Consistently show respect to the student through the steps you take to manage their behaviour and the contracts you develop with them (see Chapter 5).

2 Encourage every small effort and step toward cooperative behaviour. Make such encouragement situation specific.

3 Don't excuse aberrant behaviour but apply consequences when the 'heat' goes down. I once watched a principal trying to get a student to wipe spit off a window. In full view of a third of the school, the almost apoplectic principal tried to drag the Year 6 student's hand to the spattered window. He couldn't make him however hard he pulled. The student was dragged swearing, back to the principal's office. Who won?

We can't make the student do anything

What infuriates many teachers who have to deal with difficult students is the sense of powerlessness that such students create by their resistant behaviour. In disciplining such students, in balancing corrective and supportive adult direction, we need to grasp the fundamental premise first. We can't *make* a student do anything. We can direct, restate, ask, encourage, challenge, but the more we use traditional teacher force, the more we lose (face, contact, temper).

Some of these 'hard' students have a long-practised repertoire that sees them baiting or setting-up teachers. It gets them what they want — reaction, attention, in short, 'belonging'. If we are going to be effective, we will need to be aware of their deeper problems as well as the acting-out behaviour they present when an audience is available.

WAYNE

Wayne is persistently noisy at his desk. When asked to move, he replies with 'No', or 'Why?', or 'Why are you always picking on me?' What can the teacher do? Drag him bodily, kicking and screaming, two metres to an isolation desk? He is aggressive and sullen by turns. He swears, argues and is persistently defiant.

This type of situation is best handled by a basic plan communicated to the student prior to class and *backed up by colleagues*. Such a plan was used in Wayne's case.

The teacher had to resist his first impulse (thump him!). When students like Wayne seek to belong by aberrant power-seeking, it is totally ineffective to meet them with a win or lose strategy. The teacher was clear in his own mind that he would decide how he would behave in *response* to, rather than as a reaction to Wayne.

The teacher was assured that if Wayne was overly disruptive, a colleague would support him with a time-out approach. He was encouraged to see that such a process in no way suggested failure on his part (male teachers are still expected to be able to effectively manage the Waynes of this world simply because they are *male*).

The essence of the plan was to make a number of points clear to Wayne (at a non-threatening time and with the principal involved).

- He was more than welcome to be part of our school and enjoy classroom life and learning.
- We could not and would not make him do the work. This took him by surprise because he was used to the task-refusing ploy to gain significant attention in class. We would not, however, let him disrupt others rights to learn or be safe.
- If he did his work we would give him all the help he wanted and needed. We wanted him to be part of our group.

The class rules were re-established and a verbal or (if the student is compliant) written contract developed to enable Wayne to take some control over his behaviour. This contract is taken from class to class. (See Appendix III.) It was made clear to Wayne that if he continued to make it difficult for others to work, or to be safe, or made it difficult for the teacher to teach, then he would be given a clear direction, a clear reminder of the rule, or invited to explain his behaviour after class. If he refused to cooperate, he would be given a choice to stay and work by the fair rules or leave the classroom and do time-out.

Of course, for low-level disturbances, the teacher may well be able to tactically ignore. If the student shows any on-task behaviour, then the teacher will give due encouragement.

Employing conflict resolution steps will minimise hostility with students such as Wayne. Even confrontational students can be effectively dealt with when a teacher (or support teacher) remains calm. Teachers can receive help from specialists (consultants and psychologists) and colleagues. On some occasions such students have been moved to another class. It is understandable that sometimes, even with the best will, a bond may not be possible between some teachers and a student like Wayne. There is no professional shame attached to this.

It can take a long time to achieve any success with someone like Wayne. In the meantime, his rights must be fairly balanced with those of his peers. We cannot change Wayne's home environment but we can do a lot about how he is treated at school.

What happened to Wayne? He left school happier, although still disadvantaged by having poor literacy and numeracy skills, and poorly developed social skills. His teachers being tougher would not have improved those skills. At least his school, and its staff, never gave up. They could easily have suspended him, and continued to suspend him until an inquiry drove him to yet another school. At least the school gave him a sense of belonging, kept him off the street (had we suspended him there was no one to 'look after' him at home) and communicated that the school was able to show him respect, offer him help and barrack for him.

With extreme cases like Wayne we may never win. It is the hard reality that can, at times, make teaching a frustrating profession. However, we can work together, develop a joint plan, and minimise the unnecessary stress.

TRISH

Trish, a Year 3 student (and a ward of the state), displayed strong attention-seeking behaviours which included throwing off her shoes and socks (sometimes at the teacher); spitting and swearing; constant calling out; task-refusal and avoidance. She came from a severely disturbed and broken home life and was in transit in an institution awaiting foster parents.

The school decided on a joint teacher plan. With regional support, a behaviour modification schedule was drawn up and Trish had a book with weekly target behaviours. Those behaviours were rehearsed with two teachers and Trish (see Chapter 5). A discipline plan was worked out with a series of steps or processes (see Chapter 3) so the teachers knew when and how to intervene. When Teacher A's frustration reached a significant level, Trish was taken to Teacher B's room (with her behaviour modification book). In this way she was gently shared between two teachers. With consistent, firm, calm treatment she progressed remarkably well and in four months had settled back into some sort of steady routine. Routine, consistency and a firm, caring adult are crucial when dealing with deep-seated and on-going disruptions.

Effective teachers working with such students are marked by:
- their willingness not to give up (or in)
- their basic calmness
- their willingness to respect the unlikeable
- their consistency of treatment within the group so that the disruptor is not seen to have markedly different treatment (getting away with it)
- their encouragement, regularly expressed, for the smallest effort (They expect positive change, but not overnight!)
- their provision of opportunities for success
- their willingness to enlist the help of others
- their judicious sense of humour and refusal to take all such acting-out behaviour as personal attacks on them

Aggressive behaviour in the classroom

When I taught art in a very large primary school I had to move from class to class with my art materials. I was new to the job and, moving from room to room, came across a wide range of students.

Teaching a Year 3 class one afternoon, I had finished explaining the object of the lesson, and had asked some students to hand out materials, when suddenly, apparently 'out of the blue', Richard raced for the door.

I grabbed him quickly as one student said, 'Watch it Sir, he runs off sometimes!'. As I held him by the arms, as firmly and calmly as I could, he struggled and grunted and kicked. I had no idea why he had exhibited this explosive anger — his teacher had given me no prior warning. I had no idea how she might have handled his behaviour or whether this was characteristic of Richard.

He finally calmed down and I led him back to his chair and explained the task. He sat sulking, arms crossed, head down — dumb insolence. I already knew that pleading, arguing, fighting (power struggles) or plain male aggression was ineffective so I left him in 'dumb-insolence' mode and, as a safety measure, moved my chair near the door and taught from there. A few minutes later Richard jumped off his chair, ran for the door, head down like a bull, and charged into me to get to the door. I took hold of him and held him with my arm around his chest and arms as he kicked, screamed and struggled. I spoke calmly to him as he tried to escape. 'Don't worry Richard, I'm holding you till you stop being angry.' As he relaxed, I relaxed the hold until he was quiet and I led him back to his seat. Six more times he made the bolt for the door and he was a strong boy to hold down.

I later found out about his extraordinarily twisted home environment (including bashings from dad) and the fact that I was the only male teacher he had had at that school. Had I known about Richard I could have sent for senior teacher support for time-out (see Chapter 5). As it was, I was still able to teach; as calmly as one can holding a child while speaking to other students. 'Maria, that's developing well, can you hold it up so I can see.' 'Sandra, could you hand out the charcoal at your table.' 'If you've finished Paul, you can clean up and read a book.' All this *while* holding Richard until he calmed down enough to be led back to his chair. Tiring.

Many children cannot say to us, 'I am angry about . . .' 'I am angry because . . .'. They tell us they are angry by *acting* angrily. They rarely foresee the outcome or predict the consequences. In dealing with aggressive behaviour it is important to be well prepared.

Find out about any predisposing factors. Where possible, get parent support. In Richard's case we felt that such 'support' should be minimal for the child's safety.

Develop a maintenance plan.

1 Establish when and under what conditions the disruptions tend to occur; who with, time of day, what is happening in the lesson. Accurate records assist in diagnosis, strategy and evaluation (see Appendix I).

2 Develop a plan with *all* the teachers who come into contact with the child. Consistency is especially important with such students. If one teacher ignores, another screams and yet another tries to ameliorate, the child will either end up confused or play one teacher off against another. A team approach ensures consistency *and* stability. Where possible also enlist professional assistance.

3 The plan should have steps to deal with any conditions leading up to the conflict (seating, curriculum, directions); steps to deal with the actual disruptive behaviour itself; a contingency plan if the child's behaviour is overly disruptive or distraught. It is crucial that, where aggressive behaviour (to self or others) is concerned, a teacher acts quickly.

- Speak calmly but firmly. With lower primary age children it may be necessary to hold them to establish the importance of your direction. This is especially important if the child is hurting others (pencil jabbing, persistent pinching, biting or hitting, hair-pulling).

- Give clear directions and reminders about the rules.
- Apply consequences rather than punishments (we don't excuse their behaviour). There is a belief amongst some teachers that we should just 'be hard' with kids like Richard. 'It's the only language they understand!' That, in essence, is the trouble. We need to teach them another language.
- Use time-out. Colleague assistance is essential with aggressive students of any age.
- Develop a contract with such students to enable them to more successfully deal with the frustration that triggers such behaviours. Such contracts may include behavioural contingencies (see Chapter 7) as a short-term mechanism to get success into the child's social and learning behaviour. An important part of any contract is the designing of 'escape-hatch' mechanisms. 'Next time you feel you are getting angry I want you to tell yourself that it's okay to *be* angry then go and sit in the cool-off corner or come and tell me.'

Reward all positive attempts at management of anger. Above all, find ways to show respect and care at times when the student reveals reasonable social behaviour. It is so easy to alienate such students. Barracking for them is hard work and requires plenty of collegiate support. They have 'failed' miserably and their self-esteem is nil. While we should not ignore their anger, we should help them to redirect it.

Sexist remarks, innuendo or touching

This includes crowding, pinching, touching, provocative gestures and is largely a problem for female teachers and can be quite debilitating to those unprepared for it. It can include everything from comments about boyfriends to parts of the body. No teacher should ignore this or excuse it. We have a right to personal dignity. Of course, like all conflict, the way it is managed will affect the nature and extent of the resolution.

Assertive messages

Be clear in your own mind about unacceptable behaviour. 'Gee you've got a great figure, Miss!', is different from specific remarks about body parts. If it is offensive say so. 'Dave, I don't want you to touch me please.' 'Excuse me, I don't like that touching — stop it now.' 'I find that remark offensive.' Move away, or block with your hand those crowding behaviours students sometimes exhibit. Keep the response firm, brief, clear and intentional. Don't labour the point but make it unambiguous.

RULES

Discuss appropriate treatment behaviours during rules formation if necessary.

CHOICES

If the student continues with their offensive behaviour give a clear choice to work by the fair rules (the way we treat one another) or leave the classroom. Make the consequences clear. Be sure to have an exit plan as a contingency measure for such students.

CONFERENCING

Ms M. had heard the words 'slut' and 'pro' dropped behind her back during the Year 9 history class. She knew which of the boys were 'setting her up'. She had tried confrontation only to meet denials. 'We never said anything, Miss!' Upset, and naturally angry, she let it go for a couple of weeks only to break down, crying, at a faculty meeting. Only then did the offer of support come. A meeting was convened with the three boys, a support colleague (male) and the teacher. (Unless the teacher is too upset she should participate.)

When using this approach, it is important that all parties affected know what is going on. Get the facts straight. Give due right of reply. Explain, again, the affected rights of the aggrieved party. Expect appropriate apology. Work at a mutually workable solution with consequences clearly outlined for future behaviour.

How we deal with sexism will depend on how provocative the student has been. If it is clearly light-hearted, a rule reminder, a brief defusion may be appropriate but if it borders on the sexist put-down, deal decisively with it or get support. Most schools have a sex-discrimination policy.

Some questions to consider

- What are some of the classroom behaviours, circumstances or situations that make you angry?
- Can you pin-point them? When do they occur? In what subject areas? With which students?
- Are you able to specifically recall what you *currently* do in managing high-level conflict (conflict that sees you highly frustrated or angry).
- What sort of things do you find yourself saying? Can you recall?
- What sort of things do you think (or say to yourself) when you are angry?
- If you have angry or aggressive students, how do you deal with them?

To change, we need to be motivated to see our professional obligation to more effective management.

- What behaviours do you want to change?
- What specific alternatives can you propose to your current approach?
- What specific verbal approaches can you design as alternatives to over-reaction at the one extreme or non-assertion at the other?
- List some practical alternatives to address *your* particular situation. (More effective use of middle-management personnel, a clear policy for conflict resolution with students, a clear policy on the use of time-out across the school.)

In answering these questions it can often be helpful to work with a colleague; no doubt they too (like all of us) struggle with the emotional climate of conflict.

Summary

Frustration and anger are dominant emotions (anxiety is prevalent too) among teachers. Anger is a normal, even healthy emotion. When situations are dangerous, hurtful, or severely affecting others' rights, we are bound to get frustrated and are properly employed utilising that anger. As an emotion, we will better handle it when we understand it. What signals it? What do I characteristically think, say and do in anger-arousing situations? Can I do it better? Like any teacher behaviour it can only be more professional when, at the end of the day, we take some responsibility for it. By discussing it with our peers and making better plans, both conflict, and the attendant emotions, can be utilised towards resolution.

CHAPTER 9

Peer support for teachers

> *A winner takes a big problem and separates it into*
> *smaller parts so that it can be more easily manipulated;*
> *a loser takes a lot of little problems and rolls them*
> *together until they are unsolvable.*
> Harris, 1973

The need for peer support

Peer support is fundamental to staff well-being. While such support
may take many forms, a particular approach is discussed here that
links support to professional development.

In a post-primary school staff room, some issues that were stressing
staff in the late 1980s were being discussed. We went over the usual
issues of pupil disruption, time and work-load pressure, the pace of
change brought about by the Ministry of Education and so on. Statements of frustration were being freely thrown around. 'What do they
care? The Ministry sit on their arses all day!' 'Ministry doesn't give a
damn for us!' 'The Union doesn't care!' We made a whinge list (rather
facetiously) of those who didn't care, or didn't understand our plight:
the principal, the union, the Ministry, that year 10 class, the unfair
timetable, parents.

At the end of the whinge list I asked, 'What's left?'. We agreed we
couldn't really change many of the factors outside our control (student

background, the timetable, directions from the Ministry). We are left with what? You and me! We recognised that at the end of the day, if we don't do *something*, we'll easily slip into whinge mode and still not get anywhere. We realised that we had to work together on many of the issues over which we can have some control.

What do we have control over?

- Our classroom organisation (seating, aesthetics, classroom rules, the routines and procedures that allow smooth running in a classroom).
- Specific lesson planning and curriculum in general.
- The way we communicate a lesson and prepare for the likely rough spots (lack of equipment, early finishers, mixed abilities, variability within the lesson).
- Our management behaviour. (How does my bearing, my body language, tone of voice, what I say, motivation and encouragement affect student behaviour?)

Ask yourself:

- How do I begin and end lessons?
- How do I deal with a particular student's disruption?
- How do I enforce rules?
- How do I keep students on task?
- How do I administer consequences for rule breaking?

S.O.A.R.

Teaching is a strange profession. We advocate a curriculum to our students which is based on cooperation but leave ourselves open to the Shag-On-A-Rock syndrome.

By its very structure, a school often promotes the S.O.A.R. syndrome. It is easy to be left alone in room 17 (or that noxious portable). There is still a kind of collective consciousness prevalent in our profession, that it is all right to isolate ourselves from our colleagues and never admit we are struggling or finding it difficult to cope. S.O.A.R. can be exacerbated by senior staff members who walk past and glare at teachers whose classes seem 'over the top' — just when *they* walk past.

Teachers often have little time to share their concerns given all the demands that teaching entails. Many male teachers find it difficult to admit they are struggling with a difficult class. Staff meeting times offer little opportunity for effective sharing and faculty meetings are often taken up with the organisational elements of teaching.

To cope with the feeling, 'I must be the only one who feels this way', schools are being encouraged to set up peer-support.

Peer-support groups

Essentially peer support is a school-based program that invites and encourages peers to:

- meet regularly in order to discuss common concerns affecting their professional life
- provide opportunity for reflection on their practice and problem solving
- exchange ideas on curriculum teaching methods, use of materials, ways of dealing with student misbehaviour
- develop some peer-assisted approaches based in classroom management

The main point is to generate a climate where the issues and problems of teaching, and classroom management in particular, can be pursued in a positive, supportive and practical fashion. With thoughtful guidance, such groups can be a forum for showing those concerns that really are common to us all without feeling that failures equal 'I am a failure'. As Kyriacou (1981, 1986) has noted, 'The degree of social support available in a school is a crucial factor in mitigating the level of stress'.

The practice of peer support for teachers has shown that it decreases feelings of isolation and levels of teacher stress, and increases the level of professionalism of the group members. Each group, of course, will have its own priorities (curriculum, alternative teaching strategies, group approaches or classroom discipline), but the general focus is fundamental; the group is formed for the mutual support and professional development of its members.

The merits of peer support should be canvassed with staff members and opportunities for group formation made available according to interest level or invitation.

Forming a group

When developing peer-support groups concentrate on several key points.

1 Make the group formation totally elective; no one should be forced to join 'yet another' group.
2 Locate and involve people with facilitating skills to organise and give direction to the group/s.
3 Build opportunities into the group for the learning and practice of new skills. We can dramatically improve the quality of our teaching by accessing new skills. Peer support is an ideal forum for developing such skills.
4 Part of a group's goal may be to develop mutual (peer) observation of one another's classes as a means of identifying areas where change may be required.

Stage one: inviting members to form a group

Through staff meetings, workshops or in-service programs, staff are encouraged to consider the benefits of peer support as a forum for practical problem solving and professional development. Groups are formed in several ways.

- direct invitation (in larger schools) by key facilitators
- open invitation at a staff meeting (Staff are given time to consider the proposal and meet with designated facilitators during the following week.)
- a notice-board list for interested persons where facilitators' names are listed and interested persons fill in the list
- *ad hoc* groupings
- naturally forming groups within faculties

The important point about group formation is that its members feel comfortable with one another. Members should be absolutely free to move in or out of the group as they feel comfortable and able to participate. Generally, most members will elect to stay on once they get to know one another.

Stage two: facilitation of the group

Effective progress of the group rarely occurs by chance. To experience any success it will need guidance and direction.

Whether the facilitator is an allocated person such as a senior teacher or a member of a naturally forming group, they will need to have basic human relations skills. They will need to be able to:
- draw people out
- encourage and support others
- focus and unite the group
- direct others from their strengths
- keep the group on track with its shared goals

Where a whole school has a focus on peer support, there may be several groups in existence, all meeting at separate times as they feel comfortable.

The facilitator will assist the group to focus in on common concerns with a view to professional problem solving. While it is important for a group to be able to share concerns, to often whinge and moan, it will need to move to the level of practical support if it is going to be of long-term assistance to its members.

Stage three: forming an agenda

While each group will provide opportunity for general sharing, specific agendas will vary with group needs. These may involve:
- set topics for discussions each week
- inviting ex-officio people in who can share and demonstrate specific skills
- practical workshops on strategies for classroom management such as small group approaches or classroom meetings
- specific curriculum development
- gentle role-play sessions to rehearse new skills
- general weekly discussion where people share concerns and conclude with shared solutions

Of course, being able to say, 'You have problems with 8D too!' is a great benefit. Many first-year peer-support groups that I have worked with have benefited enormously from realising that they are not the only ones who are 'failing'; are 'worn out by it all'; have problems with recalcitrant students; can't work out the lottery system behind a large school timetable; have lousy furniture; can't get senior teacher support; have little equipment.

Often the group will invite a staff member in to discuss an approach, idea, or method that has been found helpful (alternative curriculum approaches, classroom management strategy, room organisation). On some occasions, the group may call on expertise outside the school.

Stage four: peer observation

A further level of support can be developed through colleagues giving feedback on classroom observation. It is ironic that we can go for years, in a management profession like ours, without significant or effective feedback.

While we can learn an enormous amount, and receive benefit, from a mutually supportive group, we may be unaware of how the actual dynamics of our behaviour are affecting, say, classroom management. To focus more actively on professional development, it can be highly beneficial to observe a trusted colleague in their 'natural' setting, the classroom. It is possible for teachers to hear about new ideas in a group and then say 'Well, I've done all that and it didn't work'. It may be different if they *see* the new ideas in practice.

Because a classroom climate is emotionally charged, it is not easy to be self-reflective, especially about the effect of our behaviour on student discipline transactions. Teaching is a multi-task activity and *conscious* appraisal is not easy; it is easy for us to under-report our behaviour. The 'new' skill may not have worked because of poor or inconsistent approximations. Peer feedback can assist in enabling a better application of new skills.

MATHS YEAR 7

The class was noisy but they settled down when the teacher called for order. She didn't smile and she forgot to say good morning.

She spent twenty minutes trying to explain algorithmic approaches to common fractions. The boredom curve peaked after ten minutes. The rest of the lesson was noisy, the students called out, were repeatedly off-task, engaged her in futile discussions and bolted as soon as the bell went.

- Perhaps this teacher was unaware of the tiny writing on the board; the lack of concrete examples (especially important when operating fractions).
- Perhaps she was unaware she reinforced almost all calling out by over-attending to it.
- She was certainly unaware that her rules were unclear, as was her enforcement of fair behaviour.

- She evidenced great uncertainty about what to do *when* students were disruptive (task-refusal/avoidance; procrastinating students; students out of seats; students without equipment).
- The room organisation and seating didn't make management easy either (four class clowns sitting together down the back).
- The lack of catering for mixed abilities affected the on-task behaviour of students.

Peer observation enabled this teacher to quickly address the fundamentals like:

- positive, clear class rules
- seating procedure (In time she was encouraged to try groups with the assistance of a colleague.)
- blackboard skills
- up-front explanation

After several discussions, and observing two other colleagues in the group, she picked up new skills in classroom management (see Chapter 3). Over two terms her participation in the peer-support group had assisted in the development of observational skills of her own and other teachers' practice. Knowing *what* she was doing that was ineffective helped her to know where to concentrate on areas where she needed help. She received that support, and the courage to try out new approaches, from her peers.

A traditional in-service may never have been able to offer the type and level of assistance this teacher needed. Whatever our present practice, we can all benefit by mutual observation of a trusted colleague's practice. When did you last sit and actually watch another teacher teach?

After a workshop on developing classroom management strategies, a teacher explained she had used the question and feedback approach (see Chapter 3) before — it didn't help!

The teacher invited a colleague in to observe her class. It was the Year 6 library class. Several girls, grouped around a table, began moderate chatting about a television program. The teacher marched over, extended the pointed hand, glared and loudly asked, 'What are you doing hey?'

That was not the approach we had discussed in the workshop. She *thought* she was managing the group by asking a question when actually she had increased the level of hostility between herself and the girls. The context often has to be seen to know what is actually happening. Without specific feedback teachers may be unaware of what their characteristic behaviour is. It is hard to recall actual words when one is anxious or angry. We may feel we responded to calling-out effectively but perhaps we weren't aware of the dynamics in the same way as an observing colleague was. He was there, down the back, he could *see*, *hear* and *feel* the context in a way we could not and his feedback can help fine-tune or change our practice if it is clearly counter-productive to effective classroom management.

Peer observation, as a feature of peer-support groups, would normally occur when group members feel comfortable with one another. Groups go through several phases during their life cycle and the broaching of peer observation is most effective when several meetings have secured a group cohesiveness. The most important feature of any peer feedback is the ownership by the willing colleague, without which it will be an ineffective process.

Apprehension is natural. Our self-esteem is, in a sense, under challenge. 'What will they think of my teaching?' 'What will they think of my room, my curriculum, my way of dealing with disruptions?' It is a sad commentary on our profession that we have so easily built up these isolationist practices where even a trusted colleague's presence can instil such concern.

Few teachers will find having an observing colleague in the room a natural, or easy experience. In developing peer observation the following points are important.

- Choose a colleague you can work with, someone you feel comfortable with. No one should be put 'on the spot'; the professional and personal aspects of team observation are central to any successful outcome.
- Colleagues should elect to work with a partner from within the general support group. (Sometimes a trio will form to conduct observations).
- Partners may be from cross faculties, or the same year level or from different year levels within the same faculty.
- Partners (or trios) should choose mutually agreeable times and the number of visits, and what they will observe.
- There is no 'superior' or 'inferior' relationship in the observation role. It is peer-support.

Gathering data

The facilitator should explain that the purpose of peer observation is the building up of successful classroom practice by getting feedback about current practice over several observations. After several visits most teachers begin to feel comfortable about the presence of a colleague and actually look forward to it. 'I just wasn't aware of what I was doing', is a commonly heard response. Observers give feedback on a range of issues that have been mutually agreed on.

Observation

The host teacher should introduce the colleague to her class by a brief acknowledgment, 'You all know Mr D., he'll be working in our class from time-to-time over the next few weeks'. It is better, then, for Mr D. to smile and casually wander off while the host teacher carries on with her normal lesson activity.

The observing partner is not involved with the class during the up-front part of the lesson, but merely observes. They may, during the on-task phase, move around and give assistance but are principally there to observe. Some teachers are initially bothered about students changing their behaviour because another teacher is present. However, if the visiting teacher moves quietly away from the front, the class will usually revert to its normal life cycle.

While the visiting teacher may feel like interrupting the host teacher, it is important to simply observe. If students try to involve the visiting teacher, they should be referred back to their classroom teacher. During later observations, the visiting teacher may observe and mingle as is appropriate. Taking notes, or using the Observation Information Record (see Appendix IV) can help to focus the observations. Above all, the agenda for observation needs mutual agreement prior to any visit to the class.

The observation should be two-way. Host and visiting teacher observe and are observed. Once or twice a week (no more) is generally enough.

Some groups I have worked with have developed a journal approach as well, to record their feelings, impressions, perceptions, progress, and shared this as they have felt comfortable.

Feedback

Given time for personal reflection, the two (or three) teachers agree to meet over coffee to go over their observations. This is, initially, the hardest task. It is important to:

1 *Share common feelings.*

Begin the feedback by discussing how the host teacher felt about the observation. The observer may concentrate on a specific incident. 'Wendy, how did you feel when Nathan kept rolling around on the mat during morning talk?' Alternatively, you may simply have a general conversation about the class. The observations will include many positive elements which, apart from such feedback, may not have been noticed before. We get little positive reinforcement in our profession.

Classroom observation by peers

2 *Specify observations.*
To make the feedback useful, the observer should then locate a few issues for discussion using phrases like: 'This is what I heard . . .'; 'This is what I saw . . .'; 'This is how I felt . . .'; 'Were you aware that . . .'; 'Did you notice when . . .'; 'Have you thought of . . .'.

Non-judgemental feedback is never easy, but merely giving agreement about difficulties won't help specify areas where change may be needed. This approach to feedback is non-judgemental but is specific. It clarifies the classroom situation by giving constructive feedback as data. It is given in a supportive context.

Teachers have to learn to both give and receive feedback. If it is given in a supportive context (preferably not in a busy staff room), the observed teacher can then use the observations to clarify the behaviour and situations observed. They can see whether any of their goals have been reached; indeed it may serve to clarify the need for goals.

It is important to listen to the observer, without taking personal affront, and to discuss the observations. The discussion can then form the basis for any changes that might be made in classroom practice. 'How can I modify, fine-tune, or change my practice? Where, how can I start?' 'David, I noted you said "Shh" twenty times during morning talk. Were you aware of that, Dave?' This is not an easy thing to say. It will be no less easy for Dave to say to Margaret, 'Margaret, were you aware that Nick and Dimi were play fighting in the library corner while you were moving around the room marking?' Nonetheless, these are the sorts of questions we must be prepared to ask ourselves and each other.

We may comment on organisational procedures, voice tone and the kind of directions or questions a teacher uses, seating or curriculum (see Appendix IV), general body language, etc. Feedback enables change to occur because it provides data from which we can work. It gives a framework within which realistic self-appraisal can take place.

Being an observer

Because we are after data that will enable the change process to begin, we will be observing in four broad areas.
• procedural/organisation matters
• teaching method/curriculum

- verbal behaviour (relative to inter-personal discipline)
- body language (relative to inter-personal discipline)

Post-observation discussion

Because you have already agreed about what you will observe, it is easier to sit and share your comments. Share a few things at a time and ask your colleague to comment. Some of the questions you might ask each other are:

- Are the class rules clear?
- What, exactly, are the class rules?
- Are there general consequences for rule-breaking?
- What are they? Do they logically fit the behaviour?
- Does the class teacher have any basic 'step' approach to disruptive-behaviour management?
- Is there a clear exit procedure for unmanageable behaviour?
- Is there need for help in lesson organisation? Room organisation? Method of presentation? Routines within the room?

From the data collected, make an action plan to decide:

- What can (if necessary) be easily changed? (Rank these in order, plan priorities, and then seek out the help that may be needed.)
- Which discipline/management issues should be tackled first?

Don't attempt to take too many changes on board. Likewise, be prepared to take a few risks. Change takes time and building up new repertoire is not an overnight job.

Professional development

Any effective change in our classroom management practice (or any facet of teaching) requires:

- knowledge of *current*, and typical, classroom behaviour and organisation
  (I need to become an active member in analysing my practice.)
- time to reflect on and discuss that practice with colleagues
  (Peer feedback is one mechanism.)
- knowledge and demonstration of new, or improved repertoire
  (Peer-support groups are an ideal adjunct to workshops or in-service.)

- an opportunity to practise or rehearse new repertoire (see Appendix V)

  (Classroom management ideas, or practices, can be demonstrated in the relative safety of a small group. Often, group members will offer to come into a classroom and do some team modelling to trial a new program or approach which is then followed with feedback.)
- encouragement and support during the learning and application of new skills

  (Peer-support groups and peer modelling can provide a supportive context for such a process. As such, they can productively extend the more traditional approach of in-service or workshops.)

Through the mutual discussion that follows several observations, the participants may then agree to team teach; to mutually model their new agenda. The new agenda will cover areas where the teacher agrees change is possible. An example may be the manner in which a teacher communicates with socially disruptive students. She may move from 'Don't you dare to call out like that!' to a firm 'David, you know the fair rule for asking questions — use it thanks'. Even such an apparently simple change requires a fairly powerful change in attitude and planning and skills. To move from hostile confrontation to non-hostile rule restatement requires the team seeing the value of a teacher:

- using non-confrontational verbal behaviour
- using a brief, clear step approach to discipline
- reassessing attitudes and perceptions relative to managing students (especially reassessing the extremes of management styles)
- learning how to use assertion instead of aggression
- making an increasingly comprehensive discipline plan that covers verbal behaviour, aspects of room organisation, curriculum, support structures etc.

Team-teaching

This phase involves teaching together and consciously acting by the plan. The team-teaching phase sees teachers mutually running a lesson, and mutually evaluating how effective the new repertoire is. Feedback continues through the team-teaching phase.

The larger peer-support group will, over a term or two, work through a range of classroom management strategies that can feed into the one-to-one peer support. If we 'fail' in the new approaches, or make a complete mess of running, for example, a classroom discussion together (see Chapter 5), then at least we 'fail' together; such failure is easier to take when shared. It becomes a learning experience. In this way we are learning *on the job* by:

- setting up target behaviours
- practising the new repertoire (target behaviour)
- getting feedback so we can finely tune the repertoire

Evaluation

Like most programs, peer support needs evaluation. Running records, diaries, discussion, even a final report that relates to the original goals, are all useful strategies to use when determining how effective the process was.

Peer support and first-year teachers

First-year teachers have enough problems without being 'thrown in at the deep end' as so many are. There is that twin 'culture' to break into: the culture of the school itself (each school has its own idiosyncratic culture of timetables, lines of communication, policies, routines/procedures, etc.) and the culture of teaching with its special language, bureaucracy, hierarchies, and literature.

So many first-year teachers are given a brief pep-talk and then left to negotiate these twin 'cultures' with little or no structural or professional support. It is also important not to organisationally 'slug' the first-year teachers. That common practice of timetabling the toughest or most unpleasant classes (8D for a double maths period on Friday afternoon!) indicates a singular lack of concern for first-year teachers. This is the beginning of their career! This common practice is often cynically passed off with the comment, 'Well, we had to wear it, we had our turn, why can't they?' This attitude ignores completely the practical welfare issue. Surely the 'harder' or 'tougher' classes should be taken by the more experienced teachers. It might even be valuable, for professional development, to invite beginning teachers into 'harder' classes to see how experienced teachers manage.

Using the peer-support model, first-year teachers are invited into a regular group meeting at set times (generally weekly for the first few sessions, then fortnightly). A senior staff member (or two if the first-year intake is large) facilitates the meetings which have these general aims.

- To make the beginnings of a teacher's professional life as smooth as possible (instead of the basic handshake and 'Here's the toilet, there's the timetable, you've got 10E for double maths and there's a staff meeting every Monday').
- To assist in ironing out and giving support with routines, procedures, policy matters, etc.
- To guide the group through some of the pitfalls that can occur in one's first year, especially in the area of classroom management.
- To provide a focus for sharing of common needs, problems, concerns, ideas, etc.
- To provide a climate for moral support and the opportunity to offer 'structural' support if needed, especially for the exit of difficult students, contracting with students, and parent conferences.

Many groups with whom I have worked evidence a genuine sense of being supported. Comments like 'not being isolated'; 'feeling that others care'; 'we can laugh with each other'; 'learning not to take things so seriously' are common. We begin to realise that teachers are fallible and that we can learn together from our mistakes, problems and shared concerns.

Leadership

Such a group needs clear and compassionate leadership. While the development of a peer-support group will seek to develop skills, share responsibilities and collaborate and 'own' the process, such notable aims don't just occur by inviting members into a group. Group spirit, group dynamics and the climate necessary for sharing, growth and skill development arise when effective leaders build such groups; leaders who have demonstrated skill in relationship building, communication and effective modelling skills.

Group facilitators will have to build a group spirit from disparate personalities, drawing out weaker members, encouraging and building up others, allowing non-judgemental comment on displayed attitudes and ideas inimical to positive teaching practice. Some teachers, for example, feel that it's all right to embarrass, humiliate, ridicule, put kids down, or scream. Group facilitators will encourage effective discussion on bad practice without putting down such members.

Groups will cover several areas within the stated aims.

1 How to make effective and positive rules with our classes. (Chapter 4)
2 How to make a discipline plan (building and rehearsing some basic management techniques). (Chapters 2 and 3)
3 How to use and apply logical/behavioural consequences with students. (Chapter 5)
4 How to handle conflict without getting into no-win situations.
5 How to follow up on major disruptions beyond the classroom (consequences, conferencing, contracting). (Chapter 5)
6 How to use group approaches:
   - cooperative groups
   - self-esteem groups
   - groups based around selected leaders
   - reinforcement approaches (Chapters 5 and 7)

7 How to create a positive class climate. (Chapter 6)
8 How to interface curriculum and discipline.

These areas should be explored in workshops throughout the year which are interspersed with in-service programs. Speakers may be invited to work with the peer-support group as they workshop these areas.

Peer observation

To develop professionally, it is important to receive feedback. Apart from student-teacher observations teachers rarely receive positive, helpful feedback from their peers. As a feature of on-going professional development, members of the first-year, peer-support group are encouraged to mutually observe one another's classes. Through an agreed agenda and focus, they can give feedback on what they heard, what they saw, how they felt in their colleague's class (see Appendix IV). This feedback provides valuable data for generating change. Peer-group members may also elect to rehearse skills prior to classes and ask their 'peer observer' to give feedback. This observation phase forms an invaluable link between workshop discussion and modelling, and the application in class. Many members, after several peer-group meetings, feel comfortable enough to share their experiences (often with judicious humour!) with the whole group.

Evaluation

At the close of the year the group should meet to evaluate its progress in the light of its aims. Often this can be carried out through a half or full-day 'retreat' from school where experiences and reminiscences are shared and evaluated. These can be written down and shared with the incoming teachers the following year.

The success of the peer-support process relies on:
- effective and committed leadership (embracing enthusiasm and willingness to persist in the long haul)
- support and back-up from the administration
- clear objectives, timelines for meetings and a trusting and positive attitude engendered by the facilitator/s
- opportunities for practical, professional development through regular workshops

- opportunities to give assistance to members of the group by linking up members to help, bringing in other support persons where required, and giving assurances to struggling members that the school can and will provide whatever assistance is available.

The first year of a teaching career can be somewhat bruising. We needn't have to go it 'alone'; there is much that a school can do to provide practical support. The peer-support model is one way of doing just that; peers supporting peers.

Some responses from teachers involved in first-year peer-support groups

'Peer Support saved my sanity. It was through the program that a group of us were able to work on effective strategies to enable us to teach effectively, discipline fairly, and remain sane at the same time.'

'There were three things that I found most useful as a result of our meetings. The first and probably the most crucial is for teachers to get together with their students as soon as possible to establish a set of fair rules around which the class will operate. These must range from behaviour to movement and to anything else and must be accomplished with clear consequences and be followed by the teacher as well as the students. The second most useful technique was so simple yet so brilliant. The two "magic" questions: what are you doing and what should you be doing? In my experience this year they have not failed me. It does not matter how many times you say them or how repetitive it sometimes feels — it works! Peer observation was another crucial element of my success and I believe should be examined in college before we are sent into the "jungle". The procedure is simple. Take a trusted peer or two and go into each other's "nightmares", I mean classrooms. You simply observe then discuss. Not only does it reaffirm your beliefs but you can be constructively criticised without awkward, embarrassing feelings that often go hand in hand with being told "you did it wrong!"'

'Possibly the most significant thing that I have learned during these meetings is to analyse students less and analyse myself more. I have found that once I began to honestly criticise and accept my short-comings as a teacher, then work determinedly to eradicate those short-comings, my stress level, anxiety, anger and frustration slowly receded.'

'As one aspect of my teaching improved I realised that I could spend more time and conscious thought upon improving other aspects of teaching, but it was the recognition of the need for me to change that helped me.'

'Through my observation of my colleagues' classes, I was clearly able to see a great many aspects of teaching (not child-minding as I was tending to do) that I had not really seen, felt or practised since my teaching rounds (which I had enjoyed).'

May the force be with you

'Because of this program I feel I have changed from a child-minding, assignment-feeding, aimless machine, to someone who tries and at times succeeds in actually providing the means with which students can learn and/or experience something new, different or worthwhile.'

'Peer group support — although initially yet another onslaught to the battered ego ... has proven very useful.'

'I found it de-mystified the "successful" teacher, offering objective advice, techniques and skills.'

Conclusion

Teacher stress will not go away. With the increasing demands on teachers and the difficulty of maintaining classroom management around traditional role authority, teachers are clearly in need of a more united team approach. Emotional coping increases significantly when we feel supported, when we know that someone else is expressing similar concerns. Professional development that seeks to access a new, or improved, repertoire is also more effective when we are supported. Even 'failure' is better handled together.

It has been my experience that where peer support has been a regular feature of school life, supported by senior administration, the results in staff morale and professional development have been significant.

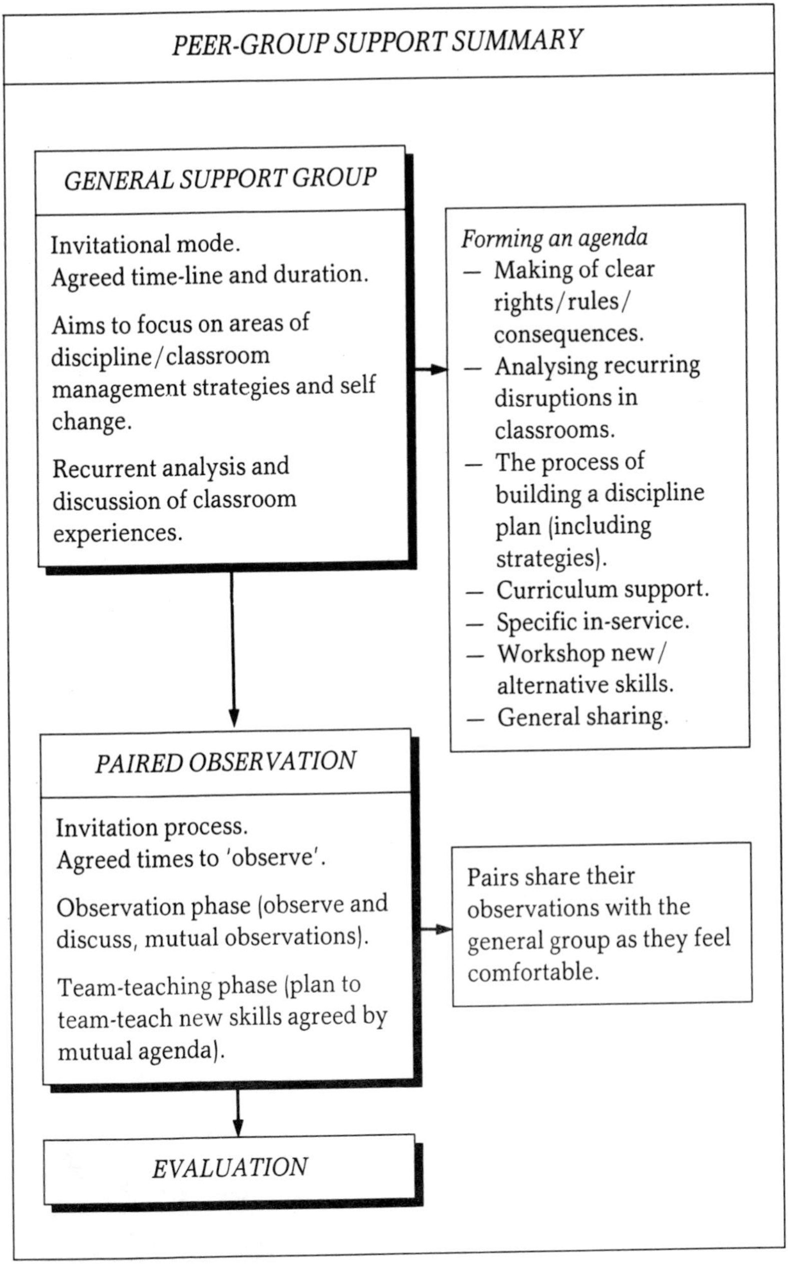

PEER-GROUP SUPPORT SUMMARY

GENERAL SUPPORT GROUP

Invitational mode.
Agreed time-line and duration.

Aims to focus on areas of discipline/classroom management strategies and self change.

Recurrent analysis and discussion of classroom experiences.

Forming an agenda
— Making of clear rights/rules/ consequences.
— Analysing recurring disruptions in classrooms.
— The process of building a discipline plan (including strategies).
— Curriculum support.
— Specific in-service.
— Workshop new/ alternative skills.
— General sharing.

PAIRED OBSERVATION

Invitation process.
Agreed times to 'observe'.

Observation phase (observe and discuss, mutual observations).

Team-teaching phase (plan to team-teach new skills agreed by mutual agenda).

Pairs share their observations with the general group as they feel comfortable.

EVALUATION

Fig 9

CHAPTER 10

Conclusion

No one, no one who is a teacher that is, pretends that discipline and classroom management is an easy task. Schools, more and more, are expected to have the widest of curricula from the 3Rs to bike education, social skills training, human relations education, computer and information technology, environmental education. How often do we hear the hue and cry, 'Why don't schools teach them ...?' We are required to cope with wide individual differences, cater for the emotional needs of our students as well as provide the best learning environment for all. We are also expected to pick up the unfinished tag that some parents leave behind. Most teachers do this with diligence, hard work and good humour.

In this demanding role of teaching there are some situations over which we have minimal control: the students' home background; the particular school we were sent to; the regular changes that proceed from the Ministry of Education; limits to funding; the 'portable' we got landed with; the timetable. There are, however, some areas of our practice that we can have significant and effective control over.

- The kind of curriculum we organise and present in our room.
- How we organise our classroom.
- The kind of rules we make with our students.
- The way we cater for mixed abilities.
- The support network we can build with our peers
- The control we can exercise over our discipline and management style.

A teacher once said to me, 'I understand all this discipline skill stuff but you know you can't teach an old dog new tricks'. 'But you're not a dog! You're a person.' We *can* change. Like most significant change it won't come about by accident, without some 'failure', or hard work, or support. Developing more effective, and positive, school discipline will require the same reflection, effort, and rigour that we apply to any area of the curriculum.

Today, personal dynamics in classrooms are subject to high emotion and fallibility but that only increases the need to plan for the sorts of things we ought to say and do when we discipline. It is possible to develop personal and schoolwide discipline (see Appendix VI) that is more decisive and less reactive without losing that fundamental humanity that not only makes teaching bearable but even enjoyable. If this book can stimulate that kind of change, based on strong peer-support, it will have achieved its purpose.

Appendix I

Personal Running Records

Personal Running Records are important regarding management and discipline for the following reasons.

1 They assess the kind, number, and content of disruptions. So often teachers will say, 'He always calls out'. Now we know that's probably hyperbole, but it's helpful to know actually how many times and when. Such records are diagnostic data much as we would use running records for literacy and numeracy.

2 They are a useful record if support services are called in (either a fellow teacher, senior teacher, psychologist, special education teacher or consultant).

3 They give a guide as to whether or not our intervention programs are effective. We can look back at particular occasions of disruption and see whether the discipline plan is working. This is especially important when using behaviour modification approaches.

4 They assist teachers in reflecting on their practice. What they are

doing; how often a given method or process is tried and whether there is a successful outcome. It is important that, as teachers, we become more reflective and appropriately critical of our actual discipline. We need to appraise what we say, how we say it, when we say it and what effect such discipline has on student behaviour.

5 They provide a focus for problem-solving discussion with our peers.

Disruptive behaviour analysis record

Incident (Brief description)	A.M. P.M. or lesson time	Gender	Task student is undertaking	Is behaviour directed at particular students?	Teacher's action

Appendix II

The 4W Form

For use as a form of logical consequences for significantly disruptive behaviour.

NAME .... CLASS ....

What I did (against our class rules).

....
....
....
....
....
....

What rule (or right) I broke or infringed.

....
....
....
....

Why I did it (my explanation).

....
....
....
....

What I think I should do to fix it up.

....
....
....
....
....

Teacher/Parent Comments

....
....
....
....
....
....

Signed ....

Date ....

Appendix III

Contracts

1 Formal contract form

I have discussed my behaviour with the following persons

....

....

....

and have agreed to work with them in changing my behaviour.

Behaviours I have agreed to work on.

Be specific here. Focus on the class rights and rules.
It is better if the student uses their own language,
with teacher assistance, 'What do you want to try to
do?' 'What do you need to work on?'

How I will do it.

Again be specific.

How my teacher/s will support me.

This aspect is often left out of a contract. It is
important to include it.

Comments on the student's progress.

Keep comments as positive as possible.

Signed ....Student

Signed ....Class Teacher

Signed ....Parent (if necessary)

Checked by ....

2 A self-monitoring contract

This can be tied in with the 4W form.

Keeping tabs: *Jason*			Year *7B*			
Week .... Monday						
How I behaved	Period 1	Period 2	Period 3	Period 4	Period 5	Period 6
1 Hands up without calling out. 2 Stick to my task, or the work set. 3 Completed the task.						
* * * I'm happy with the way I went. * * Just Okay. * Not Okay. I'm not really happy with the way I went.						

- This contract can be adapted for use with younger (from Year 3 onwards) students. They should be encouraged to write any extra comments on the back of the card.
- Use the phrase 'keeping tabs' to highlight behaviour ownership, and self-monitoring.
- The teacher, student, and teacher-support (level coordinator, home-group teacher, school counsellor) will have discussed how Jason can 'keep tabs' by working within fair rules; giving himself clear messages of encouragement; asking whether he has achieved the goals and whether his behaviour is helping him or not.

- Each teacher who has this student needs to be aware that he is trying hard to manage his behaviour. They should be encouraged to support and maximise his efforts and assist in the program of behaviour ownership and change.
- The 'contract' should be reviewed as the group feels necessary (at least twice a week).

Appendix IV

Observation information record (for peer observation)

These are provided as guides only. The groups or pairs may choose their own to assist classroom observation.

Lesson organisation/procedures	Comment
Opening remarks Lesson clear Notes enough Notes clear Chalkboard writing — visible — well-spaced Was there a welcome/introduction	

Instructions — clear
    — unclear
    — adequate
    — inadequate
Early finisher's provision
Mixed ability provision
Other

On-task teacher help given to students	Amount	Comments
Male		
Female		

General body language	Comments
Confident Upright/slouching Use of hands: direct/indirect; assertive/ non-assertive Moving around the room Time up-front Smiling Frowning Proximity to child when verbally disciplining	

Verbal Behaviour	Amount	Comments
Tone of voice Firm/confident/decisive		

Unclear/mumbling/not confident/indecisive		
Monotone		
Variation		
Too soft		
Too fast		
Too sharp		
Other		

Eye contact	Amount	Comments
Roving		
Darting		
Clear/direct		
To individual		
To group		
Looking down		
Frown		
Glare		
Uncertain		
Other		

Handling disruption	Time delay	Effective/Ineffective

Time — ignoring
    — attending to
      disruption		

Student-teacher conflict	Comment
What did the teacher actually do? How did they speak (the tone, manner)?	

How long did they speak for?
How did they enter the conflict?
How positively (or not) was the conflict
  dealt with?

Style of discipline	Number of times	Comments
Simple ignoring of student		
Moving close to the disruptive child		
Eye contact (brief, direct stare)		
Frown (firm, brief)		
Defusing statement		
Deflective statement		
Rule restatement or reminder		
Simple direction		
Assertive statement		
Choices		
What? How? questions		
In-class time-out		

Note specific helpful (positive) or unhelpful phases.

Appendix V

Gentle, assertive role-plays (GARPS)

I have used GARPs as a teacher-training tool for students at university and college as well as at school workshops. Positive discipline skills are workshopped for two weeks then the GARPs provide the testing ground for application. Teacher-training courses tend to treat discipline *practice* minimally. I believe it is possible to be far better prepared not only by knowing what we should do, but trying out how we might actually do it. We are more comfortable in discipline, and less stressed, when we have a discipline plan. A plan helps us to juggle the multi-task demands that teaching and discipline create in any one session, on any one day. Combined with in-servicing, teacher-support networks and the willingness to try a new approach, GARPs can be a highly useful vehicle for effective learning.

To improve their professional practice teachers need three things.
1 Some realistic assessment of their current practice either by self-monitoring or by peer observation.

2 A clear understanding of a possible, achievable new or improved repertoire.
3 An opportunity to model the new repertoire and get feedback.

A GARP is a gentle, assertive role-play. No one is pushed into the unknown or put into an embarrassing situation — the facilitator will ensure this. Teachers are encouraged and expected to act in appropriately assertive ways as the disruption demands. The role-plays are scripted so that those playing the disruptive students don't overplay the behaviour which is being managed. When used in the context of trusted peer-support, GARPs can provide a basis for getting a handle on new repertoire in the safety and security of a role-play situation.

Action and feedback

Teachers know how important 'hands-on' learning is; to be involved in *doing* the learned thing. Whenever we try to learn a new skill, or improve existing skills we can turn to books, or current research, or attend an in-service or college course. Important as these agencies are, they cannot reproduce the emotional climate. We can, of course, practise discipline skills in front of a mirror, or mentally rehearse an approach ('What will I say, how will I do it?'). These are valuable ways of internalising new repertoire and giving confidence. What a GARP does is simply create enough of the classroom conditions to make the practice of a skill as realistic as simulation can allow. This is followed by immediate feedback. Teachers often miss out on *targeted* feedback which is the link in the learning chain. It is fundamental to the impact of new learning on actual practice.

Feedback hits the spot when:
- it concentrates on specific behaviour
- it is non-judgemental
- it is as immediate as is possible (following the trial of the new skill)
- it encourages and builds on strengths
- it uses the feedback to 'fine-tune' the skill again as soon as is practicable

GARPs have been used at all levels of the teaching profession to enable such feedback. It goes without saying, of course, that GARPs are a voluntary teacher activity. They can be enormous fun (when facilitated with care), and can provide a simple opportunity to try new discipline and classroom management skills.

Organising GARPs

GARPs can be part of an in-service, a training course at a tertiary institution, or part of a peer-support group within a school. They need willing volunteers, a facilitator, full knowledge of the process, and a small element of risk. The facilitator should embrace the basic qualities of good humour, experience, the ability to get on well with a disparate group of personalities, and know how to give feedback. The facilitator should also be thoroughly familiar with the skill repertoire being practised; its theoretical base as well as its methodology. (See Chapters 2 and 3.)

The sorts of disruptions teachers want to role-play in a GARP vary. These are the ones commonly used.

The up-front phase of a lesson

The following behaviours would be role-played:
- students who haven't got equipment or who say 'What do we have to do again?'
- students who call out across the classroom to get the teacher's attention *while* the teacher is working with other students
- students talking loudly and who are off-task
- arguments over property ('She's got my pen Sir!')
- aimless wandering about the classroom
- students who refuse to do the task
- students who demean the task ('This work sucks')
- low-level swearing between students (or frustration-engendered swearing)
- teacher baiting ('You can't make me do anything.')
- swearing at the teacher
- play fighting
- time-out situations

In a GARP we are trying to simulate the level and extent of a typical disruption (even multiple disruptions) but with the teachers' cognisance. We are therefore looking for specific verbal and non-verbal teacher behaviour which can be exercised when managing that disruption.

'Scripted' disruptions

As suggested before, an open-ended role-play can be a debilitating task. Give teachers the licence to role-play disruptive students and they will easily go 'over the top'. If a role-play is going to be a learning experience (in this case primarily for the person role-playing the teacher), then it will be important for that learning to have boundaries within which the learner can feel secure.

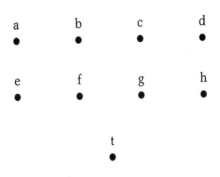

A group of 8   t = teacher
a–h = the class of students

During the GARP, one member of the group elects to play the teacher. The primary learner in the role-play is required to deal with disruptions occurring during the up-front phase of a lesson (3–5 minutes is plenty), then to move around the room dealing with on-task disruptions (another 5 minutes). The time may be extended to suit the needs of the group. The teacher will be aware of what *kind* of disruptions will occur and will be ready to try out new skills. She will have to decide what to do to manage the disruption, count to 3 and try the new skill.

The 'students' are seated at desks in any way the group feels comfortable (see diagram).

Student A has a card scripting his disruption. 'Call out twice to get the teacher's attention. If she ignores you, fold your arms and sulk. Throw in a snort as you go into sulk mode. That's all. Ten seconds later put up your hand and wait, without calling out.'

Student B has a card that says 'Call out with your hand out. "Miss! Miss! I've got a question." Do this for a count of five seconds. Stop.

If the teacher doesn't respond, do it again thirty seconds later. And again one last time. If she still doesn't respond do it again. If she does — comply.'

Students C and D have cards which say, 'Turn to your mate and whisper while the teacher is teaching. Do it until the teacher says something to you'.

Student E has a card which says 'Put up your hand and wait until the teacher notices you'.

No student is to role-play beyond the clear script. Other variations on up-front cards can be:

'Click your fingers with your hand up to get the teacher's attention. Do it for a count of eight to ten seconds.'

'Butt in and say, ''We did this stuff last year in Mr Davies' class!'' Then look around to get peer approval, lean back slightly in your chair and wait.'

The main thing is to script what you want in the disruption and then tailor it to the skill the learner-teacher is wanting to develop. The teacher knows that there will be, for example, calling out, tapping, and whispering while she takes a mini-lesson up-front for three minutes. The teacher begins a mini-lesson on applied numbers, ready to handle three students calling out, two whisperers, and a tapper. The limit of disruptions is decided by the learner-teacher and the group. The facilitator may stop the GARP during the process and get feedback, asking the teacher, 'How did you feel when Michael was calling out and clicking his fingers?'.

General questions for feedback

'Were you conscious of what you were doing?'
'Were you clear, in your own mind, what you wanted to say?'
'Do you want to try it again?'
'How will you approach it this time?'

Specific questions

'Were you aware of the *actual* words you used to Michael and Dianne? Try to recall them.'

Feedback questions for the 'students'

'Michael, did you feel Maria was assertive enough?'
'Was eye contact established?'
'Did she make her intentions clear?'
'What did you understand by her non-verbal actions?'
'Any other comments?'

Fine-tuning

The teacher should now utilise the feedback to try again (she may do this more than once). The facilitator may say, 'Maria, this time try tactical ignoring of Michael but use a clear direction to Dianne. What do you need to say? Okay, rehearse it. When you want to make a point, try extending the hand like this. Let's try it'.

The goal is to build up a repertoire that is modelled in the teacher's behaviour towards a disrupting student. This should include:

- the expectation of compliance (direct eye contact, brevity of direction or instruction, tone of voice)
- a non-argumentative stance
- general assertive (non-aggressive) body language
- matching of teacher assertion to the level and extent of the disruption
- rule-focusing and *conscious* verbal repertoire
- effective eye-scanning skills
- re-establishment of working relationships as quickly as possible
- minimal attention to off-task behaviour, maximum attention to on-task behaviour

In short, the modelling of decisive teacher behaviour.

It is better for the teacher to try again, on the spot, several times (if they feel comfortable) to get that tone of voice or gesture right. The facilitator will assist in this fine-tuning by modelling the desirable behaviour if necessary.

The on-task phase of a lesson

The same process is used when role-playing the on-task phase of a lesson. During the role-play, the teacher tries to decide what to deal with next — the student wandering out of his desk or the one calling out from three desks away? Prior to the GARP, members of the group will have discussed the sorts of skills they want to practise.

Student B's card reads, 'Go into task-refusal mode. Sit at your desk with your arms folded and do no work. Look around you. No noise'.

Student C's card reads, 'Call across to the teacher every ten seconds or so. "Miss, Miss, come over here!" If she says anything, keep quiet for a while and try again. Stop after two or three times. If the teacher ignores you, *finally* put your hand up and wait.'

Student D's card reads, 'Get out of your seat and wander over to a mate. Start a discussion whispering, "You are clearly off-task" '.

What the teacher knows

In managing the disruptions, the teacher knows what sort of disruptions will occur but not necessarily who has the cards. If the teacher wants to try out an approach more than once, the cards may be shuffled around to increase the sense of realism. At any point in the GARP, the facilitator or teacher can stop to reassess and get feedback and use this feedback to try again.

> 'This time, Maria, see if you can *tactically* ignore Michael. Give him no eye contact and only go over when you are aware (using effective eye scanning) he is on-task. Otherwise, your directions were clear and decisive. You may need to lift up the eyes a bit and give a general eye-sweep of the class if you are at a student's desk for more than a minute. Want to try it again?'

A GARP can take from five to twenty minutes. It's then a good idea to swap roles. The time can be extended, of course, as people feel comfortable.

Included here are some examples of the sorts of scripts which can be used. These need to be varied to accommodate age and setting. For example, we can model a prep child hiding under a table and refusing to come out, as easily as a Year 8 procrastinating student — as long as the behaviour is scripted and agreed on by group members. It is the facilitator's role to plan the GARP with the 'trainees', to facilitate immediate feedback during the role-play, and to debrief and guide discussion on what has been learned from it.

While the teacher is up-front, take a piece of paper and screw it up into a ball and toss it up and down in the air. Quietly giggle to your mate.

Call out three times, then sulk.

While the class is working, get out of your seat and start a conversation with a friend. The teacher will redirect you. Argue slightly, go back but sulk. After a while pick up your pen and start work.

You are a noisy pest. When the students have been asked to get back to work, turn around and start a discussion (with moderate volume) with another student. The teacher will warn you. Settle down, but resume after twenty seconds. The teacher will restate the rule. Settle down but resume after twenty seconds. You'll be given a choice, but resume. You'll be asked to move. Initially procrastinate with 'Why should I?', then move off.

You are day dreaming, and have not started work. It is during 'work' time. Start talking to your friend. If the teacher gives you a direction, stop talking. Resume a few minutes later. If he comes back, stop. Resume. He may ask you to move.

Click your fingers and call out several times. Then go quiet. Try again by clicking your fingers and loudly calling out. Stop when the teacher disciplines you. Then put up your hand using the class rule.

You are a mobile student. When the students are working, get up out of your seat. Go back. Get up again. If the teacher redirects you, initially argue and then back down and resume your seat.

You are a task-refuser. You decide not to do the work. You argue *slightly* with the teacher, then comply.

Your task is to call out during class time. Do it twice (you'll probably be ignored). Give up and put your hand up to wait.

You are a task-refuser. The teacher says, 'Okay, let's get to work' or some other similar phrase. You sit and do nothing. When the teacher redirects you, start complaining, then give in sulkily and settle down within a minute or two.

You are a pain in the neck. As an attention-seeker you click your fingers and call out several times. If the teacher corrects you, you will shut up but you'll sulk and give a few grunts turning away to sulk mode.

Appendix VI

Discipline survey

One way of developing a whole-school approach to discipline is to use a survey. Teachers are asked to observe their practice for a week or two. The answers can be used to help formulate discipline policy in the school.

Sample survey questions

1 What types of disruptive behaviours are presently occurring in the school?
   - Can you rank them from most to least pressing?
   - Can you note how regular such behaviours are?
2 What disciplinary procedures are you presently using to cope with these identifiable behaviours?
3 Which disciplinary procedures do you think are helpful and effective?

Note: Disruptive behaviour can, of course, range from tapping on the desk to the antics of the class 'strangler'. In one way or another it will be behaviour that disrupts another's right to work, safety, movement, security and so on. The data you collect will, therefore, seek to:

- describe the disruptive incidents accurately
- note their frequency
- note the specific action taken
- note year level, sex, curriculum area, time of day and location
- rate the 'incident/s'

In developing a whole school approach to more positive discipline, it is helpful to survey current practice to ascertain what teachers are currently doing regarding management. Such a survey requires plenty of discussion before it is conducted and an assurance that the data will be used to improve discipline across the school.

1 Effect a systematic appraisal of what teachers perceive as 'disruptive behaviour'.

2 Determine what present actions and procedures teachers are using which they find effective and ineffective when dealing with such disruptive behaviours.

3 Identify which teachers note undue strain from disruptive behaviours and what support is being offered, in a positive way, to address their concerns?

4 Note year levels or particular classes that seem to be overly disruptive.

5 Note particular students who appear to be causing problems and in what lessons.

6 Note any relationship between curriculum areas or time, and disruptive incidents.

7 Use the data collected over a four-week period as the basis for a discipline and welfare policy review.

Bibliography

Axelrod, S. 1977, *Behaviour Modification for the Classroom Teacher*, McGraw-Hill, New York.

Barrish, H.H., Saunders, M. & Wolf, M.M. 1969, 'Good behaviour game: Effects of individual contingencies for group consequences on disruptive behaviour in the classroom', *Journal of Applied Behaviour Analysis*, vol. 2, pp. 119–24.

Bernard, M.E. & Joyce, M.R. 1984, *Rational Emotive Therapy with Children and Adolescents: Theory, Treatment Strategies, Preventative Methods*, J. Wiley and Sons, New York.

Biggs, J. & Telfer, R. 1981, *The Process of Learning*, Prentice-Hall, Sydney.

Boer, B. & Gleeson, V. 1982, *The Law of Education*, Butterworths, Sydney.

Borba, M., & Borba C. 1980, 1982, *Self-Esteem: A Classroom Affair*, vols 1 & 2, Winston Press, Minneapolis.

Brown, D., Reschly, D. & Sabers, D. 1974, 'Using group contingencies with punishment and positive reinforcement to modify aggressive behaviours in a "Head Start" classroom', *Psychological Record*, vol. 24, pp. 291–496.

Bryant, B.K. 1977, 'The effects of the interpersonal context of self- and other-enhancement behaviour', *Child Development*, vol. 48, pp. 885–92.

Canter, L. & Canter, M. 1976, *Assertive Discipline: A Take-Charge Approach for Today's Educator*, Canter & Associates, California.

Charles, C.M. 1985, *Building Classroom Discipline: From Models to Practice*, 2nd edn, Longman, New York.

Coopersmith, S. 1967, *The Antecedents of Self-Esteem*, Freeman, San Francisco.

Cowin, M. et al. 1985, *Positive School Discipline: A Practical Guide to Developing Policy*, Parents and Friends of Monnington Publications, 1985.

Cranfield, J. & Wells, H.C. 1976, *100 Ways to Enhance Self-Concept in the Classroom*, Prentice-Hall, New Jersey.

Dalton, J. 1985, *Adventures in Thinking: Creative Thinking and Co-operative Talk in Small Groups*, Nelson, Melbourne.

De Bono, E. 1986, *Conflicts: A Better Way to Resolve Them*, Penguin, Harmondsworth.

Discipline in Schools: Report of the Committee of Enquiry 1989, Her Majesty's Stationery Office, London (The Elton Report).

Dobson, J. 1970, *Dare to Discipline*, Tyndale House, Wheaton, Illinois.

Dobson, J. 1974, *Hide or Seek*, Fleming H. Revell Co., New Jersey.

Dodge, K.A. 1981, Social competence and aggressive behaviour in children, Paper presented to the Midwestern Psychological Association, Detroit.

Donaldson, M. 1978, *Children's Minds*, Fontana, London.

Dreikurs, R. 1968, *Psychology in the Classroom: A Manual for Teachers*, 2nd edn, Harper & Row, New York.

Dreikurs, R. & Cassel, P. 1972, *Discipline without Tears: What to Do with Children Who Misbehave*, Hawthorn Books, New York.

Dreikurs, R., Grunwald, B. & Pepper, F. 1982, *Maintaining Sanity in the Classroom*, 2nd edn, Harper & Row, New York.

Erikson, E. 1960, 'Youth, fidelity and diversity' in *The Challenge of Youth*, E. Erikson (ed.), Anchor Books, New York.

Erikson, E. 1968, *Identity: Youth and Crisis*, Norton Press, London.

Fannin, L. & Clinard, M. 1965, 'Differences in conception of self as a male among lower and middle class delinquents', *Social Problems,* vol. 13, pp. 205-14.

Froyen, L.A. 1988, *Classroom Management: Empowering Teacher-Leaders,* Merrill Publishing Co., Columbus, Ohio.

Ginott, H. 1972, *Teacher and Child,* Macmillan, New York.

Glasser, W. 1965, *Reality Therapy,* Harper & Row, New York.

Glasser, W. 1969, *Schools Without Failure,* Harper & Row, New York.

Glasser, W. 1985, *Control Theory,* Harper & Row, New York.

Glasser, W. 1986, *Control Theory in the Classroom,* Harper & Row, New York.

Gordon, T. 1974, *Teacher Effectiveness Training,* P.H. Wyden, New York.

Harris, S.J. 1973, *Winners and Losers,* Argus Communications, Illinois.

Harter, S. 1985, *Self-Perception Profile for Children,* University of Denver, Denver, Colorado.

Hook, C. 1985, *Studying Classrooms,* Deakin University Press, Victoria.

Kounin, J. 1977, *Discipline and Group Management in Classrooms,* Holt, Rinehart & Winston, New York.

Kounin, J. & Obradovic, S. 1968, 'Managing emotionally disturbed children in regular classrooms: A replication and extension' *Journal of Special Education,* vol. 2, no. 2, pp. 129-39.

Kyriacou, C. 1981, 'Social support and occupational stress among school teachers', *Educational Studies,* vol. 7, pp. 55-60.

Kyriacou, C. 1986, *Effective Teaching in Schools,* Basil Blackwell, Oxford.

Lewin, G.W. (ed.) 1948, *Kurt Lewin: Resolving Social Conflicts, Selected Papers on Group Dynamics,* Harper & Row, New York.

Lewin, K. 1935, *A Dynamic Theory of Personality: Selected Papers of Kurt Lewin,* McGraw Hill, New York.

Lewin, K., Lippitt, R. & White, R.K. 1939, 'Patterns of aggressive behaviour in experimentally created "social climates" ', *Journal of Social Psychology,* vol. 10, pp. 271-99.

Lewis, C.S. 1978, *The Abolition of Man,* Collins/Fount, Glasgow.

Lewis, R. & Lovegrove, M.N. 1985, 'Students' preferences for discipline practices in schools', *Teaching and Teacher Education,* vol. 1, pp. 325-33.

Lokan, J. & McKenzie, P. (eds) 1989, *Teacher Appraisal: Issues and Approaches*, A.C.E.R., Hawthorn, Victoria.

Lovegrove, M.N. & Lewis, R. 1985, 'Students' views of discipline in the classroom', *Educational Magazine*, vol. 42, no. 1, pp. 29-31.

Maccoby, E.E. (ed.) 1966, *The Development of Sex Differences*, Stanford University Press, California.

Maccoby, E.E. & Jacklin, C.N. 1974, *The Psychology of Sex Differences*, Stanford University Press, California.

Maccoby, E.E. and Jacklin, C.N. 1980, 'Sex differences in aggression: A rejoinder and reprise', *Child Development*, vol. 51, pp. 964-80.

McCarthy, P., Freeman, L., Rothwell, C. & Arnheim, B. 1983, 'Is there life after 8D?: Group reinforcement at the post primary level', *Interview*, no. 11, Ministry of Education, Victoria.

Morgan, D.P. & Jenson, W.R. 1988, *Teaching Behaviourally Disordered Students: Preferred Practices*, Merrill Publishing Co., Toronto.

Milgram, S. & Shotland, R.L. 1973, *Television and Antisocial Behavior: Field Experiments*, Academic Press, New York.

Mortimer, J. 1987, *Character Parts*, Penguin Books, London.

Papaplia, D.S. & Wendkos Olds, S. (eds) 1982, *A Child's World: Infancy Through Adolescence*, 3rd edn, McGraw-Hill, New York.

Piaget, J. 1932, *The Moral Judgement of the Child*, Routledge & Kegan Paul, London.

Poteet, J.A. 1973, *Behavior Modification: A Practical Guide for Teachers*, University of London Press, London.

Powell, J. 1976, *Fully Human, Fully Alive*, Argus Communications, Illinois.

Reading, H.F. 1977, *A Dictionary of the Social Sciences*, Routledge & Kegan Paul, London.

Rex, J. 1981, *Social Conflict: A Conceptual and Theoretical Analysis*, Longman, London.

Roberts, R. 1988, 'School yard menace: school bullying', *Psychology Today*, February, pp. 53-6.

Robertson, J. 1989, *Effective Classroom Control: Understanding Teacher-Pupil Relationships*, 2nd edn, Hodder and Stoughton, London.

Rogers, W. 1985, Conflict resolution among pre-adolescents, MEd thesis, University of Melbourne.

Rogers, W. 1986, *Discipline and Student Welfare: A Policy Approach*,

Ministry of Education, Western Region, Footscray, Victoria.

Rogers, W. 1989, *Making a Discipline Plan*, Nelson, Melbourne.

Rosenthal, R. & Fode, K. 1963, 'The effect of experimental bias on the performance of the albino rat', *Behavioural Science*, vol. 8, pp. 183–9.

Rutter, M. *et al.* 1979, *Fifteen Thousand Hours: Secondary Schools and their Effects on Children*, Open Books, London.

Rutter, M. 1981, *Maternal Deprivation Reassessed*, Penguin, Middlesex, U.K.

Safran, S.P., Safran, J.S., & Barcikowski, R.S. 1985, 'Differences in teacher tolerance: An illusory phenomenon?', *Behaviour Disorders*, pp. 11–15.

Slee, R. (ed.) 1988, *Discipline and Schools: A Curriculum Perspective*, Macmillan, Melbourne.

Smith, M.J. 1981, *When I Say No, I Feel Guilty*, Bantam Books, Toronto.

Stanford, G. 1980, *Developing Effective Classroom Groups*, Hart Publishing Co., New York.

Szaday, C. 1989, *Addressing Behaviour Problems in Australian Schools*, A.C.E.R., Hawthorn, Victoria.

Topping, K. 1987, *Educational Systems for Disruptive Adolescents*, Croom Helm, London.

Vernon, M.D. 1969, *Human Motivation*, Cambridge University Press, London.

Williams, J., Bennet, S. & Best, D. 1982, 'Awareness and expression of sex stereotypes in young children', in Papalia, D.S. & Wendkos Olds, S. (eds), *A Child's World: Infancy through Adolescence*, 3rd edn, McGraw-Hill, New York.

Wilkes, R. 1981, 'Fly me to the moon: A classroom behaviour management program to enhance learning', *Interview*, no. 3, Ministry of Education, Victoria.

Wragg, J. 1989, *Talk Sense to Yourself: A Program for Children and Adolescents*, A.C.E.R., Hawthorn, Victoria.

Resources

Rogers, W. 1986, *Helping Us, Helping Them: Discipline*, Western Metropolitan Regional Educational Technology Unit, Footscray, Victoria. (Videorecording)

Rogers, W. 1989, *Decisive Discipline: Every Move You Make, Every Step You Take*, The Institute of Educational Administration, Geelong, Victoria. (A video learning package: two videos and a workbook.)

Index

Page numbers in italics refer to anecdotal
material in the text.